ETHICAL DII

MW01483963

This work investigates the complexity of ethics as a field of inquiry and practice across a principal's career. Fully contextualized, and thus carrying the contradictions and requirements of any school, the issues realistically do not usually lead to a single, beat-all answer, as any solution will likely have positive and negative consequences. Drawn from the authors' experiences and studies of schools over decades, the central figure is a fictional principal of a magnet school, whose dilemmas reflect the questions educators must be prepared for. Each decision takes into account the principal's and staff's identities and values because they are all humans and their opinions influence the outcomes. The work injects analytic, virtue, feminist, care, deontological, and critical theory insights as Deweyan ethics provides a lens for examining dilemmas. This accessible work blends reflective theory, the ordinary worlds of schools, and engaging pedagogical practice to guide those planning to enter the education sector.

DOUGLAS J. SIMPSON is Associated Professor in the College of Education at Texas Christian University, and Helen DeVitt Jones Chair in Teacher Education Emeritus at Texas Tech University. He is a past president of the Canadian Philosophy of Education Society and the American Educational Studies Association.

DONAL M. SACKEN is Professor Emeritus of Education in the College of Education at Texas Christian University. He has taught at all levels, mostly in the areas of administration and educational foundations. He has served as a legal consultant for school districts, and now is chair of the board at a local charter school.

ETHICAL DILEMMAS IN SCHOOLS

Collaborative Inquiry, Decision-Making and Action

DOUGLAS J. SIMPSON

Texas Christian University

DONAL M. SACKEN

Texas Christian University

CAMBRIDGE
UNIVERSITY PRESS

CAMBRIDGE
UNIVERSITY PRESS

University Printing House, Cambridge CB2 8BS, United Kingdom

One Liberty Plaza, 20th Floor, New York, NY 10006, USA

477 Williamstown Road, Port Melbourne, VIC 3207, Australia

314–321, 3rd Floor, Plot 3, Splendor Forum, Jasola District Centre, New Delhi – 110025, India

79 Anson Road, #06–04/06, Singapore 079906

Cambridge University Press is part of the University of Cambridge.

It furthers the University's mission by disseminating knowledge in the pursuit of education, learning, and research at the highest international levels of excellence.

www.cambridge.org
Information on this title: www.cambridge.org/9781108491471
DOI: 10.1017/9781108868853

First published 2021

A catalogue record for this publication is available from the British Library.

Library of Congress Cataloging-in-Publication Data
NAMES: Simpson, Douglas J., 1940– author. | Sacken, Donal M., 1948– author.
TITLE: Ethical dilemmas in schools : collaborative inquiry, decision-making, and action /
Douglas J. Simpson, College of Education, Texas Christian University (2013-P) and
Emeritus, Helen Devitt Jones Chair in Teacher Education (1213-P), College of Education
Texas Tech University, Donal M. Sacken, Texas Christian University.
DESCRIPTION: New York, NY : Cambridge University Press, 2021. |
Includes bibliographical references and index.
IDENTIFIERS: LCCN 2020019671 (print) | LCCN 2020019672 (ebook) | ISBN 9781108491471
(hardback) | ISBN 9781108798334 (paperback) | ISBN 9781108868853 (epub)
SUBJECTS: LCSH: Moral education. | Teachers–Professional ethics.
CLASSIFICATION: LCC LC268 .S56 2021 (print) | LCC LC268 (ebook) | DDC 370.11/4–dc23
LC record available at https://lccn.loc.gov/2020019671
LC ebook record available at https://lccn.loc.gov/2020019672

ISBN 978-1-108-49147-1 Hardback
ISBN 978-1-108-79833-4 Paperback

Contents

Figures

Foreword

Casuistry is probably not a word you employ in your everyday vocabulary. But I suspect that the practice of casuistry is nonetheless part of your ethical repertoire. What I mean to suggest is, you make use of actual cases of shared experience to generate ethical principles of care, justice, and responsibility *and* you apply already available ethical principles to new cases as they arise in an infinite and perhaps imperceptible cycle. This is a practice John Dewey learned from Aristotle and one that Doug Simpson and Mike Sacken learned from Dewey. It is a practice deeply woven into the fabric of *Ethical Dilemmas in Schools: A Collaborative Approach to Inquiry, Decision-Making, and Action.*

In fact, Simpson and Sacken have, in a sense, written two books here. The first is captured in the subtitle, "A Collaborative Approach to Inquiry, Decision-Making, and Action." This is a careful and complete academic exegesis of Dewey's ethical theory. Key concepts like habit, experience, value, inquiry, and responsibility are analyzed and represented in a pragmatist vein and then brought together in a vision of ethics that focuses on responsibility to one's self and one's community rather than focusing on liability and blame.

The second is a detailed rendering of the professional and ethical life of the hypothetical but clearly experience-grounded principal Maria De La Garza, her colleagues, her students, and other constituents. The essence of this effort is captured in the main title, "Ethical Dilemmas in Schools." What Simpson and Sacken call "in-text vignettes" are much more than that. They are seemingly discrete cases interspersed with relevant Deweyan theory but woven together to capture De La Garza's professional and ethical practice and the dilemmas that challenge her. Those cases prompt us to imagine ideals, values, and principles – but we are also prompted by the discussion of Dewey's ethical theory to analyze and weigh the range of possibilities for right action that each case presents.

By fully developing each of these two phases of their work and by weaving the two together, Simpson and Sacken are "doing Dewey"; that is, they are living and thinking the reality that theory and practice are dialectically connected. They are two sides of the same coin, two views of the same reality. Thus, the authors avoid both the criticism of casuistry as relativistic and narrowly focused and the criticism of theory as absolutist and abstract. They invite, no, they *compel* us to come to the dilemmas that arise in our lives as educators with a theorist's eye *and* a practitioner's heart. Principles matter, but so too do consequences. Justice is required, but so too is caring. The habits that constitute ethical virtues will carry us, but just so far. When the situation demands more than our virtues easily allow, we must shift into full-blown ethical inquiry, and in the process, reconstruct new, more adequate virtues, principles, and habits.

As Simpson and Sacken tell us,

> only by engaging in ethical investigation, reflection, and action as a complete person is one enabled to avoid what Dewey terms "the great moral tragedy" that separates "warm emotion and cool intelligence" (MW 14, 177). Emotions and intelligence, not scorching passions or arid reasoning, are especially useful in collaboratively discussing polarizing school issues. Appreciating the affectional ties of participants facing ethical quandaries may surface reasons for students' and colleagues' choices and actions.

This is Dewey's "pragmatic experimentalism," an approach that emphasizes deliberation about "viable choices and actions, a scientific approach to ethical inquiry and development, and an evaluation of the likely and actual consequences of moral decisions and actions" (LW 7; Martin 2002). The "good and bad, right and wrong, virtue and vice, and prudence and imprudence" (LW 5, 279–88) all come into play.

That this is a book for educators, present and future, is clear from the opening bell. The title proclaims it, the structure marks it, and the thread of cases highlight it. Simpson and Sacken show their cards clearly when they tell us that "addressing ethical concerns is an intrinsic, not intrusive, part of being a teacher and leader." They lead us from expectations to empathy, from principles through care and on to specific problematic situations, and finally, to the ethical educators who navigate those problems within the confines of good schools (and too often, not so good schools). In the process, we come to understand that educators' basic ethical responsibility requires the capacity to recognize when an issue is ethical and to examine such problematic situations thoroughly – always

x

Foreword

doing so in the face of doubt, conflict, disequilibrium, and complexity. Rushing to judgment is unethical; it leads to misdiagnosed situations and unwarranted conclusions and outcomes. Instead,

> inquiry is [to be] exacted: observation of the detailed makeup of the situation; analysis, into its diverse factors; clarification of what is obscure; discounting of the more insistent and vivid traits; tracing the consequences of the various modes of action that suggest themselves; regarding the decision reached as hypothetical and tentative until the anticipated or supposed consequences which led to its adoption have been squared with actual consequences. (MW 12, 173)

This is intellectually difficult and demanding. It calls on and calls out our inquisitiveness, our ethical imagination, and our creative deliberation. It requires that we confront what Dewey calls "the prevalence of prejudice" (LW 5, 397).

It is also emotionally difficult and demanding. Simpson and Sacken clearly convey what interpreters of Dewey sometimes miss: thinking well is as much an affective as a cognitive endeavor. As they remind us: "To ignore the emotional aspect of ethical inquirers and participants, for Dewey, was to disregard a vital part of the human personality and ethical inquiry. In the end, such neglect is similar to disregarding acts or outcomes: unthinkable." Empathy and sympathy are not merely prosocial feelings; they are the affective markers of our capacity to rightly understand students' and colleagues' emotions, thoughts, values, and challenges. They provide a window into personal and cultural narratives.

A hidden strength of the Simpson and Sacken collaboration is the book's direct engagement with matters of ethical absolutism and ethical relativism. In my experience, this is the issue that divides well-intentioned persons of all cultural and political stripes. Some of us want, need, and are committed to answers that are absolute and uncompromising; others of us tolerate, welcome, even wallow in ethical ambiguity. Some of us believe that there is no ethics if there are no inviolable rules; others of us are painfully aware of the subtle difference that context and conditions make even in similar situations and wonder if rules are not made to be broken. It is hard to make sense of the reality that while having rules is clearly better than not having any, sometimes following the rules does substantial harm.

Simpson and Sacken do not back away from this conundrum. They speak the pragmatist "truth": principles are not rules. The fact that particular rules are not inviolable does *not* mean anything goes. They quote Dewey:

Rules are practical; they are habitual ways of doing things. But principles are intellectual; they are the final methods used in judging suggested courses of action. . . . [T]he object of moral principles is to supply standpoints and methods which will enable the individual to make for [her]himself an analysis of the elements of good and evil in the particular situation in which [s]he finds [her]himself. (LW 7, 280)

There is no substitute for ethical judgment. Unlike rules which are followed or applied – often unthinkingly – principles are a powerful tool for judgment in problematic situations. We use them to help us "think about attitudes, acts, and consequences." But no act can be judged based on principles alone. We need situational variables, ethical continuities, and prospective consequences to flesh out our judgments. Moreover, principles are not "given." They are "constructed, discovered, justified, and used when thinking and deciding."

I bring this up at this juncture because some argue that casuistry – using cases not just to illustrate or apply rules but also to generate principles as new habits of thought, feeling, and behavior – is specious and unhelpful. Their position is that relying on cases opens you up to the dangers of relativism. However, this need not be the case, as Albert Jonsen and Stephen Toulmin demonstrated in their 1988 book *The Abuse of Casuistry: A History of Moral Reasoning*. Using cases to develop and ground principles is the one approach that can dissolve what appears to be a contradiction between moral absolutism and moral relativism.

Deweyan pragmatism acknowledges that "we are justified in using" repeatedly verified truth claims "as if they were absolutely true" but cautions that each as if absolute claim is a provisional claim "subject to being corrected by future consequences" and new research (LW 2, 12). There *are* "relational universals" (that is, claims that everybody – across cultures and political chasms – takes for granted). There are "practical certainties" (that is, claims of all kinds that function as useful "rules to live by."). They work to get us through the day. They should not be lightly discarded. At the same time, as we have known since Hume first posited the problem of induction, they are likely to be true, but never certain – and each could be undercut with the next wave of experience.

Dewey's willingness to take cases seriously – and to resolve those cases by "working collaboratively, thinking empathetically, deciding deliberatively, and acting reflectively" – does not lead to a simplistic relativistic ethic. It leads to an ethic of constancy *and* flexibility. It leads to the possibility of living as an authentic self in community.

In the face of conflicting desires, obligations, and virtues, we are called by Dewey to *investigate* first and foremost. That investigation is an embodied experience, thought, felt, and enacted. The challenge is to take on as a new habit of ethical reasoning "a rhythm of seeking and finding, of reaching out for a tenable conclusion, and coming to what is at least a tentative one" (LW 10, 183). In the light of each tentative, tenable conclusion, we act – and test our conclusions over and over and over again, reframing new principles, new virtues, new habits in what will always be a multigenerational, multi-entity, and multinational endeavor (Garrison, Neubert, and Reich 2012, 103).

Like Maria De La Garza, each of us is regularly asked to take stock of "the ethical forum" of our own minds. We are required to face the forces that influence us and to recognize and acknowledge how those forces limit the ethical possibilities of another. We are prompted to make choices, and "the cumulative force of [serious and] trivial choices" determines who each of us is and who we are all together becoming.

For those of us who call ourselves educators, we ask only this: that our understandings, affections, and choices are in the process of being transformed into "habits of refined moral sensitivity, discernment, and perception – habits analogous to those of an artist" (Fesmire 1995, 592). If these habits take hold, then, in Dewey's words,

> the school becomes ... a form of social life, a miniature community and one in close interaction with modes of associated experience beyond school walls. All education which develops power to share effectively in social life is moral. It forms a character which not only deems the particular deed socially necessary but one which is interested in that continuous readjustment which is essential to growth. Interest in learning from all contacts of life is the essential moral interest. (MW 9, 370)

We can all be indebted to Doug Simpson and Mike Sacken for reminding us of this principle so central to the pursuit of our work as educators.

Barbara S. Stengel
Professor Emerita
George Peabody College
Vanderbilt University

Preface

Democracy is belief in the ability of human experience to generate
the aims and methods by which further experience will grow in
ordered richness. Every other form of moral and social faith rests
upon the idea that experience must be subjected at some point or
other to some form of external control; to some "authority" alleged to
exist outside the processes of experience. Democracy is the faith that
the process of experience is more important than any special result
attained, so that special results achieved are of ultimate value only as
they are used to enrich and order the ongoing process. Since the
process of experience is capable of being educative, faith in democracy is all one with faith in experience and education.
—John Dewey, "Creative Democracy – The Task Before Us" (LW 14, 229)

In order to clarify the focus of *Ethical Dilemmas in Schools*:
A Collaborative Approach to Inquiry, Decision-Making, and Action, it is
useful to explain that it is, foremost, an introduction to democratic ethical
inquiry and reflection and is designed for professors in educator preparation programs and, thereby, for their students, especially K–12 administrators, teachers, and related staff. But policymakers, parents, and
guardians should find the work beneficial too. In fact, the work may be
more beneficial than one initially assumes. While our focus is on John
Dewey's understanding of ethics and his approach to addressing ethical
dilemmas and issues, we suggest readings that enrich, question, and
diverge from his orientation. We raise questions and engage other ethical
theories, especially, but not exclusively, those that are often familiar to
professors and educators, e.g., deontology, care ethic, consequentialism,
and virtue theory. We did this because Dewey himself examined features
of many theories and culled from them ideas that he found insightful and
warranted. But he went further too, assessing and reconstructing aspects of
other theories to incorporate into his own philosophy. His views, therefore, represent at least a partial appreciation and critique of a variety of

ethical theories. Likewise, his ideas are sometimes precursors to aspects of other ethical theories, especially those that have emerged more recently, e.g., contemporary care, feminist, and, if one focuses on social justice, critical theories. Understanding well the distinctiveness of Dewey's ethical theory and its implications for educational leaders, whether classroom teachers or school administrators, then, means understanding certain features of the theories he examined and anticipated. Interestingly, Dewey (LW 7, 337–9) states that the teacher is an "intellectual leader" of classrooms and students. By virtue of her or his professional and experiential knowledge, she or he should be welcomed into nearly any ethical discussion of educational issues.

A general goal, then, is to present Dewey's ideas selectively, concisely, and, on occasion, comparatively without offering either a complete historical contextualization or a sustained evaluation of them. Happily, implicit critique of his views from different viewpoints is found herein and explicit criticism is found elsewhere in a plethora of works. In addition, systematic contextualizations of his ethical views are provided by many scholars, including Robert B. Westbrook's *John Dewey and American Democracy* (1991) and Gregory F. Pappas's *John Dewey's Ethics: Democracy as Experience* (2008). In short, then, we introduce aspects of Dewey's ethical views, illustrate them, and encourage readers to discuss and test his ideas by analyzing and applying them to actual and imagined professional ethical challenges. Our hope is that many education preparation scholars, moral educators, and educational researchers will also examine Dewey's ideas so that their specific interests are informed by his thought. In turn, their evaluation of Dewey's ethical thinking – scientifically, experientially, and philosophically – can strengthen the field of ethics and education and, thereby, the areas of moral development and education. In addition, researchers can test Dewey's hypotheses in order to clarify which aspects of his thinking can be confirmed, which ones need reconsideration, and which merit rejection.

A second clarification concerns the structure of *Ethical Dilemmas in Schools*. We use several methods to advance an understanding of the chapters' themes and, thereby, ethical reflection and action. Securing a finer grasp of a Deweyan-informed ethic involves engaging in ethical deliberations and problem-solving, analyses that deal with the problems of societies, schools, educators, and students. The methods employed in each chapter include: (a) an epigraph to introduce chapter topics; (b) in-text vignettes to demonstrate the relevance of Dewey's ideas; (c) "Stop and Think" pauses to stimulate thinking and, if desired, discussions; (d) graphic illustrations to enhance understanding of strategic concepts; and (e) a set of end-of-chapter materials (discussion questions, related readings, and case studies) to foster broader thinking.

The epigraphs offer a series of snapshots that reveal several key features of Dewey's ethical themes and deliberations. Building on the epigraphs and related ideas, the in-text case vignettes focus largely on Maria De La Garza's ethical challenges. Maria, a fictional character, is the principal of the Academy for Civic Responsibility, where our illustrations and vignettes are situated. Collectively, these vignettes constitute Maria's story. The illustrations illuminate Dewey's ideas as they are employed to clarify ethically challenging issues, which are found in many schools and communities. Maria's story, with its assorted permutations, is an implicit, oblique, and thin excursion into narrative ethics. The Stop and Think pauses are designed to slow one's reading of the material and to guide one's thinking about and discussions of pertinent issues. These pauses, in a sense, broadcast Dewey's call for reflective breaks when a person is facing ethical quandaries. In *How We Think*, Dewey claims that:

> The working over of a vague and more or less casual idea into coherent and definite form is impossible without a pause, without freedom from distraction. We say, "Stop and think"; well, all reflection involves, at some point, stopping external observations and reactions so that an idea may mature. Meditation, withdrawal or abstraction from clamorous assailants of the senses and from demands for overt action, is as necessary at the reasoning stage as are observation and experiment at other periods. The metaphors of digestion and assimilation, which so readily occur to mind in connection with rational elaboration, are highly instructive. *A silent, uninterrupted working-over of considerations by comparing and weighing alternative suggestions is indispensable for the development of coherent and compact conclusions.* Reasoning is no more akin to disputing or arguing or to the abrupt seizing and dropping of suggestions than digestion is to a noisy champing of the jaws. (LW 8, 335–6; emphasis added)

Stop and Think pauses, then, are not primarily intended to encourage dialogues. Dewey's intent is to cultivate times of reflection, digestion, and assimilation. He suggests at least an intellectual retreat to think about some ethical challenges. On the other hand, when a Stop and Think pause is used to stimulate class discussions, Dewey's claim about conflict is particularly relevant: "Conflict" – disagreement in the language of some – regarding ideas and opinions, especially if not emotionally dominated, "is the gadfly of thought" (MW 14, 207). In our case, then, his reflective device is used as a pedagogical device and is designed to foster private and public understanding, reflection, and inquiry into everyday school and life affairs.

A third point we wish to note is that the end-of-chapter materials employ Dewey's and others' ideas as tools to analyze a case study. Additionally, we recommend his and others' writings for a broader and deeper look into ethical issues and paradigms. The related readings include pertinent material from Dewey's and other ethicists' writings that inform or challenge an emphasis of the chapter, sometimes giving alternative perspectives. The end-of-chapter cases, occasionally created by blending fragments of actual experiences with imaginary ones, are anonymized and designed to be provocative but not necessarily solvable problems. Dewey, in fact, believes that some problems cannot be solved because they and their situations are too complex and resources are too few. Even so, they need to be addressed and ameliorated in ways that are ethically feasible and warranted. Leaving complicated situations simply as they are encountered runs counter to the desire to at least better life for everyone. Besides, how can problems be deemed insolvable if they are not seriously examined and addressed through the lenses of different paradigms and experiments?

We encourage readers to anonymize and fictionalize their own experiences for ethical analysis. In this way, employing Dewey's analytical method of problem-solving can begin immediately. One's immersion in a personal past, present, or prospective problematic situation helps meet Dewey's ideal of engaging the whole person in problem-solving. For, only by engaging in ethical investigation, reflection, and action as a complete person is one enabled to avoid what Dewey terms "the great moral tragedy" that separates "warm emotion and cool intelligence" (MW 14, 177). Emotions and intelligence, not scorching passions or sterile reasoning, are especially useful in collaboratively discussing polarizing school issues. Appreciating the affectional ties of participants facing ethical quandaries may surface reasons for students' and colleagues' choices and actions.

A singularly important feature of the volume requires attention; for, we have done more than provide a series of ethical issues and dilemmas in the book. We provide a narrative for ethical analyses; our scenarios, examples, and cases are situated in a particular school, with details and circumstances that remain relevant throughout the volume. Thus, the principal, Maria De La Garza, is, first, an observer of and, now and then, a participant in, problematic situations, analyzing and responding to events in the Academy. But, for some, she may also be seen as a creator of problems. The problems situated in the Academy occurred during her twelve-year principalship, although their presentation herein may leave the impression of being clustered in a shorter period. The ethical scenarios are not necessarily in chronological order. The Academy is a K–12 school of choice that draws its population from the Harbor School District. The Academy is a theme-based school: Academy for Civic Responsibility. The specialized focus of the curriculum is geared to nurture habits of ethical conduct and decision-making by students.

Among the Academy's distinctive curricular and pedagogical features are community service-based experiences, adult mentors, inter-age student collaboration in project-based learning, democratic decision-making experiences, social justice engagements, and a variety of intergenerational experiential learning activities across the entire curriculum. The social studies, history, and literature courses draw upon the realities of how many nations have been populated by waves of immigrants and repopulated by episodic migrations (MW 13, 295–305). To enhance these studies, the Academy, with parental alternatives, has third-grade DNA analyses to inform students of their ancestry.

The school is organized into ten vertically arranged or all-grade houses of equal size, each with vertical faculty. Co-curricular activities within the Academy are often based on the house as the unit of membership for teams or other representative activities apart from school- or district-wide activities, which are more typically based on age or other characteristics. Likewise, houses are intended to be an essential base for welcoming newcomers, nurturing community, facilitating friendships, and providing microgovernance and leadership experiences. Each house participates in academy-wide governance experiences too.

Students are drawn from applicants across the district and the demographics of the Academy are intended to more or less mirror those of the district as a whole. The Academy is one of two theme-based schools in the district, and the newest one to open. A majority of the district's secondary students now attend specialty middle and high schools, but the only other K–12 school is the Fine Arts Academy. Both schools are experimental and evaluated accordingly. The Academy for Civic Responsibility is capped at a total of 800 students, which is near the upper limit of small schools that are sometimes shown to be effective academically with an inclusive student population (Lee and Smith 1997). The school is centrally located in a refurbished high school near the city's center. The city's population is slightly over 100,000; the district's student population is around 12,500.

When the school was organized, its faculty and staff positions were opened to all eligible district employees and then positions were filled by the newly appointed school administrative staff. After selecting 30 percent of the teaching staff, three teachers were added to the selection committee. The district sought to have a demographically diverse staff to fit the expected student body and families that joined the school. Like the district itself, the school's staff is disproportionately white and female but is diverse, particularly in the elementary and middle grades. And because this school was viewed by many faculty and staff as a new and attractive opportunity, the faculty and staff were skewed toward more experience than averages across the district. There is age diversity as well, with the elementary and middle school faculty younger and less experienced on average than the high school. In view of the Academy's organization, problematic ethical situations arise in classes, within houses, and across the entire school, not to mention before and after school and in the hallways, restrooms, cafeteria, and gymnasium.

When the school was planned, the Design Committee chose the idea of dividing the students and faculty into a set of houses. Given the impact of Hogwarts on the world at that time, the idea was pervasive and persuasive. Indeed, the first complex decision was what to name the houses once some members of the committee understood that the names of Hogwarts' houses belonged to J. K. Rowling and could not be appropriated. The alternative of using names of the country's early explorers and founders was unappealing due to the prospect of having nearly all houses named after white males. The eventual consensus was naming the houses after wild animals; to wit, houses were named after various breeds of big wild cats (in the Felidae family). In time, some lower grades of Academy houses pushed to have small- to medium-sized wild cats (in the Felinae subfamily) approved as names or co-names. In fact, it was the pre-eleven-year-old students in the Lions House that argued successfully that their house would better represent their interests if it were named the Black Footed Cats & Lions House, especially since all lion symbols to date had been roaring males. The group's first request for the name Rag Doll Cats and Lions House was denied because the Rag Doll is a domestic cat. By accident, then, the wild cats of the world instantly became collateral curriculum, leading to a better understanding of their animal and human neighbors and their ecologies.

The houses were populated vertically, with members from every level assigned. Once a child enters the school, they are assigned to one of the houses and, apart from unexpected situations, remains in that house for their entire time at the Academy. The vertical configuration ensures younger students have mentors and role models to help socialize them and allows students of all ages to participate in various civic programs and volunteer work. Also, within each house, students play a meaningful role in policy formation and governance with leadership operating in a horizontal manner for some issues and a vertical manner for others. The same process extrapolates out from the houses to an academy-wide governance process. Participation in decision-making is universal, albeit shaped by developmentally appropriate roles that coordinate with curriculum and co-curricular experiences.

Consistent with Dewey's thinking (EW 5, 84–95), the Academy does not prepare students for predictable, adult worlds. Instead, studies are essential parts of students' daily lives and their experiences and are designed to enhance student understanding of and participation in the life and dynamic work of society. Being engaged imaginatively and fruitfully in the present world is considered the best preparation for any future world. Hence, the Academy is forward-looking in its curricula. Obviously, a central component of student development is framed in both personal and social ethical growth. But this is readily pursued because Dewey (LW 2, 282–7) conceives of social and ethical development being practically identical.

The concerns of the Academy for Civic Responsibility are streamed throughout Chapters 1–7. Chapter 1, "What Can Educators Expect from Ethics?" provides a brief examination of some conflicting views of what many existing and aspiring educators may expect from a study of ethics as well as hints of how Dewey does or does not meet their expectancies. Dewey's thinking is injected into the expected discussion, sometimes with a dialogical flavor. In particular, the importance of Dewey's emphases on reflective experience, inquiry or investigation, the nature of problematic situations, the rhythm of seeking and finding pertinent data and arguments, and the development of tenable and tentative conclusions are introduced.

Chapters 2–7 provide more details about Dewey's thinking, especially how his emphases on the roles of sympathy and empathy (Chapter 2), the nature of ethical principles (Chapter 3), the principle of regard for people (Chapter 4), the nature of problematic situations (Chapter 5), the qualities of ethical educators (Chapter 6), and the characteristics of good schools (Chapter 7) fit together to help inform board members, superintendents, central office personnel, principals, teachers, support personnel, and parents about how to envision and make ethical decisions. Therefore, everyone needs to be involved when decisions are made about building ethical schools and districts and addressing ethical controversies. But more is embedded in these chapters: We explore Dewey's thoughts about the importance of developing a comprehensive picture of a good, meaningful, satisfying, or flourishing life. We discuss this sphere of his thought because he argues that the ethical person is a stronger, more engaged, reflective, happy, and caring person than she or he would be otherwise if he or she unifies the multiple dimensions of one's self and life, including the aesthetic, social, emotional, vocational, scientific, natural, and spiritual. But as a social philosopher and public intellectual, Dewey was also interested in everyday life and ordinary people. Thus, he discusses how a good society is formed through ongoing contributions by people from all walks of life. Conversely, he rejects the idea of intimidating students, educators, and parents into ethical conformity.

The Epilogue is both a threadlike summary of the previous emphases of the chapters and a new infusion of Dewey's thoughts. In keeping with Dewey's philosophy, the conclusions he reaches are hypotheses that are subject to further research, experience, and deliberation.

Dewey (LW 7, xxxv) considers his ethical theory to be dynamic and subject to change, for it is tied to "the growth of knowledge." Thus, he (xxxv) encourages warranted revisions and improvements "as knowledge grows." His growth-of-knowledge orientation is an explicit feature of his thought.

Acknowledgments

As researchers understand well, they are deeply indebted to numerous people. Those who study John Dewey often thank Southern Illinois University Carbondale, its Special Collections Research Center of the Morris Library, the University Press, and the Center for Dewey Studies too. In particular, we thank the SIU Press for permission to quote from *The Collected Works of John Dewey* and *Unmodern Philosophy and Modern Philosophy*. Our indebtedness to the late Jo Ann Boydston for her masterful editorial work on the critical edition of *The Collected Works of John Dewey, 1882–1953* and to Larry A. Hickman for his superb editorial leadership on the electronic edition (2008) is also enormous – difficult to overstate. The recent work of Phillip Deen (2012) in identifying, editing, and securing the publication of Dewey's long-misplaced manuscript *Unmodern Philosophy and Modern Philosophy* is also appreciated. Moreover, without permission to quote frequently from Dewey's works, we would have been less able to stimulate readers with his own words and, thereby, entice them to read further, especially in his and Tufts' *Ethics* (1932 edition), and his *Democracy and Education* (1916), *Reconstruction in Philosophy and Essays* (1920), *Human Nature and Conduct* (1922), "Qualitative Thought" (1930), "Three Independent Factors in Morals" (1930), and *Art as Experience* (1934).

We also acknowledge our depending on research that was originally published elsewhere: (1) "The Sympathetic-Empathetic Teacher: A Deweyan Analysis" (2014) in the *Journal of Philosophy & History of Education*; (2) "The Ethical Principle of Regard for People: Using Dewey's Ideas in Schools" (2015) in the *International Journal of Progressive Education*; and (3) "Ethical Principles and School Challenges: A Deweyan Analysis" (2016) in *Education and Culture*. The theoretical elements of these articles inform sections of this volume, particularly Chapters 2–4. Our thanks are extended to the editors and publishers of these works for granting permission to draw from them.

We are deeply indebted to Cecilia Silva in ways that would be stunning if we did not know her well as a colleague and friend. She first surprised us when she volunteered to read an early draft of the manuscript and to provide extensive feedback. She amazed us when she later offered to read and discuss the manuscript and to assist with concluding details. Our debt to her is beyond expression.

Importantly, we want to thank the students, colleagues, editors, and reviewers who provided feedback on earlier discussions, presentations, and manuscripts that deal with Dewey's ethical theorizing. Like current reviewers and editors, they appraised aspects of our work and helped us clarify Dewey's views. Simply expressing thanks to these people is manifestly inadequate, but not recognizing their generous influence seems incalculably worse. In addition, we cannot fail to thank a select group of people who read portions of earlier manuscripts that laid a foundation for this book. That is, we are immeasurably indebted to Eric Bredo, Nance Cunningham, Joe DeVitis, Jim Garrison, M. Francyne Huckaby, Michael J. B. Jackson, Bruce Maxwell, Brandy Quinn, David Snelgrove, and our anonymous reviewers for their helpful comments as this work evolved. Their suggestions significantly informed the work, enabling us to provide greater depth, balance, and relevance. Tammy Riemenschneider deserves a separate word of thanks for her contributions, including earlier feedback on two related publications, as well as for making suggestions for the incipient volume. Similarly, we thank Paige Tooley for her early editorial feedback and Jenny Moore for her graphic design suggestions.

Appreciation is extended to John P. Portelli, University of Toronto, for inviting the first author to serve as an external member of a dissertation committee on Charles Taylor's educational theory and to discuss the nascent scope of this project with a cadre of faculty and graduate students. The timing of the visit and discussions crucially shaped the direction of the project. In addition, William Hare and Cornell Thomas each devoted considerable time to examining in depth separate chapters of the book. We greatly appreciate Peggie Price's sharing of her time and research expertise with us. Molly Spain expertly oversaw the final editing and preparation of the manuscript before we forwarded it to our Cambridge University Press editors. Molly is a master editor and a major reason we completed the work. Finally, we wish to express our gratitude to Niranjana Harikrishnan, Penny Harper, Jessica Norman, David Repetto, and Emily Watton, who were enormously supportive of the work. Of course, we alone are responsible for the contents and infelicitous remarks in the work. Finally, we happily thank Barbara Stengel for contributing the Foreword to the book.

Her generous reading of the work often says more elegantly what we ourselves attempted to convey.

In closing, we want to express our appreciation to four extraordinary supporters. First, our indebtedness to Mary Patton, former dean of the College of Education, Texas Christian University, for her support is gladly acknowledged. Her unwavering encouragement of this project has been exceptional. Likewise, we appreciate the consistent encouragement of Nowell Donovan, former provost of Texas Christian University, who enabled us to complete the work. Judy and Nancy also have our sincere appreciation and unending admiration for their support, personally and professionally. We treasure their tolerance of our consumption of temporal and psychic resources.

CHAPTER I

What Can Educators Expect from Ethics?

In reflective experience as such, in investigation called forth by problematic situations, there is a rhythm of seeking and finding, of reaching out for a tenable conclusion and coming to what is at least a tentative one.

—John Dewey,[1] *Art as Experience* (LW 10, 183)

Introduction

Many future and current educators – teachers, leaders, counselors, and allied professionals – probably have more than a single expectation of the contributions of ethics to their educational theory and practice.[2] Unsurprisingly, they have insights and cautions to offer about the field, especially in diverse schools and societies (Hansen 1988). The cautions are offered, in part, because opinions and expectations are so numerous and diverse that they frequently collide. Moreover, ethical claims and concerns can sometimes be off-putting because they are confusing now and again as certain ethical ideas are encountered (e.g., subjectivism, relativism, emotivism, pluralism, particularism). These strands of thought, however, are readily distinguishable (Pappas 2008; Ruitenberg 2007). Beyond wanting clarity and offering caution, then, many educators think that a study of ethics should offer ways of determining the differences between right and wrong and wise and unwise choices and actions as they interact with students, colleagues, and others. In short, they think ethics ought to offer clear paths to a fair, responsible, and caring way to teach and lead. Equally, they may think of

---

[1] John Dewey and James Hayden Tufts coauthored *Ethics*, but each focused on a select set of chapters although they jointly wrote the 1908 and 1932 edition prefaces and 1932 Introduction. Dewey is the primary author of chapters 10–17. When referencing *Ethics*, we refer only to Dewey's primary chapters. Hence, our citations from the volume list Dewey only.

[2] Readers will note that we blend expectations for both ethics and ethical theory. While these topics can be distinguished, this work is based on the premise that ethics encompasses ethical theory.

ethics as a set of intellectual tools that enable them to address and contribute to the resolution of school moral quandaries so that they can quickly refocus on their teaching and leading, not realizing, perhaps, that addressing ethical concerns is an intrinsic, not intrusive, part of being a teacher and leader (Fenstermacher 2013; Goodlad, Soder, and Sirotnik 1990). Relatedly, some people wish to learn more about ethics so that their ethical reasoning and choices become more consistent and integrated with their religious ideals and professional codes of ethics. Others, both religious and nonreligious educators, may expect ethics to affirm and help them refine a swath of ethical givens, if not absolutes, that run through their transcendental thinking. Obviously, the above-mentioned expectations may commingle in complex and even contradictory ways.

Expectations and Dewey

Still, other aspiring and practicing educators may indicate that they expect little, if anything, worthwhile from a study of ethics. Their expectations may be shaped by historical, social, economic, political, and personal experiences and events that cause them to doubt the usefulness of ethics as a field of inquiry. Among these educators are those who think ethical claims are either an entirely personal matter or that they stem exclusively from one's cultural or religious beliefs. The choice, as they see it, is one of deciding which, if any, ethical values they prefer to observe or practice: their cultural ethic, religious ethic, or, perhaps, their personally designed eclectic ethic. Others (e.g., Gorecki 2017; Harris 2010; Stengel and Tom 1995), however, want to go beyond an inherited ethic to add an epistemic or knowledge concern: What are the intellectual grounds or warrant of ethical claims? That is, many proponents of diverse positions add to the what-to-expect-from-ethics discussion that ethical claims – whether cultural, religious, rational, scientific, or otherwise – need more than personal affinities to justify an acceptance and practice of them. They may argue too that a form of political or democratic legitimacy or social tolerance needs to be examined (LW 15, 170–83; Fine 1993; Heft 1999).

But those who want to examine the epistemic warrant or credibility for ethical assertions often differ on whether and to what degree there is a knowledge base for making ethical decisions. Some argue there are logical, scientific, religious, historical, practical, and experiential grounds for making many ethical decisions. Yet, others argue that there is little, if any, epistemic warrant or authority for ethical decision-making. Plus, they may add that a number of ethical claims have become tools for familial, cultural, religious, political, and economic coercion and oppression (MW 14, 208). They think people with much to gain or lose – an autocratic family, a wealthy social stratum, a political elite, a religious oligarchy, a privileged profession – use ethical frameworks as tools to justify their manipulation, coercion, miseducation, and domination of others; they rely on undemocratic power rather than open deliberations, public data, and noncoercive persuasion to foster beliefs and practices. Moreover, whatever the practical or philosophical roots of ethical positions, those who are influential and powerful often reinterpret beliefs to their advantage, whether that entails defending the status quo or changing practices to advance their interests. Hence, many educators, like noneducators, think that ethics is often an instrument that is employed by the influential and powerful to retain and extend their cultural, educational, economic, religious, and professional advantages over others. In short, ethics has been corrupted, frequently, perhaps incorrigibly, in the interest of the powerful (Apple 1982, 2002; Freire 1973; Taylor 1996). Inside this evaluation of ethics may be an unarticulated assumption that there are both defensible and indefensible forms and uses of ethics.

Are there other reasons for studying ethics? Perhaps there are others who wish to understand how advantaged groups and individuals use ethics as a tool for control and dominance. These inquirers, rather than rejecting a study of ethics because of its frequent association with exploitative power, prefer to understand how people in power positions may employ ethical theories and arguments to give their personal or group agendas an advantage. Studying ethics from this angle, therefore, may provide opportunities for those interested in the economically and politically underprivileged to develop counterarguments to the claims of the overprivileged. On this point, Dewey (MW 14, 208) implies that multiple theories need to be studied because there is no one ethical position of those who seek "a monopoly of moral ideals, to carry on [their] struggle for class-power."

Beyond the aforementioned diverse expectations for studying ethics are many others, including Dewey's approach and expectations.[3] He, like

---

[3] While Dewey is known for being interested in moral struggles that result from "sincere doubts" and "moral perplexities" that are "between values each of which is an undoubted good in its place" (LW 7, 164–5), our interests as educators lead us to approach ethical inquiry more inclusively. That is, we employ Dewey's method to address both ethical dilemmas that involve undoubted goods as well as ethical conflicts that seem, at least to some, to be between questionable goods and possible evils for at least two reasons. First, many, using multiple ethical lenses, begin analyses of reported ethically problematic situations without knowing whether anyone has acted ethically or unethically. They simply see problems and seek to address them. As they enter the inquiry process, it seems

ethicists with multiple backgrounds, is familiar with the contributions, limitations, and distortions of ethical theories, not just the strengths and limitations of his own orientation. Thus, he references, directly or obliquely, other theories (e.g., deontological, virtue, consequentialist, utilitarian, Marxian, Islamic, Jewish, Christian, Buddhist, Hindu, Confucian, and Taoist). He anticipates elements of other theories too, e.g., critical, feminist, and care approaches. Incorporated into his philosophizing are references to many of the aforementioned expectations people have for studying – or not – ethics. Regularly he enhances his own ethical theory by recasting the strengths of others' theories, but he appraises these theories, seeking to select and employ warranted ideas.

Fortunately, there are critics (Gouinlock 1993; Horrigan 2015; Margolis 1986; Miller, Fins, and Bacchetta 1996) who respond to Dewey by evaluating his strengths and limitations. Collaborative evaluation of one another's ethical theories and arguments, therefore, is an intrinsic part of thinking ethically. As Peters (1966, 8) somewhat humorously states, "Philosophy [and ethics] is essentially a co-operative enterprise. Advances are made when two or three are gathered together who speak more or less the same language and can frequently for the purpose of hitting each other politely on the head." Dewey (LW 1, 298) clarifies that collaborative ethical evaluation or "criticism of criticism" is rooted in ordinary experience and has "its distinctive position among various modes of criticism in its generality" (298). Hence, ethics as "criticism of criticism" constitutes "discriminating judgment, careful appraisal" of any matter that involves goods, virtues, and obligations (298).

Dewey (1859–1952), of course, is a pragmatist or experimentalist, who profits, at least in part, from understanding many of the aforementioned ethical ideas and theories that arose before, during, and near the end of his life. He had the opportunity to construct, evaluate, and reconstruct his own thinking from almost the time of the US Civil War (1861–5) into immense cultural, political, demographic, epistemic, technological, and scientific change through both World War II (1939–45) and the Chinese Revolution (1949). He was noticeably influenced by numerous intellectuals, including thinkers like Plato, Aristotle, Hegel, Kant, Darwin, and James. His first wife, Alice Chipman, friend Jane Addams, and numerous

---

worthwhile for them to learn to employ Dewey's method of inquiry, even when they disagree with aspects of his thought. Second, as people enter the inquiry process, they often learn that, at least on many occasions, an ethical conflict is indeed between two undoubted goods, e.g., providing more resources to better serve students on the autism spectrum or providing more resources to better serve students with English as a second language needs.

colleagues and students at the universities of Michigan, Minnesota, Chicago, and Columbia likewise deeply influenced his ideas (Martin 2002; Menand 2002; Ryan 1995). As an international figure, he was influenced by audiences and acquaintances who heard his lectures, raised questions, and answered his queries in China, Japan, Mexico, Canada, South Africa, Turkey, and Europe (Martin 2002). His ideas, however, do not constitute a nomadic ethical eclecticism but a pragmatic experimentalism that emphasizes a deliberation of viable choices and actions, a scientific approach to ethical inquiry and development, and an evaluation of the likely and actual consequences of moral decisions and actions (LW 7; Martin 2002). But his views are also greatly informed by the ordinary people who live in multiple forms of community as they communicate with one another and develop commonalities and differences (MW 9, 11, 17).

Dewey, along with William James (1842–1910) and Charles Peirce (1839–1914), produced a largely original philosophy and ethics that continue to inform philosophical and ethical deliberations, research, and evaluation worldwide (Martin 2002). His final articulation of ethics, while only a facet of his immense body of writings, is worth examining for several reasons. For K–12 educators, it is particularly relevant because he maintained a career-long interest in ideas, which continue to influence schools and students, e.g., (a) educational philosophy and practice; (b) democratic principles and values; (c) children, pedagogy, and learning; (d) curricular development and educational outcomes; (e) scientific inquiry and school assessment; and (f) social and school change and continuity. While many of his detractors and proponents have made claims about his ideas that range from the fanatical to the fantastical, there are also many carefully reasoned evaluations of his thought.

We explicate and employ Dewey's ideas in order to provide a way of addressing educators' ethical quandaries and dilemmas suitably for contemporary times (Pring [2007] 2017). His voice can help provide insights into a public ethic that welcomes the full public, including the Other (Abowitz and Stitzlein 2018; Stengel 2009), to share ideas and arguments. Of course, attention needs to be directed toward public problems and challenges using inquiry, laws, data, and deliberation rather than privileging certain opinions. But listening to others to understand their interests and to expand one's own is considered an essential ethical duty and virtue (Rice and Burbules 2010). Moreover, policies and expectations regarding ethical development and practice by public school educators and students in liberal democracies are regularly based on publicly accessible reasons and grounds. Everyone, including those of different faiths (Kunzman 2006), should be welcome to participate in the development of policy proposals, explain why a proposal is or is not deemed acceptable, and argue why their identities, if they are not, should be respected. What is more, any critic of public school policy or practice, in whole or in part, should be free to express their criticism with the aim of reconstructing or replacing it, whenever merited, with a more clearly stated, valuable public ethical practice that attracts the support of diverse citizens.

We start our discussion of the above epigraph and this chapter to clarify the emphasis Dewey places on (a) reflective experience, (b) investigation, (c) problematic situations, (d) the rhythm of seeking and finding pertinent data and relevant arguments, and (e) tenable and tentative conclusions. These ideas represent a partial answer to the question, What can educators expect from Dewey's ethical theory? and provide a skeletal overview of certain aspects of his broad ethical theory. This glance at Dewey's ethics focuses on Problematic Situations and Reflective Experience and, later, on Aesthetic Experience and Investigative Conclusions.

Problematic Situations and Reflective Experience

What can educators learn by examining Dewey's ethical views? While his answer to this question is partially, if obliquely, implied earlier and in the epigraph, further clarification is merited. For explanatory purposes, the epigraphic order of concepts is modified below. Of course, the discussed strategic concepts remain ultimately connected; they overlap and, sometimes, fuse but can also be distinguished. The epigraph opens by giving attention to problematic situations and reflective experiences.

Problematic Situations

For Dewey, ethical issues and dilemmas arise in everyday school experiences and situations that are characterized by specific practical, local problems yet not isolated from broader life settings. He labels these typical encounters and circumstances, variously, as contexts, environments, and situations. Importantly, he argues that no problematic situation is ever an exact replication of another but that ethical precedents and historical continuities are frequently informative when one encounters moral challenges in new surroundings (LW 7, 329–30; Garrison, Neubert, and Reich 2012, 58–64). Each situation, then, is unique but not an isolated or disconnected experience. Every situation is embedded in a context that includes more than the obvious concerns of interacting participants. Participants – students, educators, and parents – are unique and remain unique, because they are in a never-ending process of development, whether positive, negative, or both. Contexts include elements of social, material, and emotional cultures; they contain rudiments of prior and continuing emotions, beliefs, values, and conduct; they promote diverse desires, intentions, goods, evils, and obligations; they retain considerable historical and ethical continuity that informs new situations; and they involve both ethical uncertainty and conflict regarding equally feasible proposals of good. They too are distinctive as they change. The potential solutions that ideally lead to tenable and tentative solutions in situations, therefore, emerge through participants' everyday experience and thinking, interactive and reflective inquiry, not by a simple reflexive recall of opinions, beliefs, and truth claims.

Take, for example, the situation of Irene Sebastian, a third-grade teacher at the Academy for Civic Responsibility,[4] who is reported for suddenly screaming at her students. The appropriate response to Irene's problem, according to Dewey, is not a reflexive reaction and quick reprimand based on a code of ethics, relevant laws, desirable virtues, or ethical principles. Instead, a cycle of "seeking and finding" facts and answers to pertinent questions is merited, a "reaching out for" Irene's and others' explanations and for tenable solutions to the problem, and, then, a narrowing of options to tentative explanations is necessary. But the consequences of the tentative resolutions should be determined (a) hypothetically by focused deliberations or dramatic rehearsals and (b) actually after a specific tentative solution has been carefully examined and tested. Plus, thoughtful attention, if Dewey's analytic strategy is acceptable, needs to be given to Irene's present problem, her formative growth and future responsibilities, not on her discipline for unprofessional behavior. This is not to say that her troublesome conduct is ignored; it is not. Instead, her actions should be investigated and, if appropriate, addressed with the intent of better serving students and enabling Irene to grow personally and professionally.

But important questions for the Academy, Maria, and others, are: How should problematic situations be investigated? Should the inquiry process always be the same or, alternatively, be situation specific? That is to say,

---

[4] We strongly encourage the reader to read the Foreword and Preface if they have not already done so. Each is central to understanding the volume. The Preface not only introduces the book as a whole but importantly it also clarifies how the Academy helps contextualize Dewey's theorizing, related vignettes, and case studies. Likewise, the Foreword by Barbara S. Stengel helps situate the work in the context of contemporary ethical deliberation.

should each inquiry process be overseen by a senior teacher, a house coordinator, an assistant principal, the principal, or a school or district committee? Or by a variety of processes? How will solutions be constructed to ensure the well-being of individuals, classes, social groups, and the Academy? How will fairness in processes and outcomes be created, safeguarded, and expanded? To be more specific, who should do the "seeking and finding" and "reaching out for" and "coming to" the relevant details of Irene's situation (LW 10, 183)?

However, there is much more to be said about what ethics may offer educators. Thinking back through Dewey's concept of a problematic situation offers insight. First, ethics offers both broad and deep perspectives on how to address problematic situations. This is fortunate since problematic situations are inescapable and ubiquitous. They may also multiply if they are not addressed thoughtfully and expediently. Thus, Dewey claims, decisions and actions should be examined in a contextualized and holistic fashion, not in an isolated and atomistic way. Inquiring into ethical situations, moreover, is a crucial endeavor and not to be pursued haphazardly if a broad and deep perspective is to be gained. Any information – data, facts, outcomes, intentions, desires, and emotions – that offers insight into a practical problem and helps resolve the problem needs to be uncovered and considered. Indeed, Dewey conceives of educators' involvement in ethical problems as another way they help one another and students to dissolve, resolve, or solve practical problems and problems of practice (EW 4, 54–61; Garrison 1999; Hansen 1998). But he goes further to suggest that ethical imagination, inquiry, and living should lead to an enjoyable and meaningful life (LW 7). He is not recommending a narrow ethic that just helps educators identify, analyze, disentangle, and adjudicate ethical infractions. To the contrary, he tries "to discriminate the fundamental instrumentalities requisite to our achieving and sharing the most intrinsically satisfying life" (Gouinlock 1972, vii). Thus, studying Dewey opens a window on multiple ways educators may wish to live broadly and fruitfully.

In Irene's situation, she and her students appear to be the concerned participants. But does the obvious serve to mislead the inquirer? Are the obvious participants the only participants? Are there unidentified onlookers or participants? If yes, who are they? Seeking to address a complete problematic situation, therefore, means that ethical inquiry raises questions that may lead to more fertile interpretations of a problematic incident. For example, if the question, Who were the participants in Irene's situation? is not raised, only a limited picture may be obtained and, thereby, result in a skewed understanding of Irene's actions. Overlooking participants – or their importance – and other elements of a situation can be catastrophic, undermining what could have been a fair, responsible, and future-oriented outcome. In such cases, a problem becomes compounded by inadequate inquiry and may evolve into a series of related problematic situations. Dewey, therefore, concludes that one of an educator's basic ethical responsibilities is to examine thoroughly problematic situations. Fact-finding is an initial and ongoing responsibility of educators, parents, and students. Rushing to judgment is unethical and frequently leads to misdiagnosed situations and unwarranted conclusions and outcomes.

Studying ethics, then, helps educators understand the nature of ethics and ethical inquiry. In particular, studying ethics usually clarifies a set of concepts and questions, such as: What is ethics? What is an ethical problem? What does it mean to be ethical? When is a teacher or student ethical? How are ethical issues examined and resolved? What counts as warranted conclusions or cogent arguments in ethics? Why should I be ethical? Who am I becoming when I make a decision or set of decisions? Dewey approaches these questions from several angles. To begin, he observes that ethics involves "should questions" and wrestles with what an individual, group, society, or a teacher, parent, or principal should or should not do in a particular problematic situation (LW 7, 214, 229, 246). Dewey's emphasis, of course, is on specific situational problems, not on issues that are irrelevant to a board, student, teacher, school, or district. To work on the problematic details of a school-related situation, Dewey thinks ethical imagination and creative deliberation are likely as necessary as inquisitiveness. Or, better, he argues that imagination and deliberation are embedded in insightful inquiry. For instance, Maria needs imagination when she first hears of Irene's outbursts. As fair-minded and caring professionals, Irene's colleagues need imagination when they consider how they should respond to accounts of her behavior. How should they determine what is well-advised? Who needs to be involved? Why?

Moreover, Dewey claims that ethics is concerned with the emotions, actions, conduct, and habits that have a bearing on the well-being of one's self, others, groups, and, ultimately, the common good (LW 13, 18). How, from a personal-groups-common-good perspective, will Irene's situation and its resolution affect her, students, staff, administrators, and, maybe, the district as a whole? What do the likely outcomes of the situation imply about the development of desires, attitudes, and dispositions that will have an effect on the welfare of students and teachers?

To ignore the emotional aspect of ethical inquirers and participants, for Dewey, is to disregard a vital part of the human personality and ethical inquiry. In the end, such neglect is similar to disregarding acts or outcomes: unthinkable. The whole person is and should be involved in thinking about and learning to feel and act as an ethical person, including deciding what needs to be learned about a problematic ethical situation.

Most ethical decisions that are made in schools may seem to affect only the relationships of administrators, teachers, students, or a mixture of these participants. Yet, nearly every decision or behavior that affects anyone in a school has the potential to affect other district personnel, school volunteers, and parents because all are together part of the time (LW 13, 65–79). Thus, all principal-teacher-student-guardian interactions and collaborations can easily roll over into other situations. This rollover potentiality, for us, means the outcomes of situations are rarely self-contained, for many initial outcomes link to later ones. Situations, therefore, are not only unique; they are interconnected, dynamic, and can mutate into expanded or new situations. As a result, personal and group deliberations or dramatic, imaginative rehearsals need to consider the current whole situation as it exists and how that situation may be transformed in the future by reflective decisions (MW 14, 132–8). Indicators of potential undesirable changes in the lifecycle of a situation, therefore, are invaluable markers for school communities, e.g., unanswered questions, stubborn doubts, and pervasive uneasiness.

Dewey notes too that those who examine problematic situations explore and interrogate claims of good and bad, right and wrong, virtue and vice, and prudence and imprudence (LW 5, 279–88). He emphasizes that the meanings of these concepts and other ideas are unusually important and, frequently, controversial. Thus, they should be clarified as often as needed, e.g., situationally, culturally, and generationally. In many multilingual and multicultural situations, the need for conceptual clarity is heightened: seemingly simple words like the Spanish "respeto" and the English "respect" can have both similar and dissimilar meanings. The concept of equal respect of persons, therefore, can easily lead to different shades of expectations and misunderstandings. Similarly, Dewey recognizes that one of our earlier imaginary objectors to studying ethics is correct: many – perhaps most – people use ethical claims to impose, at least occasionally, their personal preferences and purposes on others, children, and adults (LW 13, 5–10). Imposing values on others, he observes, is itself an ethical issue that merits ongoing investigation. The grounds for opposing – but occasionally approving – imposition require examination and evaluation (LW 11, 345–7).

Finally, Dewey explicitly addresses two questions – Who should decide what is right and wrong? And how should people decide what is right and wrong? – that have long challenged, if not obscured, legitimate steps to address ethical concerns (LW 7). While his full answers to these two questions cannot be provided, a couple hints are merited: (a) the who question is partially answered when he notes that everyone who has a stake in a problematic situation should have a voice in its resolution, and (b) the how question is partially answered when he observes that anyone who has or desires a voice in a problematic ethical situation is obligated to inquire into its epistemic status the same way she or he is obligated to explore an educational, economic, historical, political, religious, or scientific dispute. To do less than be involved in ethical concerns and explore the issues that impinge upon us leaves others to both identify the questions and decide on how the questions will be answered.

Stop and Think

Is imposition an underexamined concept in school decision-making? If yes, illustrate your thoughts. If no, why did you conclude imposition is not a problem?

Reflective Experience

Unlike many, Dewey (LW 13, 1–62) highly values the ordinary experiences and practical problems a person has during her or his intellectual and moral development. Through everyday experience, people learn, to varying degrees, how to speak, understand body language, interpret events, interact socially, think, evaluate the importance of others' observations, and appraise their decisions and actions. Indeed, without such experience, people would be virtually incapacitated. So, ordinary ethical experience and solving practical problems provide numerous benefits, including many otherwise irreplaceable ones. But life, Dewey reasons, includes miseducative as well as educative experiences, leading to a mixture of beliefs and values that are both counterproductive and productive. Miseducative experience, for Dewey (LW 13, 11–16), includes interactions that influence a person to adopt faulty assumptions, absorb antisocial attitudes, use unreflective decision-making habits, and act in ways that negate present and undercut future growth opportunities. Educative experiences, including experimental inquiry, foster reflective thinking, generous feelings, people-regarding decisions, and life-enhancing activities. Ordinary experience nurtures both educative and miseducative attitudes and habits and "promotes or retards growth," especially if left unevaluated (LW 13, 19). Stated positively, reflective, educative experience can and should foster "mutual responsiveness," a vital element in ethical development, individually and socially (Rogers 2009, 146, 148).

Dewey's thinking regarding experience and growth is both simple and complex. Experience is at times, or at least appears, random, disconnected, and meaningless. But experiences are always within the life space of a social being and, therefore, are regularly being pulled together and, ideally, reflectively evaluated and integrated. In these experiences, a person can become better prepared to make judgments and decisions whether formally educated or not. In best-case scenarios, thoughtful experience in ordinary life complements reflective formal educational activities. Neither ordinary nor formal education experiences, however, guarantee educative interactions or growth; for, educative and miseducative experiences know no spatial or experiential boundaries. A reflective, experimental approach to life, however, enhances the possibility of educative experiences and reflective growth.

Stop and Think

Dewey suggests that a dogmatic position is revealed when a person does not personally investigate and does not allow others to examine the "underlying principles" of her or his beliefs (LW 13, 9). Do you disagree with Dewey's claim? Explain why.

Aesthetic Depictions and Investigative Conclusions

That Dewey is described as examining ethics through two interconnecting lenses – the scientific (Hickman, Flamm, and Skowronski 2010; Johnston 2009) and the aesthetic (Abowitz 2007; Fesmire 2003; Shusterman 2000) – is rather well-known. Still, the level of awareness of his employment of the aesthetic lens needs elevation.

Aesthetic Depictions

Dewey's depiction of aesthetics and ethics is regularly communicated via his vocabulary and discussions, particularly through metaphors. Steven Fesmire (2015, 203) notes that Dewey's reconceptualized "aesthetics of

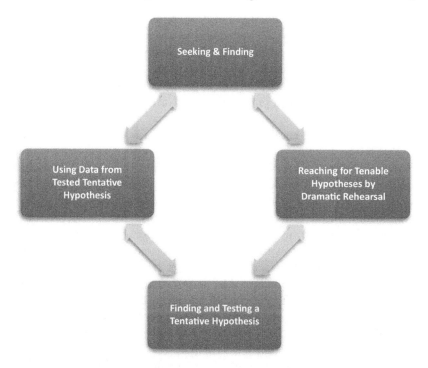

Figure 1.1   A fourfold rhythmic pursuit of understanding

the moral life" makes connections with the arts and sciences. First, Dewey (Fesmire 2015, 203) asserts that art includes active, intelligent inquiry much as does scientific inquiry. Second, he (203) claims that aesthetic experience and scientific inquiry often occur simultaneously. Third, Fesmire (2015, 203, 205) argues that Dewey found that artistic imagination and sensitivity deepen consummatory experience. In short, Dewey, Fesmire argues (204), thinks "Art shares in inquiry, and inquiry at its best attains to art" (204). Of course, Dewey appears influenced by the ancient Greeks' appreciation of "grace . . . [and] harmony" as important qualities of ethical conduct (LW 7, 271).

Dewey's aesthetic approach to ethics is also manifested in the rhythmic element found in his description of research. His almost poetic depiction of inquiry from fact-finding through hypothesis testing is portrayed below in Figure 1.1, "A fourfold rhythmic pursuit of understanding." The fourfold activity of a "seeking and finding, of reaching out for a tenable conclusion and coming to . . . at least a tentative one" is necessary for much ethical inquiry to be productive and deliberations to be fruitful (LW 10, 183). Rhythmic inquiry, Dewey suggests, occurs as individuals, groups, classes, and schools – people holding diverse interpretations of problematic situations – are involved in raising questions, seeking answers, testing hypotheses, rethinking tenable and tentative conclusions, and repeating the inquiry process as appropriate. Nearly as soon as a partial answer emerges in an initial search, other questions may arise from newly gained insights and require another round of inquiry. Each step of the process likely leads to testing or challenging ideas or hypotheses to determine their merits or warrant. The conscious testing may take place, first, hypothetically via what Dewey describes in cinematic terms. In this imaginary scenario, an ethical conflict between habits, impulses, and desires is foregrounded: "Each conflicting habit and impulse [which reveals one's desires] takes its turn in projecting itself upon the screen of imagination. It unrolls a picture of its future history, of the career it would have if it were given [freedom to act]" (MW 14, 133). This seeking, finding, projecting, and testing process, while not a lockstep activity, may continue for extended periods of time or just during an encounter in a corridor. The process may of necessity be abridged in some time-limited situations. For example, should I call the emergency number to alert security, request medical assistance, or both?

The pressures brought by multiple personalities, multilayered realities, and child and adolescent participants make ethical decision-making both weighty and pressing on occasions but should lead to tenable conclusions in expeditious, yet not irresponsible, ways. The obligations of fair-minded procedures, inquiry, deliberation, and conclusions, therefore, outweigh district and community convenience. But this may mean that some multifaceted problems need both immediate and extended attention. Educators, during exigent situations, may need to work as healthcare professionals frequently do: first, they may work somewhat like emergency medical services personnel to treat a situation almost instantly; second, when needed, they turn the matter over to or assume the role of emergency room-type personnel for additional attention; and, third, if necessary, still other educators may need to work on an ethical problem somewhat like chronic care medical specialists do with patients that need long-term interventions. Of course, many, perhaps most, ethical concerns arise in nonemergency contexts. Inquiry, nevertheless, is often ongoing, if not continuous, because the consequences of decisions constitute tests of their usefulness, fairness, and worth. Seeking and finding, of course, may continue after the welfare of students and the judgments of teachers are discussed. Principal De La Garza, for instance, could no doubt ask herself as well as confidantes: Will Irene, her students, and the school be well-served by our planned decisions, or will they stimulate spinoff problematic situations?

Stop and Think

Since schools usually focus on daily teaching responsibilities, how can they reasonably be expected to engage in research regarding the outcomes of their ethical interventions? Or, if you prefer, answer this question: What kinds of ethical research are both doable in and useful to schools?

Dewey refers to this rhythm of seeking and finding – and reaching out and coming to – as reflective thinking, scientific thinking, and, simply, thinking. In *Democracy and Education*, his educational magnum opus, he mentions the process of ethical inquiry in slightly different language but with the same focus: "Thinking includes ... the sense of a problem, the observation of conditions, the formation and rational elaboration of a suggested conclusion, and the active experimental testing" (MW 9, 158). Fesmire shares a valuable insight about the power of well-selected hypotheses used in experimental testing: "Ethics at its best" tests "hypotheses that enlarge perceptions" (2015, 124). Thinking about the potential range of a hypothesis is, therefore, part of the hypothesis construction process, and Maria regularly encourages such questions as: How will the suggested hypothesis enlarge the Academy's perception of ethical data and its relationship to district responsibilities? Will this hypothesis enlarge our perceptual range of ethical priorities?

Investigative Conclusions

Tenable, reasonable, or even tentative conclusions regarding ethical situa-tions often arise quickly. Talent, experience, and education often combine to enable a person to recognize quickly problematic ethical situations and offer reasonable ways of addressing them (MW 9, 158). Thus, an almost instantaneous scan of a particular situation and the identification of the dominant situational qualities may be filtered through an ethical grid or framework for immediate discussion. Intuitively, then, many teachers and administrators rapidly reach conclusions – and often, although not always, correctly. But immediate impressions or intuitions – even when supple-mented by reviews of pertinent factors, interactions with others, and recall of similar ethical experiences – can be misleading. In particular, insufficient attention may be paid to (a) the novelties of a situation, (b) the recent maturation of participants, and (c) the discovery of supplementary relevant facts. Hence, educators wisely consider their first impressions as tenable or plausible interpretations, not as settled conclusions. Impressions and intuitions, therefore, may be where many ethical judgments begin, but this is not where they should necessarily end.

Seeking and finding, when pursued collaboratively, will in time enable inquirers to identify novelties, clarify concepts and issues, and make better-informed decisions that may or may not agree with one's first impressions. When first impressions and inquiry outcomes conflict, this should lead to new questions and inquiry. For instance, those involved in the discovery of details in Irene Sebastian's situation might ask (even though they think they know she would not scream at anyone): Who reported Irene's screaming? Were there staff or volunteers present in her classroom when the incident occurred? Are there specific facts that the tenable conclusion does not explain well? Are there other plausible, even compelling, explanations? When in the discovery process did Maria solicit Irene's explanation? Does the hypothesis that Irene screamed at the class help us understand why no parent or student mentioned the incident until being asked about such?

Similarly, it may be helpful to ask: Does the proposed solution to the situation involving Irene fit into a pattern of school decision-making that ignores or supports either the common good or the good of a particular person or group? Adjusting the lens of biocentrism for human inquiry, a person (Fesmire 2003) may query: Why are we so concerned with Irene as an individual when we should care about everyone in the class and about ourselves as a school too? Does the tenable conclusion contribute to the potential well-being and growth of the students and Irene? Are there other reasonably well-supported tenable options? Are there any research studies about possible interventions in this type of case? Is the proposed intervention likely effective both immediately and later? In Irene's situation, the seeking and finding cycle may need to be repeated several times. Figure 1.2 below captures the spirit of Dewey's thinking about both tenable and, soon to be examined, tentative conclusions.

Stop and Think

In some circumstances, reasonable doubt plays a significant role in a jury decision. The preponderance of evidence is decisive in other situations. The cogency of argument serves well in many academic situations. What epistemic standards should be expected in an ethical case like Irene's?

Figure 1.2   Seeking tenable and tentative conclusions

Tentative Conclusions

As the seeking and finding cycle provides greater warrant for some hypotheses and conclusions, reaching out for and coming to one or more tentative conclusions should emerge as the goods and the evils of a situation become clearer. Revisiting Irene Sebastian, the anxious and harassed teacher who reportedly screamed at her students, reflexive reactions caused most colleagues and administrators to sympathize with her. She is not only highly respected as a professional and person, but also it is widely believed she simply would not scream at anyone, much less students. If for some inconceivable reason she did scream, the children must have been uncharacteristically disruptive. But that speculation did not seem possible.

But when, you may wonder, did the phrase "harassed teacher" arise? Actually, Irene used the label in her first post-incident meeting with Principal De La Garza. She admitted shrieking or groaning near two students on Monday morning but said she had never done such before or after that moment. She readily apologized for her spontaneous behavior and said it would not happen again. Although guarded and embarrassed, she almost immediately disclosed that she needed to take a brief leave so that she could recuperate from the stress of a difficult winter and recent events. When asked about recent events, she hesitantly mentioned that her stress had risen precipitously because of her husband's seemingly rapid onset of Lewy Body Dementia and, recently, because Dante Venturelli, the assistant principal for evaluation, talked with her about two students' unsatisfactory achievement test scores. Dante said that she could look for another job if similar outcomes reoccurred. He stressed that she was not serving students well, was failing the school, and was jeopardizing its ranking and incentive funding. His conclusion, according to Irene, was: "You cannot expect any sympathy from me. My leadership style is official and direct. Research indicates that business-like leaders are more successful than warm, fuzzy types. You must ensure that all students are served well."

Rethinking a situation is required when the only tenable conclusions are strongly questioned or even contradicted. Fortunately, Dewey's method of analysis takes into consideration the idea that so-called facts are not purely facts but data selected and interpreted through particular lenses. These lenses mean, therefore, that people, without exception, are "biased beings, tending in one direction rather than another" (MW 14, 134). Yet bias does not mean that everyone is completely blind, for "the scientific attitude and method [broadly described by Dewey as any form of rigorous inquiry, experimentation and evaluation] are at bottom the method of free and effective intelligence" (LW 13, 279). Yet, a free intelligence is virtually always partial and needs to interact with intelligent others. A community of inquirers is often recommended because a collective of partially freed intelligence may be likelier to self-correct, grow by reinterviewing people, reexamining data, and testing additional tentative hypotheses (Ioannidis 2012).

Stop and Think

When someone says something akin to, "Research indicates that business-like leaders are more successful than warm, fuzzy types," should you be inquisitive? Why?

Happily, at least for Irene, her portrayed situation is not the final resting place of Maria's ethical inquiry. But Maria recognizes that when minds – hers or others' – are made up like well-arranged bedding, they may be difficult to unmake and remake them. Yet it is safe to claim that Maria's willingness to remake her mind – or remain open-minded in the face of pressure to address a matter quickly – is an ethical disposition of incalculable worth. Of course, the process of evaluating one's conclusions could result in a very similar outcome. In any case, Maria and others will be better prepared to answer critical questions and, ideally, make warranted decisions if their minds remain open. But, Dewey cautions, one does not need to create an excess of hypotheses to test, which can lead to "too much thinking," too little action, and, thereby, professional paralysis (LW 8, 147). Balance, again, is needed, to avoid both too much and too little inquiry and too much and too little reflection (147). Adequate time, of course, should be spent considering "real connections" when inquiring into data but none on "embroidering upon the given facts a tissue of agreeable fancies" (147).

Conclusion

In conclusion, we ask three questions: What does Dewey expect from a study of ethics? What attitudes and actions does he encourage? What may a reader expect from a study and use of Deweyan-informed ethical theory? The advantages of studying ethics for Dewey are, for the moment, embedded in his encouragements to educators. He encourages, for example, educators to employ a recursive form of inquiry and criticism when examining problematic situations; examine an entire problematic situation so that all relevant data and opinions are considered: ask how solutions to or ameliorations of problems can and should be achieved so that additional problems are avoided and new insights are gained; pay attention to the desires and the goods of the diverse participants in problematic situations; aim for a proactive outcome or for the future ethical growth of everyone involved; forecast the potential consequences of conceivable solutions, decisions, and actions; consider the well-being of one's self and others as individuals, groups, and the common good when making decisions; pursue tenable and tentative conclusions until a consensus, if possible, develops; analyze the outcomes of decisions to determine if the actual consequences of actions are the desired and desirable ones; recognize that everyone has biases that need to be acknowledged and countered by empathetic analysis of others' views; work open-mindedly, humbly, deliberatively, and collaboratively with colleagues and students to examine and address problematic ethical realities.

Looking to the future, it is clear that Dewey similarly encourages teachers and administrators to reflect on the changes that are taking place in themselves as they think with and act on ideas being examined and incorporated into their ethical frameworks and contemplate how doing ethics enables them to help themselves and others to live better lives as they cultivate democratic communities, especially at school but in the broader parts of society too (LW 7, 340–50). Edel and Flower's conclusion (in their Introduction to LW 7), therefore, seems apropos: "Dewey's ethical theory is freshly relevant with its attentiveness to the particular, to change, to the incorporation of the best available knowledge, to the role of ethical theory as enlightenment, to the summoning of innovative thought and intelligence" (xxxv).

Discussion Questions

1.　Does the concluding synopsis of Dewey's ideas overlook any idea you think is substantial? If yes, what is it and why should it be added?
2.　What do you consider the most important aspect of doing ethical inquiry from Dewey's perspective? Why? Can you illustrate your choice?
3.　If you were Maria De La Garza, what would you do next regarding Irene's situation? What would you explore or verify before deciding on tentative conclusions?
4.　From your prior experience with ethical challenges, what would you add to Dewey's list of ways that ethics can contribute to the work of educators?
5.　If Dewey is correct in claiming that humans are "biased beings," does this mean that education is a waste of time and resources? Is one bias as good or as bad as another? If bias is so prevalent, should it just be ignored by teachers in their pedagogical roles?

RELATED READINGS

Campbell, Elizabeth. 2008. "The Ethics of Teaching as a Moral Profession."
   Curriculum Inquiry 38, no. 4 (August): 357–85.
Campbell's survey of ethics and teaching literature provides an informative
introduction to contemporary ethics and teaching. The main strands of modern
ethical thought are provided for both beginning and seasoned educators.
Dewey, John. 1922. *Human Nature and Conduct.* Vol. 14 of *John Dewey: The
   Middle Works, 1899–1924*, edited by Jo Ann Boydston, 1–189. Carbondale
   and Edwardsville: Southern Illinois University Press, 1983.
Murray Murphy's Introduction (MW 14, ix–xxiii) offers a concise and acces-
sible summary of Dewey's ethical views. Dewey's Introduction (1–11) provides an
intellectual historical context for his writing the volume.
Fesmire, Steven. 2019. "Ethics for Moral Fundamentalists." *The Journal of School
   & Society.* 6 (2): 66–9.
Fesmire's exploration of moral fundamentalism is filled with provocative claims.
The essay is designed to stimulate classroom discussion, immediately and thereafter.
Hansen, David T. 1993. "From Role to Person: The Moral Layeredness of Classroom
   Teaching." *American Educational Research Journal* 30, no. 4 (December):
   651–74.
Hansen's work examines moral layers of teaching in three schools: a public, a
Catholic, and an independent. Manifest and hidden moral matters are
identified and used to illustrate how moral questions pervade classroom
cultures.
Martin, Christopher. 2013. "On the Educational Value of Philosophical Ethics
   for Teacher Education: The Practice of Ethical Inquiry as Liberal Education." *Curriculum Inquiry* 43 (2): 189–209.
Martin explores the topic of how philosophical ethics can contribute to
understanding the moral dimensions of teaching. He examines why an awareness
of the plurality of normative considerations and why making deliberative judgments regarding normative considerations of teaching are invaluable.
Martin, Jay. 2002. *The Education of John Dewey: A Biography.* New York:
   Columbia University Press.
Martin's contextualization of Dewey's writings in the social, economic, political, educational, and philosophical milieu of 1859–1952 is priceless. Although he
speaks directly to the origins of Dewey's ethics (120–4), he also integrates
Dewey's musings throughout his volume.
Maxwell, Bruce. 2017. "Codes of Professional Conduct and Ethics Education for Future Teachers." *Philosophical Inquiry in Education* 24 (4):
   323–47.
Maxwell makes a case for abandoning negative stereotypes of teachers' codes
and for involving aspiring teachers in a study of regulatory and aspirational
varieties. While codes are seen as a "minimal threshold of adequacy" for the
ethical education of future teachers, he also offers insight into the work that needs
to be done to provide a rich ethics education for teachers.

Case Study: An Academy Testing Outrage

Standardized examinations are nearly always a time of stress for schools, but Maria realized that at the Academy, as a new school with a publicized focus on something other than test scores, the pressure would be amplified. Because most of the faculty had come to the Academy due to the focus on developing effective and ethical graduates, she had to keep a careful balance. While the Academy did not need to lead the district with high test scores, she had to be sure the school did not become a public embarrassment or a target for true test believers. She had to be sure teachers were committed to and focused on adequate scores, especially those whose students scored below the fiftieth percentile. However, she had to make sure not to become an ogre for tests or leave the impression the tests were ultimately more important than building socially responsible graduates in defining success for her staff and students. She knew every magnet school (except maybe for talented and gifted, exclusionary schools) had a balance issue around testing priorities.

Her teachers, by and large, accepted tests as setting the parameters for school survival, but she did not expect they had a passion for optimizing student performance, nor did they tend to define competence, much less excellence, primarily by student scores. She had to be pragmatic, however, and was very grateful to teachers who helped the most to produce the school's best scores. They were, for that time of the year, her bell cows.

Yet, the district monitor of scores was assigned, so she believed, to hold specialty schools' noses to the grindstone. And in Maria's mind, Beverly Binet was a true believer in test scores – or maybe a careerist who saw her career arc in terms of the scores she extracted from district schools. Her relationship with teachers, generally, was a bit chilly as she was openly a member of the "no excuses" mentality. Her background did not help her establish rapport with teachers – her graduate degree was in measurement psychology and she had taught only three years of intermediate grades before jumping toward the testing administration world. After listening to her, most teachers (and Maria) thought she was not able to carry good, experienced teachers' shoes when it came to performing the totality of a teacher's duties. But she was very earnest and vigilant in conducting her duties. Overly vigilant, perhaps.

It was a sudden, but not surprising, shock when Beverly brought her indignation to a meeting with Maria about following testing protocol in her building. The source of Beverly's consternation was high school English teacher, Derrick Grant.

Derrick was a superstar at the Academy. Students revered him, even the cynical and exhausted ones. He was so obviously committed to his students' success and to developing their self-confidence as students and people that even students who felt overwhelmed at times by his enthusiasm and drive would typically admit he was a "go-to teacher" for all sorts of matters. His students produced writing for him that was frequently published, and he ran a monthly coffee shop night for students to read their writing to peers and parents. Admittedly, students produced some raw stuff, but it was impossible to question the authenticity and emotional honesty of their works. Maria loved to go listen and, while she might flinch for a moment at times, at the end of the evening sessions she was almost speechless at the talent and courage of her students. Their writings, as Derrick said, spoke truth to power, often about social justice issues that characterized their lives and those of many students across the world.

Moreover, his students succeeded at a remarkable level and rate on the markedly less creative task of standardized tests required for graduation. These students outperformed any predictors given the ecology of their lives out of school. It was like a movie result – beyond what any statistical system or comparable performances for similar-situated students produced. It made her wonder why his students performed so well on these tests, particularly as many of them did not rise to such elite performances in other classes. She was pretty certain some peers asked themselves the same questions and some wondered if Derrick maybe pushed the rules. Yet, Maria saw no indication that he was coloring outside the lines as to testing, nor did his Lead Teacher, who was one of Derrick's biggest fans. Plus, there was no reason at the Academy to push students to do superbly on standardized examinations except the one Derrick gave: "I want my students to learn that they are capable of doing well on standards that are set artificially high and mostly for somewhat privileged peers."

If Maria had occasional questions, she was not surprised Beverly was altogether doubtful and was seemingly on a mission to investigate this anomaly and, if possible, pull the curtain on the mystery. She was no fan of outliers at either end of the curve. Inevitably, she arrived in Maria's office with an "Aha!" to share and, it seemed, some level of vengeance.

On the day of the tests, Derrick would bring a microwave and heat whole-grain waffles for each student to eat before and, occasionally, during the test. His rationale was straightforward: too many of his students came to school with no breakfast, did not show up for the school's free breakfast (as they explained, either because it was way too early, or it was definitely not cool in their world), and were less than energized starting the day with long, high stakes tests. He knew a waffle was not the central reason that his students did well; he was just being humane to them.

Beverly saw it altogether differently. She shared with Maria information about state-dictated testing protocols. First, the Department of Education strictly requires that teachers who proctor testing focus their full attention on monitoring students during the test. Moreover, his activities would likely be characterized by the department as distracting to students and, thus, unfair. Apparently, Maria puzzled, Derrick was wrong because he helped too much and also detracted from students' opportunities to do their best work. A bit contradictory, but it was the education department. Beverly also pointed out that given the free breakfast and lunch for qualifying students, his actions were unnecessary and gave an impression of desperation or unfair assistance.

Beverly was certain that when this came to light – and it had because she had already reported it to central administration and would soon be known by the Department of Education – it would raise serious questions and precipitate an external review of practices in the district. Even if no penalties were imposed, the publicity could be a nightmare. Beverly speculated, all too happily Maria felt, that Derrick was likely facing suspension or even a dismissal hearing if the Department was very upset.

Beverly also had advice for Maria:

> You better get on the train in this situation. As an administrator, you need to be faithful to the district administrators rather than to a rogue teacher. Whatever happens to Derrick, he is not worth your career in the district. Either you are a team player on this matter, or you do not show the right stuff and raise loyalty questions. You remember that episode when a teacher cheated on tests a year or two back and the principal and superintendent almost lost their jobs? The superintendent said then the next teacher that did anything like that would be promptly and publicly "executed." I think the superintendent's staff are ready to throw Derrick under the bus. You do not want to go there too, do you?

The meeting ended abruptly, and Maria's thoughts turned to a related matter. "Now," she said to herself, "Irene's story about Dante Venturelli's bullying her makes sense."

Schools are small towns and even as Beverly left the Academy, the story that Derrick was in trouble hit the grapevine. Maria figured a few of his peers who resented Derrick's status were spreading the story with faux sympathy. At day's end, some of his students arrived in a fury to tell Maria how wrong this situation was and that tomorrow they intended to protest the unfairness of targeting the best teacher in the building, as well as the assumption they could succeed only by cheating. The word *racism* was offered. But students were convinced to await further information.

As the students emptied her office, Maria tried to quickly list her questions: What is Derrick's view of his responsibilities to his students, colleagues, parents, the Academy, and the district? What questions will have priority for Superintendent Kennedy? No doubt, he fears that Beverly's "indignation" and an overreaching demand that Maria support the administration might have fomented an avoidable crisis. The situation, if as described, seems caused by reckless, inflammatory, and divisive behavior. Then Maria added a personal question that Kennedy might ask: "Where was Maria's frontal lobe when the waffles were being served?"

Maria had her own set of questions and plans, speaking next with Derrick and then with Kennedy. Later, she did not know what she would do.

"Should I," she asked herself, "tell Derrick now that, if we both survive this occasion and the facts are as claimed, we have to have a frank discussion of your future activities at the Academy?"

QUESTIONS

1. What are your first impressions of this situation? What information do you need?
2. What questions would you want to raise if you were employed to advise the superintendent and school board regarding the now labeled "waffle situation"?
3. If Derrick Grant has a legitimate, replicable approach to raising test scores, why would he not share the information with the faculty of the Academy and district?
4. If Derrick's approach is not legitimate, why would he risk so much when his unusual success would almost certainly draw negative attention to him and the Academy, including his own students?
5. Would you be pleased with the work of Beverly Binet if she is as depicted? Why?

CHAPTER 2

What Does Sympathy or Empathy Have to Do with Ethics?

Sympathy is the animating mold of moral judgment ... because *it furnishes the most efficacious intellectual standpoint. It is the tool, par excellence, for resolving complex situations.* Then when it passes into active and overt conduct, it does so fused with other impulses and not in isolation and is thus protected from sentimentality.

—John Dewey, *Ethics* (LW 7, 270; emphasis original)

Introduction

Examining sympathy or empathy as a part of ethics may seem odd, especially if one is accustomed to thinking that ethics is a purely intuitive, rational, procedural, or codified matter. The answer to the question of what sympathy or empathy have to do with ethics can, however, take a number of both beneficial and detrimental directions. Even so, Dewey's conclusion is that sympathy is such a crucial aspect of ethical inquiry and action that ethical reflection and maturation would be greatly impoverished without it. He holds that sympathy is pertinent to everyone but especially to those who interact regularly with children and youth and with those who are fulfilling normative responsibilities. As we pursue his thought, some details of the ethical difficulties and opportunities at the Academy are used to demonstrate why sympathy can be helpful but deserves "protection from sentimentality" and other distorting influences (LW 7, 270). In addition, it is also obvious that more than sympathy is necessary: inquiry, facts, data, deliberation, and experimentation are important too. Consequently, in districts and schools, there may be grounds to argue that there should be ongoing projects to help synthesize research about empathy and related topics. Suffice it to say, now, there is much to learn by examining psychological as well as philosophical considerations that illuminate empathy and ethics education.

Three vignettes – regarding Irene Sebastian, Derrick Grant, and Raleigh Dickenson – are foregrounded as Dewey's views are explored. Up to this point, Irene's story focuses on school staff and students: Maria, the principal, and Dante Venturelli, Academy coordinator of evaluation. The gist of Irene's story is that she has been reported for angrily screaming at her students. A second story unfolds and involves Derrick Grant, an Academy English teacher; Beverly Binet, district director of assessment; Peter Kennedy, the district superintendent; and Maria. In this narrative, Derrick is suspected of violating assessment protocols. The third story centers on Raleigh Dickenson and her son, Nigel. He is a middle school student who allegedly inflicted serious damage to a biology laboratory.

The Concepts of Sympathy and Empathy

As we revisit Irene's situation, we observe that Dewey's concept of sympathy is an interpretative tool that, as Edel and Flowers claim, offers "enlightenment," not definitive answers to problematic situations (introduction to LW 7, xxxv). Moreover, understanding that Dewey's idea of sympathy seems to embrace the two contemporary conceptions of affective and cognitive empathy (*empathy* was rarely employed by Dewey since it was introduced late into English) is vital (Simpson and Sacken 2014). He argues for what he terms an "intelligent sympathy" (LW 7, 251), or a sympathy that identifies the distortions and the implications of the concept. Dewey's views can be distinguished from but overlap with certain contemporary pragmatists who are inclined to "*integrate* empathy and rationality in a distinct concept and practice of 'sympathetic reason'" (Sorrell 2014, 68; emphasis original). Likewise, his ideas largely parallel Maxwell's explanation of compassionate empathy: "the main point is the conceptual one that compassion is not just perceiving someone's suffering or desiring to relieve someone's suffering but *caring about* their suffering ..." (2008, 54; emphasis original).

Similarly, Dewey's use of sympathy (a) indicates that one feels for or with others during times of distress and happiness, (b) responds to others' pain and pleasure in caring ways, and (c) denotes that one seeks to understand another's feelings, thinking, valuing, and behaving. The epigraph exhibits Dewey's blending elements of sympathy and identifies concepts that offer clarification, e.g., "animating," "judgment," "impulses," "intellectual standpoint," "active and overt conduct," "fused with impulses" (LW 7, 257). He suggests that sympathy provides "the most efficacious *intellectual* standpoint," not merely a passionate reaction, to someone's grief (270). Clearly,

Dewey reasons that the impulse to sympathize can stimulate an educator to feel for others; study their desires, thinking, and actions; make better informed judgments regarding problematic situations; and act in the interest of students and colleagues. Without sympathy, Dewey thinks ethical inquiry, engagement, and conduct lose a powerful ally that is not replaceable by reason and science. Thus, he concludes that prosocial affections, insights, and actions, inside and beyond schools, will be diminished considerably if intelligent sympathy is excluded from human relationships (270). Like contemporary psychologists who use the term *empathy* (Maxwell 2008), Dewey addresses both positive and negative emotions when discussing sympathy. His reasons seem at least twofold. First, he argues in his description of a good person that one should be thoughtful or caring in evaluative circumstances and that many, perhaps most, people hope for encouragement in such situations (LW 6, 285). Second, Dewey may think that children or students constitute a population of people who need affirmation even during successful and enjoyable learning activities (LW 13, 345–6).

Dewey's approach to sympathy is measured, reflective, and, yet, enthusiastic. He considers sympathy as, at first, a spontaneous affective inclination to support others in their pain and pleasure and as, second, a decisional intellectual process to examine others' feelings, thinking, and valuing. Similarly, Steven Pinker (2011) suggests that empathy can lead to scientific mind-reading, which involves reading someone's thoughts and emotions. He clarifies that empathy was originally seen as "*projection* – the ability to put oneself into the position of some other person, animal ... and imagine the sensation of being in that situation" (575; emphasis original). Hence, he concludes that empathy is the skill of "*perspective-taking*" and is achieved via a painstaking "mind-reading ... or empathic accuracy" (575; emphasis original). Unfortunately, today some seriously overstate the potency of empathy and almost turn it into a magical power (575).

Dewey's claim is far from a minor one; for he asserts that sympathy partly ignites the process of ethical interest and as it "passes into active and overt conduct ... [it is] *fused* with other impulses" to shape the entire teacher (LW 7, 257). He adds, however, that both "sentimentality" (257) and "cold-blooded thought" (269) should be avoided when affections, inquiry, and reason are intelligently combined. When an educator is involved in a sympathetic course of action, the rhythmic process of inquiry and reflection (see Chapter 1) involves "the most efficacious intellectual standpoint" for understanding others and addressing complex ethical challenges (270). Effective moral learning and growth, by educators and students, involves their "virtuous traits" interpenetrating "one another" and leading to a unified "integrity of character" (257).

As a sympathetic principal, Maria is obviously affected as a whole person too. Presently, she is stimulated to support Irene and her class. Her sympathetic qualities, as well, constitute a moving affectionate inclination to support parents. But confronted with supporting, maybe, three dozen people at once, she has to stop to ask: How do I prioritize my responsibilities in this situation? Understandably, then, Dewey claims that "the cumulative force of [serious and] trivial choices" partially determine who Maria is and the kind of person she is becoming (MW 14, 150). How she responds to the choices in front of her constitutes a part of her ongoing ethical development. But Dewey warns against becoming overly introspective and consumed by one's personal virtuousness. Hence, Maria's priority should be with classroom participants, not herself. In the process, she should attend, as needed, to balancing others' interests with her own. She can combine her care, fairness, and firmness with inquisitiveness in the current problematic situation.

More comprehensively, the virtues and actions that flourish among the Academy's staff facilitate the ongoing maturation and vitality of the school ecosystem (Simpson 2011). The vices or blemishes that remain or emerge also influence student and staff development and the school culture. Moreover, the choices of Academy students and staff are gradually changing them as persons, ideally each toward a self-, other-, and group-regarding person. But this kind of growth is far from inevitable. Therefore, collaborative learning, inquiry, and problem-solving are essential. Cooperative deliberations about problematic situations regularly help the Academy's community grow as pertinent parties participate in making decisions. One could claim, if Dewey's argument is well-founded, that neither Maria nor Irene will be exactly the same person once the current situation is addressed and that the children involved will also probably become somewhat different people. Similarly, the children's classmates and parents change to the degree they participate in or understand the unfolding situation. This "collateral learning," Dewey asserts (LW 13, 29) in *Experience and Education*, unavoidably occurs regularly and unconsciously much as Myles, Trautman, and Schelvan (2004) describe a hidden curriculum being absorbed. This admirable collateral learning provides new growth, although none of it may be listed in Superintendent Kennedy's annual report to the school board.

Sympathy, including the animating affection for moral judgment, connects to the cognitive processes Dewey describes. Unfortunately, some misinterpret sympathy and perpetuate dodgy conclusions. That is, they conclude that (a) the stimulus response process is a deterministic one, (b) the mold is a lockstep means of starting and addressing ethical problems, (c) the inquiry process is an undeviating one, (d) the distinguishable elements of the approach are not interlaced, (e) the moral judgments are largely cognitive and do not involve the emotions and habits, (f) the coalescing of impulses is primarily a conscious decision exclusive of organic tendencies, (g) the resolution of every problem is always possible even in the most challenging circumstances, and (h) the formation of character is an automatic byproduct of understanding and employing this process. Keeping in mind that when these flawed suppositions arise, it is an occasion to clarify Dewey's actual meaning regarding the relationship of one's sympathy, perception, reflection, action, integration, habituation, and character. In his thinking, evaluation of the outcomes that stem from a perceived resolution is necessary too. If the consequences of a purported resolution or solution include inequities, rigidities, prejudices, stereotypes, inefficiencies, confusions, and hostilities, the problems of the situation have not been satisfactorily resolved; they have been dealt with unsuccessfully. Irene's situation, for instance, may worsen if unsympathetically or harshly handled.

Sympathy and Ethics: Affections

Understanding how sympathy may help or hinder Maria and others as they pursue their ethical responsibilities is important. In a few words, Dewey's view is that "Sympathy instinctively transports us to ... [another's] position, and we share their glow of liking and their fire of resentment as if we were personally concerned" (LW 7, 238). An educator's sympathy, therefore, moves them to feel the pains and pleasures of students, colleagues and guardians and moves them to support others' concerns, i.e., Maria's sympathy moves her to feel for and help Irene and her students. But like Austin Phillips, the Academy's most sympathetic faculty member, Maria – or any staff, student, or parent – might be prodded to act excessively or without sufficient information. One's "glow of liking and ... fire of resentment" (LW 7, 238) can bias one against some students, teachers, and parents and favor others. Contemporary researchers like David Hoffman (2000 cited by Maxwell 2008, 85–6), also warn of "familiarity bias."

Austin is instantly transported to another's side, usually before Maria or others have an opportunity to explore fully a matter. He springs immediately to the side of anyone who is experiencing discomfort, often defending several oppositional students at once. But he has sympathetic limits or, perhaps, his biases block sympathy for certain people: administrators and economically privileged students. In the present situation, he immediately confronts Maria, insisting that she encourage students, parents, and Irene before her personal plan of analysis has crystalized. She can feel the "fire of [Austin's] resentment" toward her immediately because she needed to deal with another, even greater emergency (LW 7, 238). Maria's variously worded response to Austin is: "Information is being gathered as we speak, and decisions will be made and action taken as soon as such are appropriate. In the meantime, everyone involved is being assisted." Her unarticulated thoughts, however, are: "Oh, am I glad Dewey clarifies that sympathy should not be a 'dictator of conduct' and that 'unenlightened benevolence' and rage should not be allowed to create an administrative nightmare" (300). When Austin is in his hyper-sympathetic mood, some of his colleagues say he acts completely on his impulses and loses his wonderful mind. Almost uniformly, however, he is appreciated for being sensitive to the problems of others. He is even deemed a welcomed counterforce to the few colleagues who still callously say things like, "Get over it," or, "Pack up your emotions."

Dewey notes the aforementioned and other potential problems with sympathy. Several are worth mentioning. First, some people, perhaps like Beverly Binet, seem to have little to no active or public sympathy for others. Thus, "the abnormally callous" and the otherwise sympathetically inhibited may face challenges or create problems when they show little or no regard for the joys and, especially, ordeals of students and educators (LW 7, 238). An unsympathetic educator may be untouched and, therefore, passive when students' academic challenges, athletic inabilities, and aesthetic limitations become known. The educator who is characterized by a lack of sympathy can complicate teaching and leading, because he appears to care little, if at all, for the social and emotional well-being of participants. That person may actually escalate stress and anxiety levels in classrooms and offices. Second, the overly sympathetic person, like Austin Phillips, may be besieged with emotions to the point of being sentimental and, thereby, engage in overly affectionate behavior, making excuses for others rather than contributing to their growth. Paradoxically, they may unsympathetically denigrate and malign peers who fail to meet their excessive standards of sympathy. They may absorb indiscriminately the resentments of a colleague or student against another and, thereby, magnify rather than ameliorate problems. Third, Dewey warns that the emotion of sympathy "rarely extends beyond those near us, members of our own family and our friends. It rarely operates with reference to those out of sight or to strangers, certainly not to enemies" (LW 7, 238). Pinker (2011, 590–2) warns too of the dark side of sympathy, e.g., fairness is jeopardized when people favor those with whom they sympathize most. How, then, will new, diverse, and marginalized students, even educators, receive the sympathy, concern, and nurturing they need if their teachers, colleagues, and classmates have a selective or partial sympathy? Fourth, some kinds of sympathy may not be sufficiently strong to last more than a day or two, stalling out because the sympathizer only develops superficial commitments, attends eye-catching situations, and notices short-term needs and consequences (LW 7, 239). Fortunately, many who go into teaching seem to possess reflective sympathy and to a healthy degree. When educators are characterized by a balance of the loves Dewey emphasizes – love of others, love of contact with children and youth, and love of arousing the interests of others – there are additional people-supporting attitudes and actions in schools (Simpson and Jackson 1998).

Should Dewey's thoughts stimulate discussions about leadership appointments, staff development emphases, and evaluative feedback to personnel? The answer may be a qualified yes. Getting beyond learning just ideas to displaying ethical attitudes and engaging in intelligent sympathetic behavior appears irreplaceable. Educators, especially, need to be intelligently sympathetic, generally, and, particularly, to students who are unlike many teachers and students. If not, some teachers and principals will remain largely on the outside of some students' worlds and keep thinking that orally transmitting information or monitoring behavior is the extent of their responsibilities. Then what happens to the unlike-us students and educators?

Here the second dimension of Dewey's concept sympathy is much needed: cognitive empathy (Maxwell 2008, 33–41). Here the educator begins to understand problems and situations through the eyes of others: sympathy facilitates developing rapport with students and educators, as well as advancing effective leadership behavior and using engaging teaching activities. Sympathy that leads to understanding from another's perspective, getting on the inside of a person's thinking, feelings, and values is considered "the tool, *par excellence*, for analyzing and resolving complex cases" (LW 7, 270). Intelligent sympathy prompts one to care for a student and moves one to be a student of students and an effective guide of student development. Maxwell draws an almost indistinguishable conclusion about "compassionate empathy [being] the moral emotion par excellence" (2008, 11).

Is there a two-dimensional cyclical potentiality for sympathy? For Dewey, the answer is probably yes. An intelligent cycle of sympathy can lead to caring for students and, as a partial consequence, can lead to learning about them in order to better teach them. Likewise, understanding students can lead to caring intelligently for them. The cycle is possible in part because the two distinguishable aspects of sympathy can activate intelligent affection and action. To reiterate his definition of sympathy, it entails two distinguishable but integrated elements, affection and cognition, that activate and guide the entire person. Jointly, they are the mold and guide for intelligent, holistic responses to others' experiences, whether they are having painful or pleasurable ones. Sympathy (a) moves a person to the side of others, (b) promotes "moral judgment," (c) works toward the resolution of "complex situations," (d) displays "overt conduct," and, organically, (e) transforms one's impulses into virtues (270). To repeat, what Dewey describes is an "intelligent sympathy" (251) that enables the whole person to grow stronger ethically, elude "sentimentality" (270), and become helpful to others. Sympathy that is rigorously studied and clarified by scientific research can enable a well-prepared teacher or leader to make substantial ethical and educational progress as an educator. But these outcomes are not inevitable: they are contingent upon a variety of factors that can only be identified and contextualized by philosophical and empirical studies. After examining considerable research and related analyses, Maxwell (2008, 74) concludes that

> irrespective of the fact that compassionate empathy is strongly antithetical to . . . impartiality – its attractiveness as a focal point of moral-developmental interest and educational intervention is both explained and justified by the fact that it expresses just as strongly another – the idea of normativity or, loosely, that human needs carry with them binding practical demands on one's attentions and actions.

Dewey's terminology (e.g., intelligent sympathy) may be dated, but his concepts and arguments are often surprisingly relevant.

Stop and Think

Who, if anyone, is obligated to determine whether aspiring staff who seem accurately characterized as unfeeling and hardened or overly sensitive and demonstrative should be teachers or administrators?

In Dewey's thought, it may appear that extending one's spontaneous and/or fostered sympathy to students who are largely outside of one's own experiential territories is a responsibility required by the democratic principles of the teaching profession (MW 9, 362–3). Yet, administrators sometimes lack sympathy with the challenges of classroom teachers and vice versa. Dante Venturelli, the coordinator of Academy evaluation, may manifest behavior that displays inadequate sympathy for and, perhaps, scant insight into Irene Sebastian's situation. But is this a premature conclusion? Is enough known about Dante to merit this deduction? Could the glimpse at his recent behavior run counter to his usual inclinations? Indeed, is it already difficult to have sympathy for Dante because of the comments he reportedly made to Irene? But is the little that is reported about him correct and suggestive of dispositions? Might he have made his comment after a stressful meeting with Beverly Binet?

Sympathy and Ethics: Cognition

As Dewey focuses on the cognitive dimension of his holistic view of the "emotion of sympathy" (LW 7, 251), he notes that it

> functions properly when used as a principle of reflection and insight, rather than of direct action. Intelligent sympathy widens and deepens concern for consequences. To put ourselves in the place of another, to see things *from the standpoint of his* [or her] aims and values, to humble our estimate of our own pretensions to the level they assume in the eyes of an impartial observer, is the surest way to appreciate what justice demands. (LW 7, 251; emphasis added)

In this comment, Dewey indicates that sympathy does not work properly when it is separated from its intellectual dimension because impulsive tendencies alone are frequently counterproductive. But sometimes, an immediate response is appropriate – for example, seizing a chemical flask or beaker before it is knocked on the floor. Immediate action that is based on impulse and affection minus inquiry and reflection, however, can be mindless rather than mindful. Moreover, he observes that sympathy as an intellectual tool is partially concerned with seeing from another's place or through their lenses and is concerned with the consequences of proposed and actual actions. In *Human Nature and Conduct* (MW 14, 132–8), Dewey concludes that deliberation or dramatic rehearsal is particularly helpful when examining the potential consequences of choices. Likewise, sympathetic insight, for Dewey, is based in part on one's being able to control or set aside hubris, overconfidence, and arrogance. A contemptuousness that leads to personal tirades against others' unconfirmed misbehavior and to social media rants against someone's reported offences reveals, perhaps, a right-minded propensity that is overcome by a wrong-minded urge to castigate. Conversely, to be sympathetic means that a person begins the process of learning to see and feel through another's frame of reference by deciding that what is immediately important is not what one personally thinks but, rather, what a student or colleague thinks and how this thinking contributes to a perceived or actual solution to a problematic situation. When hubris dominates any attempted resolution, Dewey thinks participants may easily amplify problems.

But hubris need not control school relationships and ethical problem-solving if Dewey's thoughts are warranted. In *How We Think* (MW 8, 136–9), he encourages three habits – open-mindedness, pains-taking inquiry, and intellectual responsibility – that can help foster reflective and collaborative ethical development. He implies that sympathy for others and their needs should be combined with open-minded attention to others' opinions and to a fair-minded evaluation of them. Open-mindedness, in-depth inquiry, fair-mindedness, and intellectual responsibility (e.g., responsibility for the consequences of one's ideas, plans, solutions, and actions) cannot ensure complete impartiality and justice in schools, but they can establish conditions, means, and ideals for evaluating school and district procedures, policies, activities, and outcomes.

Sympathy may also have the potential to change pedagogy so that educational outcomes become more equitable and teacher-student inter-actions foster understanding that is suffused with new insights. Teachers may be privileged by having excellent K–12 and university studies and by superb teacher preparation and school-based experiences. They may also have high expectations for students, but the consequences of their teaching may be less effective than originally expected because they lack sympathy for all students. To be clear, the problem may not be that they lack preparation in diversity education, English as a second language, cultural anthropology, ethics and education, and child or adolescent psychology. Instead, it may be that they lack a native or developed intelligent sympathy for others. They may not know how to enter insightfully into the emotions, thoughts, values, and challenges of students. Or, they do not understand how to investigate sympathetically the personal and cultural narratives of individual students (McAllister and Irvine 2002; Zins et al. 2004). Whatever the reasons, school districts have a responsibility to foster educators who are characterized by intelligent, research-informed sympathy.

Stop and Think

What do the authors mean by intelligent, research-informed sympathy? How does the text provide insight into their meaning?

When considering pedagogy and sympathy, Dewey's explanation for the superior teaching of many teachers is that "they have a quick, sure and unflagging sympathy with the operations and processes of the minds they are in contact with. Their own minds move in harmony with those of others, appreciating their difficulties, entering into their problems, sharing their intellectual victories" (LW 13, 345–6). Even so, sympathy raises important questions for equitable teaching processes and outcomes in academic areas (e.g., language studies, mathematics, and art) as well as in advancing student and faculty understanding of obstacles and insights into moral situations and development. Hence, educators, in Dewey's opinion, need to understand the precise errors of thinking and the misinterpretations of experience that hinder their students' ethical and subject matter learning.

Questions about a student may also be plentiful: Is there an unusual student, for instance, who is almost literally closed-minded and, therefore, his thinking largely inaccessible except, perhaps, in one-on-one private interactions with teachers? Is he disengaged because he fears what openness will mean for him if his peers, family, or teachers learn of his thoughts? Will he be unsafe, even in his own family and school, once he acknowledges beliefs that are unwelcomed, perhaps even abhorrent? Auspiciously, Warnick, Yacek, and Robinson (2018) provide a welcomed inquiry into aspects of working with people who hold morally repulsive beliefs.

Stop and Think

Learning to ask thought-provoking questions without humiliating others is an art based, in part, on reflectively understanding others' experiences. In your judgment, are there delicate questions Maria needs to ask Irene and Dante to help them better address their situations?

The Academy Situation

As the Irene-Dante situation is revisited, it hardly needs to be said that it is similar to many other situations in that it is characterized by uniqueness, complexity, uncertainty, and, to a degree, urgency. The three main parties – teachers, administrators, and students – and their affiliations (e.g., with families and friends) make the situation somewhat urgent. The situation is, at least potentially, a volatile one in that the problem can easily escalate into a substantial challenge even though Maria momentarily thinks the matter is amenable to a quick ethical resolution; she knows the key participants well. But as an experienced principal, she also knows that best-case scenarios can unexpectedly be derailed because of participants' unknown desires, fears, and ambitions. Plus, bruised feelings, if unaddressed, can turn into hard-to-remove resentments.

If Maria has the set of qualities that Dewey deems desirable, her sympathies will be foregrounded rhythmically throughout the resolution processes. She will easily sympathize with Irene Sebastian, a long-time excellent teacher with a chronically ill husband, with Said Khan and Chen Lî, the two students closest to Irene when she yelled, and with Khan's and Lî's parents. As she seeks to understand all five people and the rest of Irene's class, a knock on her office door shifts her thoughts to another situation. Raleigh Dickenson, Nigel's mother, has come to talk with her, although she does not have an appointment. The interruption was, from Maria's perspective, a happy occasion in spite of the timing and topic. She was delighted to learn that Raleigh had come to talk about Nigel. Raleigh, a soft-spoken thirty-something person, rarely comes to campus. Her jobs and children allow her little time for other activities. So, her presence is a good sign, an indication that she has something important to share. No doubt, she is concerned about Nigel's reported behavior and the corrective discipline that was taken. Nigel had his tutorial time with a highly admired school volunteer taken away from him, a punishment he considers excessive although the damage to school property is considerable and the vandalism is his most recent incident in a string of violations of school policies.

But for Nigel, Raleigh observes, there were several reasons the punishment was inappropriate. First, she observes that, if Nigel is correct, no one had seen him throwing rocks at the biology laboratory windows; no one could have seen him, he insists, because he was not even near the laboratory at the time. In addition, Raleigh adds: "I think he is most upset because the personal tutoring by Ruth Epstein is, perhaps, the school activity he most enjoys. He can barely wait to discuss neighborhood history and related socioeconomic situations with her." Moreover, Nigel had told Raleigh that the fact that a substitute teacher had seen an auburn-haired boy throwing rocks at the laboratory windows did not mean he, Nigel, was that person. Several other students near his age and size have auburn hair too. He was accused, he maintains, because he is stereotyped as a problem student. Besides, Raleigh continues, "Nigel said Ms. Alima Anderson, his substitute teacher, referred to him as 'our fifth-grade terrorist'." If she did, she should apologize to him, not profusely but clearly, in class where her offence occurred (Ruitenberg 2017). Raleigh, offering her own opinion again, said, "Why should he lose his learning privileges with Ms. Epstein even if he did throw rocks? Why remove an educational opportunity that deprives a child of enjoyable learning experiences? This is a school." Later, as Maria and Raleigh stood up, Raleigh pauses to mention a final thought, "Nigel wants me to mention that 'Delaying justice until more facts are discovered (if they exist) and a more appropriate punishment is identified is a really good option.'" After responding to Raleigh's comments, Maria ended the session by saying she would inquire further into the matter and text her a short answer by Friday at 2:00 p.m. They could talk later when Raleigh had time.

By her visit, Raleigh reminded Maria that "A matter is not settled fairly until the Other has been heard" (Stengel 2009). Now she needs to touch base with Xiaoming Wu, an assistant superintendent, and Alima before talking with Molly, Irene's intern. But what, she asked, should I do – if anything – about Alima's reported spontaneous remark to Nigel? Dropping her as a substitute teacher seemed, to put it mildly, "overly reactive" given her unblemished record and superior talent. But what was she to make of Raleigh's wishes: an apology to Nigel? Perhaps talking a bit with the Leopards' house director would be helpful. Pausing, she concluded that it was fortuitous that Raleigh had entered her forum.

As Maria asked Kenseisha, her administrative assistant, to come into her office, a stream of priorities descended on her. Among them were the need to know what Dante had learned from Molly and what he observed in Irene's class earlier in the week. Likewise, she needed the latest draft of the mathematics grant proposal to take home. Plus, she needed a copy of her revised paper entitled "Contemporary Discussions of Sympathy and Empathy: Panaceas, Problems or Possibilities?" by Thursday at noon.

Conclusion

In conclusion, Dewey's twofold view of sympathy offers insight into ethics and education. He notes that sympathy is invaluable since it includes the ignition of interests in and concern for others; but it operates best when accompanied by intelligent inquiry, for it is a means of gaining insight into others and an instrument that fosters reflection about and with others

(LW 7, 251). Sympathy is ultimately based on highly regarding students and colleagues and, hence, their lives and thoughts. Studying and reflecting on others' goals and beliefs opens doors for mutual understanding and appreciation that can lead to intellectual, emotional, and social development. It can provide glue for class and school communities. Yet, learning to appreciate others and building communities requires a degree of decentering of one's personal priorities and interests and a recentering on the school community, colleagues', and students' interests. In this way, students' needs and interests are foregrounded, and educators' attention shifts to, among other matters, the consequences of classroom pedagogy, environments, and conditions. And, noticeably, one grows toward being a more, but never an unqualified, "impartial observer," which is, according to Dewey, "the surest way to appreciate what justice demands" (LW 7, 251). Thus, if correct, the school that fosters sympathetic educators and students also cultivates more impartial and just ones. If sympathy offers these potentialities as he argues, Dewey has provided a powerful clue about how both pedagogical effectiveness and school fairness and community can be nourished. In some measure, both educators and students develop a sense of belongingness with others who respect them, consider their values and ideas, and sympathize with their pleasures and pains and challenges and successes. Contemporary studies (e.g., Maxwell) in compassionate empathy appear to go deeper to clarify the differences between intelligent empathy and unreflective empathy.

Discussion Questions

1. What potential problems with Dewey's concept of sympathy do you see when it is applied or employed in K–12 schools? Can you also anticipate how Dewey, if he were present, might address these possible problems?
2. Given your personal observations and experiences in schools, do you think there are sympathetic scarcities and excesses? Why?
3. How might Maria De La Garza's sympathy help her address the situation that involves Irene? Clarify your thoughts.
4. If you were mentoring a new teacher on the importance of sympathy, what ideas would you discuss? Include both potential weaknesses and strengths of sympathy.
5. Given that people have varying degrees of sympathy for others, is it reasonable, ethical, and legal to encourage aspiring and practicing educators to reconsider teaching as a career if they generally seem devoid of these qualities?

RELATED READINGS

Bialystok, L. and P. Kukar. 2018. "Authenticity and Empathy in Education." *Theory and Research in Education* 16 (1): 23–39.
The authors address a series of important problems (e.g., research reliability, conceptual clarity, pedagogical effectiveness, contradictory claims, and political intentions) that compromise the usefulness of much authenticity and empathy research.
Dewey, John, and J. Tufts. 1932. *Ethics*. Vol. 7 of *John Dewey: The Later Works, 1925–1953*, edited by Jo Ann Boydston, 1–512. Carbondale and Edwardsville: Southern Illinois University Press, 1985.
Dewey explains his views of sympathy, intuition, happiness, justice, benevolence, and praise in Chapter 13.
Gerdes, Karen. E. 2011. "Empathy, Sympathy, and Pity: 21st-Century Definitions and Implications for Practice and Research." *Journal of Social Service Research*, 37(3): 230–41.
Gerdes examines the roles that empathy and sympathy play in promoting more just and caring social structures and how they can inform the work of social workers and others. The references include empirical studies that are informative to educators and others.
Maxwell, Bruce. 2008. *Professional Ethics Education: Studies in Compassionate Empathy*. Netherlands: Springer.
This work is probably the best philosophical and psychological treatment of the contemporary concept of empathy in the English language. Maxwell's discussion of historical and contemporary issues makes it convenient to position Dewey's thought in present-day research.
Simpson, Douglas, and D. Mike Sacken. 2014. "The Sympathetic-and-Empathetic Teacher: A Deweyan Analysis." *Journal of Philosophy & History of Education*, 64 (1): 1–20.
The authors employ Dewey's ideas as tools to analyze a complex case study about an imaginary classroom teacher who becomes overly attached to a student. The entangled web of affections, sympathies, conflicts, and responsibilities provides a helpful view of Dewey's thinking.
Stueber, K. 2014. "Empathy." In the *Stanford Encyclopedia of Philosophy*, edited by E. N. Zalta. Last updated Spring 2014. http://plato.stanford.edu/archives/spr2014/entries/empathy.
This critical historical analysis of philosophical and psychological issues embedded in the concept of empathy is particularly helpful in understanding scientific research and its bearing on Dewey's theory of sympathy.

Case Study: Maria in Purgatory

Simon Sycamore, a greatly admired district employee and the head coach of the boys' Academy soccer team, resigns as coach just a week before the soccer season starts. After weeks of preseason practice, he told Maria that he was retiring as coach immediately and was planning to focus on his teaching and family's needs. Maria, while aware of his wife's ongoing sciatica problems and appreciative of his priorities, was a bit annoyed by the timing of his decision. All of the information he provided had been known for three or four months. Plus, his teaching was already fantastic. How much better could he become? It was difficult to sympathize with Simon. So, she urged him to reconsider his decision and its impact on the team and school. "Remain as coach at least this season," she encouraged. Simon said that his decision, while somewhat regrettable, was final. Knowing that Assistant Coach Albert McIntosh was ready to lead the team made the decision easier for him, Simon noted.

Nearly everyone who knew Simon was disappointed with his decision. Within twenty-four hours, however, different views of him and his resignation arose. A flood of criticism was directed at both him and Maria. In many ways, critics condemned her more than him. Several argued that Maria must have yielded to pressure from a Latina/o faction who insisted that the Academy hire a Latino head coach. Others, especially Simon supporters, argued that Maria failed to support a highly successful and admired lifelong teacher, coach, and community leader. Still others opined that she was a coward who put her job and security ahead of Simon's.

After a few days, more complicated interpretations of the situation arose charging that Maria was harboring a bigot, Simon, on the teaching staff and, possibly, exposing Eric Bonhoeffer, a transgender student, to more harassment. Moreover, other critics charged that she was disrespecting LGBTQ students, staff, and faculty by wanting Simon to remain as a teacher. Simon obviously did not want to coach Eric, they stated. Maria's request that the district openly address the false accusations by releasing the facts of the situation was denied. She was told that the majority of the school board was happy with Simon's resignation as coach and, if he resigned as teacher, the board would approve a request for retirement too.

Maria inferred that several district administrators and board members would welcome her resignation too. She was becoming controversial and a liability, they believed. She considered the advice to take a paid leave with a promise to get a positive recommendation to work in another district when her leave ended. But she loathed any outcome that would allow denigrators of Simon and would-be manipulators of Latinas/os' and LGBTQ interests to be rewarded for their devious attacks. She wondered if she should confidentially discuss the issues with a reporter in San Pedro, a nearby metropolitan area. But how, she asked herself, would an open article or two serve the interests of Academy students, staff, parents, and the community? Indeed, how was the common good to be determined in these circumstances?

The outcomes for Academy personnel and students, even after a couple of articles and even if a positive shift in community support occurred, would probably still be largely the same. Freedom of the press, Maria sighed, in spite of its importance, could not protect staff or students from any strong fallout. What good does it do to attempt to fight with your voice muzzled by board policy and practice? she continued. But, she partly answered her own question: at least it would become clear that Coach Sycamore was not resigning because of any prejudice against Eric. Indeed, how could anyone forget that he and she both gradually convinced other coaches and, later, the school board to support changes in district policy that would allow the first transgendered student to play on the girls' volleyball team? Critics, at least many, will suppress the facts as long as it suits their agenda. Even so, people would be reminded that Latinas/os support Coach Sycamore as strongly as any other group. Chaos and crisis creators, obviously, do not care deeply how their priorities are achieved.

In addition, maybe Simon would share with the reporter the other reasons he had resigned. A rumor suggested that one of his daughters would be demoted or terminated by her employer if Simon did not keep Eric Bonhoeffer off the soccer team. The rumor seemed consistent with Simon's vague disclosure the day he informed Maria of his resignation decision: "More is involved than I can discuss, Maria." But it appears inconsistent with the fact that Simon had already selected Bonhoeffer for the team and his own daughter might suffer for his decision. But who would have profited if Simon had kept Eric off the team? A first-rate reporter could uncover the options quickly. Maybe the only reasonable option for her was to meet with a reporter. But what would the consequences of the news items be for Simon's daughter? Plus, Maria was certain she would be the suspected source of information for any reporter who wrote an article. Perhaps the common good in this case would emerge from a simple setting forth of the facts. Later, Maria decided that only the actual consequences could determine how common and how much good would result from any decision. Maybe good is not identifiable, much less measurable, now. No conceivable option could guarantee only positive outcomes. Sleeping overnight on the matter seemed to be a good idea (MW 5, 375–9).

By the next morning, Maria was focused on several possible actions. Her first act would be to talk to Zoe, her former professor, about the options she had identified, e.g., talking with a reporter, resigning as principal, and recognizing that the situation is too complex for her to resolve.

QUESTIONS

1. If you were Zoe, would you advise Maria to keep her thoughts limited to a couple of discreet district personnel and allow the district and community dynamics to work themselves out?
2. As a former teacher with Maria and current principal in another district, would you ask Maria why she does not want to reconsider the district's exit package?

3. If you were one of Maria's influential community friends, would you ask her if she wants you to contact other friends who could tilt the balance of conversations toward needed clarifications?
4. Should Maria reconsider Dewey's claim that some problems are too complex to resolve or solve? How might this idea influence Maria's decision?
5. If Maria were in a unionized district, how might the options change?

CHAPTER 3

How Are Ethical Principles Useful?

Rules are practical; they are habitual ways of doing things. But principles are intellectual; they are the final methods used in judging suggested courses of action . . . the object of moral principles is to supply standpoints and methods which will enable the individual to make for [her]himself an analysis of the elements of good and evil in the particular situation in which [s]he finds [her]himself.

— John Dewey, *Ethics* (LW 7, 280; emphasis added)

Introduction

When a person listens to the flow of ideas in many ethical conversations, she or he may hear some arguments largely about the facts of a situation, although participants' engagement may commence with an almost immediate impression or, perhaps, perception. Other contributors may seek to determine or unmask intentions, discover new information, and listen to others' affirmations, denials, and reinterpretations of previously claimed facts. Still other observers, while seeking to clarify attitudes, dispositions, and habits of the people involved in a situation, focus anew on answers to specific queries: What really happened? Can this problem be dissolved by clearing up the confusion caused by dichotomous and fuzzy thinking? Is there a person or small group that is most responsible for the problem? What ethical principles are pertinent to the situation? Are ethical principles merely emotional responses to situations or are there evidentiary and reasoned bases for them?

In many mixed settings, a person may wish to inject, "In Islam, this behavior is considered an affront to Allah. No one, it is believed, has the right to treat others with disdain." Another may contribute: "In my culture, we consider everyone present – including those who choose to let situations unfold and continue – responsible in part for what happens, not just the instigators and accomplices. Silent enablers do harm too."

Three others add, "I think we cannot find a solution to this problem unless we abandon absolutes." "One doesn't provide much help if all he or she says is that there is no one answer." "This isn't our problem; it belongs to them. Let them solve it by applying their cultural beliefs." Another claims, "Considering the pressure that was placed on the participants, anyone would have done the same thing."

If this imaginary, free-floating discussion were to shift to Maria's office, someone might suggest, "Dewey, I suspect, might say this is a practical situation and requires practical reasoning (Garrison 1999); we need to know precisely what happened in this situation before considering potential conclusions and resolutions." Another person may want to use his long-held-and-seldom-questioned ethical rules to offer an immediate solution. Perhaps, he says,

> The rule is clear: No Eating While Standing. Maybe we should update the website and print some copies of the rules in order to avoid situations like this in the future. But what are we going to do this time? The rule doesn't indicate the penalty and why there should be any punishment. Yet we cannot ignore the total disregard for others that occurred.

A third person adds, "Don't forget the planning and deception that is behind this." "But did they really have a choice?" a contrarian whispers.

Dewey's lifetime, as noted earlier, was characterized by enormous ethical and intellectual change and upheaval; therefore, he engages ideas similar to those expressed above and learned much from everyday and academic interactions as he crafted his own ethical theory. Intersecting with the above thoughts are other issues that he raises about whether (a) good, duty, or virtue should be considered the supreme ethical factor or principle (LW 5, 279–88); (b) specific virtues (e.g., compassion, respect, kindness, integrity) are absolute, universal, or experimental in nature (LW 7, 275–83); (c) principles like regard, trust, and honesty should be applied as a set of rules or used as reflective tools to investigate issues (280–3); (d) intentions are important considerations when making judgments (MW 9, 356–70); or (e) qualitative features of ethical situations and experiences should be considered as they are in aesthetic, political, and historical inquiries (LW 5, 243–62).[1]

---

[1] Although some treat the terms absolute and universal as synonyms, we distinguish them, in part, because Dewey seemingly did (LW 7, 270; MW 12, 260–4; MW 14, 167–70). In *The Public and Its Problems* (LW 2, 369), for example, Dewey objects to people attempting to conjure up support for the creation of communities in society by making it appear that community is "the ultimate universal, and as near an absolute as exists." In addition, absolutism is historically, although not invariably, associated with a belief in the Absolute or god and eternal values. Also, absolutism has

Using Dewey's ethical framework, then, does not always lead to immediate, simple decisions and resolutions. Yet it may at times when people are
ethically sensitive and insightful, and problems are not extraordinarily
complex. Also, when inquiry and concern do not permit solving an issue
immediately, they may still illuminate the problem and make it possible to
better cooperate, discuss, and modify problems. On the other hand,
Dewey's approach is designed to address and, possibly, handle complicated, multifaceted, and nuanced ethical situations too. As some particulars of his multilayered ethical thinking are examined below, Irene's
situation is revisited to learn how his theory informs her situation. In
addition to Irene and Maria, two of Irene's third-grade students, Said
Khan and Chen Lî, and school psychology intern, Molly Greenwood,
emerge as important figures. Virginia Lewis, a fifth-grade teacher, arrives
on the scene too. Dewey's ideas about ethical principles are interwoven
under the headings: Empirical Generalizations, Reconstruction of Universal Claims, Reconstruction of Absolute Claims, and Conclusion.

Empirical Generalizations

Dewey argues that certain philosophical and historical misunderstandings
of the nature of ethical prescriptions and prohibitions discourage substantive discussions in societies and schools. Yet many ethical discussions, like
the imaginary one in Chapter 1, contain explicit or implicit references to
absolute, universal, relative, or subjective claims. If stated with a tone of
finality, these claims often build walls that block dialogue, seeking clarity
on points of interest, and cooperating to find solutions to problems. In
addition, he argues that when ethical beliefs are wedded to the idea that
customs, traditions, and religions should not be evaluated or modified,
dialogical problems are magnified. The accidents of birth, plus socializa-
tion, often make it difficult to learn about ethically infused concerns and to
live reflectively and openly together. Although ethical development is
definitely influenced by customs, political beliefs, traditions, and religions,
one's ethical development should not simply be a byproduct of these

been associated frequently with thinking that ethical principles do not allow room for making any
exceptions. That is, an absolutist may claim that prohibitions against abortion, dishonesty, or killing
humans allows for no exceptions, regardless of temporal and contextual particularities. On the other
hand, those who make universal ethical claims may or may not make exceptions, e.g., abortions may
be acceptable if a mother's life is at risk, dishonesty may be acceptable during certain war events, and
killing may be acceptable if a peace officer has no other way to protect her or another's life.
Absolutists, nevertheless, sometimes agree with universalists on the last point.

influences. Other influences – inquiry, reflection, and deliberation – should play roles too. For comparative purposes, think of societies gradually developing healthcare practices, theories, and bodies of information that evolve over hundreds of years with significant input more recently from both experiential and scientific learning. While imperfect, the health sciences progress by open inquiry, studying Indigenous peoples' practices, investigating folk tales, testing hypotheses, and developing warranted but not final practices, procedures, and treatments. Healthcare researchers and professionals continue their inquiry as the depth and breadth of their fields are enriched.

Similarly, ethical theory, knowledge, and practice have developed, resulting in a somewhat nascent ethical or moral science that is informed by philosophy and the humanities, sciences, and arts (MW 14, 204–5). In consequence, ethical tools for analyzing problematic situations are being refined (LW 7, 280) and, in time, warranted ethical claims and principles become at least "empirical generalizations" (MW 14, 165). As intellectual tools, ethical principles (a) enlighten ethical thinking, judgments, and decision-making; (b) function as *"final methods"* (165; emphasis original) when one evaluates situations and considers possible solutions; (c) make available perspectives and procedures to analyze "elements of good and evil" in specific situations; and (d) help create hypotheses for further inquiry and experimentation (165). Hence, while there are many differences between the fields, the development of ethics as a broad field of inquiry is similar to that of the health sciences.

Dewey's method of studying ethical questions and situations, therefore, includes rigorous processes that give careful attention to experience, deliberation, data, hypotheses, experimentation , and consequences. His language regarding a moral or ethical science may not be intended literally but understood paradigmatically (Pappas 2008, 17–19), e.g., ethics should be methodologically and attitudinally similar to the sciences as human nature, experience, and conduct are examined (Pappas 1997a, 2008). In addition, Dewey (LW 5, 1–40) seems to have envisioned a transdisciplinary use of the sciences to inform ethical inquiry and decision-making much as he used the term *science of education*. Thus, he argues that "Moral science is not something with a separate province. It is physical, biological and historic knowledge placed in a human context where it will illuminate and guide the activities" (MW 14, 204). Although different in his details, Marc D. Hauser (2006, 425) affirms a similar claim: "Inquiry into our moral nature will no longer be the proprietary province of the humanities and social sciences, but a shared journey with the natural sciences."

In due course, using ethical principles to inform decision-making is personal: an understanding of them and the broader dimensions of ethics enables each person to make "*an analysis of the elements of good and evil in* ... [a] *particular situation*" (LW 7, 280; emphasis original) and to reach balanced, fair-minded conclusions. Emphasizing the personal element, including perceptions and sensitivities (Fesmire 2003, 143), Dewey asserts that decisions are nevertheless made in social contexts: "the forum of individual minds ... [are] carried into effect by individual agents, who are in turn personally responsible for the consequences of their acts" (LW 7, 317). Thus, personal responsibility is at least twofold: for inquiry into issues and for the consequences of decisions. But he observes also that too few people casually or informally learn about, utilize, and reconstruct ethical principles in reflective ways. Moreover, too many people believe that principles are merely rules to be followed or applied, not principles to be constructed, discovered, justified, and used when thinking and deciding. Too many think their involvement in making ethical decisions means they are always free to do as they prefer without any responsibility.

Dewey argues that the first forums of people's minds are populated by similar voices – those of parents, siblings, relatives, neighbors, friends, and acquaintances. Hence, early intellectual configurations are frequently developed without seriously entertaining alternative ideas (MW 14, 216). Later constructed forums, ideally, are not formed in "a closet but in the forum of intense, continued and wide-spread mutual discussion" (LW 5, 351). Ultimately, he clarifies that each person should, like George Mead, develop a mind that is "a forum of discussion with itself and a sharing" of these ideas with others (LW 6, 25). Schools, no doubt, are contributors to students' expanding deliberative forums. But while students' expanding worlds beyond schools also help shape their forums, the mind is not necessarily growing if the same voices are heard internally or externally. People who largely retain tightly laced original forums or who repetitively reinforce contemporary forums may not, in important ways, be significantly different. Cultural lag is not uniform, and the subparts of anyone's forum may be temporally not reflectively, populated (Brinkman and Brinkman 2005).

Dewey envisions, then, deliberations in each person's mind, involving, metaphorically, interactions with "Ordinary Experience," "Reflection," "Research," "Experimentation," "Consequences," and streams of "Others." Then, deliberation and decision-making are, in a crucial way, (a) personal, (b) social, and (c) historical. Hence, one should not immediately dismiss one's own experiences and traditions, the claims of others, or the historical continuities embedded in multiple forms of inquiry and creativity. The

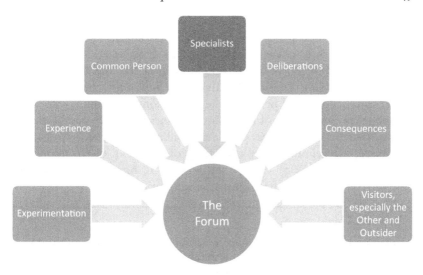

Figure 3.1   The forum of one's mind

personal dimension, as many argue, should result in a knowledgeable selection of the ideas, acts, habits, consequences, and responsibilities that help shape a meaningful and rewarding life. Ethical principles emerge in these forums as well as provide insight into how to address issues that arise. But when the principles become a part of a person's ethical tools, they do not dictate conclusions (LW 7, 279). They remain tools, thinking tools. Figure 3.1 depicts many, but not all, of the factors that are selected to contribute to one's personal ethical forum. "Visitors," including Woolf's (1938) "Outsider," refer to those who hold similar, alternative, and contrarian views in addition to others who may be cultural and ideological outsiders. From Dewey's perspective, contrarian voices should be regularly heard and analyzed via informal discussions and inquiries. In time, some visitors become regular inhabitants of one's mind. The common person, as Westbrook (1991, 153) notes, is central in Dewey's thinking because of the relevance of their everyday interest in solving practical problems. Thus, addressing practical problems should entail being alert to questions of necessity, compassion, equity, friendship, and inclusion. On the other hand, the forum of a person's mind is frequently populated also by formal studies, including but not limited to career, vocational, and professional preparation. Dewey, fortunately, made sure his intellectual forum was populated with "intelligent women, non-philosophers, odd thinkers and ordinary folk" (Stengel 2009, 92).

We turn now to focus on Dewey's views of universal and absolute ethical claims. Understanding his reworked view of universal and absolute ethical principles is crucial to clarifying his broader ethical viewpoint. Significantly, his reconstruction of the principles does not lead to a naïve ethical subjectivism, simplistic relativism, or unsophisticated contextualism (Pappas 2008), and he rejects the conclusions that ethical thinking is reducible to unchallengeable whims or unexaminable traditions. He argues, therefore, that unless people are willing to "surrender to chance, to caprice, to prejudice" they need to reconsider and, often, reconstruct moral principles (LW 7, 320). A key concern for him, therefore, is when and why principles may have epistemic warrant or merit.

Stop and Think

Think back through some recent conversations you have had. Was there an occasion that seemed to inhibit or foster the discussion? Was there a tone, word choice, intense feeling, body movement, or other factor that built conversational barriers? If the conversation recovered from an inhibiting factor, how?

A Reconstruction of Universal Claims

A casual reader of Dewey may conclude that he categorically opposes universal and absolute ethical claims. In reality, his views are decidedly more nuanced and complicated than often interpreted. Clearly, he does reject universal ethical principles as sometimes depicted, e.g., as rationalistic, transcendental, and decontextualized assertions that apply to everyone in all situations everywhere (LW 7, 275–83). Yet, he also indicates that when purported universal claims emerge in discussions one should decide whether the claims have sufficient warrant to merit retention or reconstruction. For example, many at the Academy, especially in the lower grades, originally employed a maxim – "Dishonesty is wrong and forbidden" – that might need reconstruction in order to stimulate reflective and educative discussions about a range of issues. But some teachers claimed that to change the maxim would irritate a sizable group of teachers, parents, and students. Nearly any change might be confusing, but others claimed a change would result in more reflective thinking, and students would be better prepared to engage in discussions of personal and social issues. Others claimed that using a revised maxim could become a gateway to discussing sociopolitical controversies and to learning how to deal with ideological dogmas.

Reconsidering Irene Sebastian's situation may illustrate why the maxim could profit from a reconstruction. Although Irene hesitantly admitted that she screamed in class, two of her students interpreted the incident differently. In a quick response to a carefully crafted question to a few students, Said Khan noted, "Ms. Sebastian suddenly moaned." Chen Lî, capturing the spirit of another student, added, "She was sad, almost crying." Said's and Chen's parents had nothing to add to their students' views. Virginia Lewis, the teacher who reported the occurrence to Maria, later observed that the word "scream" did not originate with her. As far as she could recall, Molly Greenwood, the school psychology intern, first used the term when she approached her the day of the incident. Molly was in Irene's classroom at the time of the reported scream – or was it a moan, as Said observed?

Maria, as usual, is pressed for time but felt she had to talk with Molly. When they met, Molly affirms that she used the word "scream" and added that Irene's scream frightened students. Sensing the state of affairs might be more complicated than initially believed, Maria asks Molly if she also mentioned the matter to staff other than Virginia Lewis. Molly answered yes and that she did so because she was concerned about the yelling and wanted to ensure that students were protected from further outbursts. Plus, she thought that if more teachers knew about the incident Irene would receive additional support from her colleagues. But, she stressed, her priority was to ensure the well-being of students. She concluded, "I was there. I know what I heard. Anyone present would describe the incident the same way." "Anyone?" Maria said to herself, as she recalled Said and Chen's words.

Maria redirected the discussion to ask if Molly was aware of Irene's family situation, the rapid deterioration of her husband's health, and the Guardian Angel's text to Irene from the hospital immediately before Irene's verbalization. Did she know that Irene's husband had just fallen and been rushed to the hospital where he was diagnosed with a fractured femur? "No," Molly softly responded. She had not known of the Lewy Body diagnosis, fall, and trip to the hospital. She indicated that she was too involved with university studies, completing job application materials, and planning her wedding to discuss nonschool matters.

Shortly thereafter, Maria reached a conclusion about Irene's situation, recommended a family medical leave for her, and clarified to relevant parties the little that confidentiality policy allowed. But she was unsure about related matters, including whether a faculty development day some-time might explore the topic "caring for colleagues and students" and discuss the relationship of truth-telling and the roles of sympathy or empathy to caring for one another. Fortunately, she had already talked with Alima about her misspoken remark about Nigel and with Dante about his fear-inducing remark to Irene. Still, she wondered: Should I also talk further with Molly or her supervisor before her internship concludes? Did Molly have a personal reason for calling Irene's moan or yelp a scream?

But then, she questioned herself, am I amplifying the importance of Molly's word selection and seeming lack of collegial interest in Irene? Am I thinking too much about nourishing a caring school culture? But, she did not wonder if there was any compelling reason to change the maxim "Dishonesty is wrong and forbidden" to an affirmative thought, perhaps something like "Honesty is an important part of community building and personal growth." However, in a flash, she concluded the old maxim might be serviceable a bit longer. The time and energy it would take to address the concern now would be more demanding than the immediate advantages. Plus, the existing maxim could be reenvisioned as a stepping-stone for guiding reflective student discussions.

Word choices, of course, are frequently momentous decisions, positively and negatively. Xenophobic, racist, and sexist terms alone underline the offensiveness of certain words. Political inaccuracies are controversial too, depending on whether one is – or wishes to be – labeled a conservative, reactionary, or fanatic or a liberal, radical, or extremist. Dewey too was greatly concerned over the selection of words and their specific meanings and, in context, used the term *principle* rather than the word *rule* when writing about ethics (LW 7, 279). For him, a rule is a practical term that usually conveys the idea of adhering to an inflexible prescription, but he thought that principle connotes a flexible intellectual instrument that helps one gain insight into an ethical situation and its resolution. He argues also that honesty is usually a crucial quality in human relationships (LW 7, 277, 279, 359) and is a significant principle in nurturing trust and democracy (MW 3, 230). That is, if citizens, including politicians, are not motivated by a desire to discover and understand the facts and data regarding a need or problem, the point of doing nearly any form of inquiry – ethical, legal, political, governmental, educational, medical – is to a significant degree undermined (MW 3, 229–30). He connects human relationships, democracy, and inquiry when he avers: "Honesty of purpose is universally recognized to be a condition of successful government, but it may be doubted whether intellectual activity has been sufficiently emphasized as a condition of the success of democracy" (LW 7, 359). Ironically, fabricated, even dated and misunderstood, information and data may have more destructive power than warranted assertions have positive power at times. The rapid distribution of information and misinformation creates ethical challenges for schools and society.

On the other hand, Dewey, like many ethicists, may think that "dishonesty" is either permissible or warranted, even virtuous, in certain situations. Imagine Harriet Tubman, the nineteenth-century US abolitionist who used the Underground Railroad to free slaves making a misleading comment to authorities or Oskar Schindler, the twentieth-century industrialist, who protected Jews in Germany by employing them in his factories during the Nazi Holocaust, providing a misleading answer to a Nazi authority. If the established authorities of their day asked either Tubman or Schindler for information they intended to use to resubjugate, torture, and/or murder blacks, Jews, and others, they did not deserve it. Any person who gave authorities information about escaping slaves or Jews in these situations seems to provide insight into one type of collaborator: one who enables others to brutalize and rob people of their lives. On the other hand, misleading people would probably be an infrequent, if not rare act, in Dewey's ethic as important questions arise and likely consequences emerge: When, if ever, is deception in the interest of the common good, a school, a district, or a community? What are the probable consequences for the school, profession, and us if we deceive impulsively, defensively, arbitrarily, and capriciously? What sort of persons are we becoming if we mislead whomever or whenever we desire? What kind of profession, society, and world are we helping to construct? Kurzban's (2010) recent research on the modularity of the mind or brain reveals interesting challenges to human consistency and truth-telling but does not diminish the need for human integrity and honesty.

On the subject of justice, Dewey's concept of and method for determining whether an act or policy is just is informative. He asserts that when justice is viewed as a principle, it indicates "the will to *examine* specific institutions [e.g., political, commercial, governmental, religious, military, educational] and measures [funding, oversight, laws, policies, practices], so as to find out how they operate with the view of introducing greater impartiality and equity into the consequences they produce" (LW 7, 79; emphasis original). What, then, may leaders reveal about themselves, schools, and districts when they are unwilling to examine their practices and operations? When consequences of policies and practices are unknown, why is there opposition to collecting data? When a leader tells their colleagues and other audiences that releasing particular data is forbidden by their supervisors, what are they implying? Being open regarding actual or desired public information does not, of course, mean a leader can divulge confidential personnel or student data.

Dewey's embedded criteria for identifying policies and practices of justice includes eight connected points: (a) reflective inquiry ("find out how"), (b) personal intention ("with the view of"), (c) individual attitude ("will to examine"), (d) particular context ("specific institutions"), (e) evaluation indicators ("measures"), (f) degrees of growth ("greater"), (g) desirable qualities ("impartiality and equity"), and (h) associated outcomes ("consequences") (LW 7, 79). Of course, much should be added to this skeleton in a thorough discussion of justice and its various forms, e.g., communicative, procedural, retributive, distributive, restorative.

Although many people may not be inclined to act completely just or fair sometimes, this does not mean they act on their inclinations. Nor does it mean people are aware of their faulty thinking, defective intentions, and ill-advised choices. Plus, recognizing one's fallibility is different from being conscious of one's specific intellectual biases and moral prejudices. Hence, ongoing public accountability and ethical development is essential in dynamic societies and professions. Thus, an improvement in many schools and districts appears likelier if Dewey's justice criteria are clarified, affirmed, and practiced. He also warns against the undue influence that stems from the "inequitable distribution of power" that can cause "intellectual blindness" by the privileged to the interests of others (LW 7, 347). Yet, this does not mean only the privileged are biased. Nor does it mean that only the wealthy are likely privileged. Democracy, therefore, needs various systems, institutions, and cultures that foster the skills, attitudes, dispositions, and habits necessary for an equitable distribution of powers, rights, and resources. Likewise, democratic societies and districts need to ask focused questions, e.g., Who is privileged in this particular situation? What are the noneconomic sources of power or forces in this classroom, school, and district? How do they use their power? Do they hoard power or cultivate equitable opportunities? What signs of powerlessness should Maria and her staff notice and address? What should they do to nurture power and responsibility distribution throughout the Academy and into the community?

Dewey indicates further that open-minded, sustained, multi-institutional, and, ideally, multinational inquiry and testing of ethical hypotheses often lead to *relational universal* or widespread general claims (MW 12, 262). That is, general agreement concerning specific relational universal standards, processes, and aims are possible (MW 12, 197–8): e.g., schools in Hong Kong, Puebla, Paris, Nairobi, and Mumbai may agree that they are obligated to ensure the safety of their students and staff as well as to foster the honesty of students and staff. Arguably, many differences in these cities are still likely, including those often found in moral development programs and in school policies. Still, Dewey concludes that when relational universal claims are found warranted by multiple parties in multiple locations, ethical principles could be used in the specific temporal and spatial contexts where these shared goods are affirmed (MW 12, 198). Moreover, he clarifies that scientific ethical inquiry and deliberation may extend out of local situations to include situations in transnational contexts (LW 7, 366–72). But relational agreements do not usually arise instantaneously and sometimes requires "a process that transcends generations" (Garrison, Neubert, and Reich 2012, 103). The time it takes for new international and multigenerational inquiry and moral agreement to occur, however, is no excuse for allowing flagrant inequities and indisputable oppressions to continue.

Of course, even in democratically disposed schools and districts, recognizing and building relational and community agreements is frequently a lengthy process and always an ongoing one. This ongoing learning process points to Dewey's emphasis on the continuity of ethical knowledge and its development. For instance, learning that the tragedies of international, regional, and local wars during the twentieth century may constitute moral knowledge that informs some twenty-first century moral development by ordinary people and political and military leaders (Pinker 2011). In the same way, educators are well-advised to ask what specific moral knowledge of twentieth-century schools should inform the development of twenty-first-century schools (Gutek 2013; Urban and Wagoner 2009; Warren and Patrick 2006).

Stop and Think

What advantages or insights do you see in Dewey's ethic? What reservations do you have about using his thoughts to make ethical judgments in schools?

A Reconstruction of Absolute Claims

Dewey also offered a reconstructed absolutist theory. To begin, he states that advocates offers absolutes often do not give sufficient attention to the realities of a dynamic universe and the progressive growth of bodies of knowledge (MW 12, 256–77). Plus, ethical thinking, like other forms of inquiry, should not be dominated by either unquestioned theoretical assumptions or a search for absolute certainty. Yet, while he thinks there are no absolutes as traditionally argued, he maintains that societies can and do arrive at reasonable, secure, and stable ethical conclusions that might be either relational universal or, as described below, practical certainty claims (LW 12; MW 14). Secure ethical conclusions exist for at least two reasons. First, some bodies of knowledge that support specific ethical conclusions are being advanced, refined, and broadened, and their warrant is characterized by greater degrees of warrant or support today than they had been in the past. Granted, some assertions are little more than poorly supported hypotheses; others have a considerable degree of support; still others have a high degree of warrant. Second, ethical knowledge grows as more hypotheses are tested and, now and again, confirmed (LW 12, 481–505). He concludes that "we are justified in using" repeatedly verified truth claims "*as if* they were absolutely true" but cautions that each *as if* absolute claim is a provisional claim "subject to being corrected by future consequences" and new research (LW 2, 12). Stated similarly, truth claims repeatedly verified over decades and generations "may have practical or moral certainty, but ... never lose a hypothetic quality" (LW 1, 123). His perspective, therefore, includes the possibility of practical certainty in making real-world choices, but not in arriving at theoretical or epistemic certainty (123).

Stop and Think

Sometimes people argue that no one has the right to keep anyone from doing as they wish, because no one knows absolutely that any act is ethically wrong. How might a Deweyan-informed teacher, principal, or superintendent respond to the claim?

When Dewey (LW 7, 242; emphasis original) states that "[we] are sure that the *attitude* of personal kindliness, of sincerity and fairness, will make our judgment of the effects of a proposed action on the good of others infinitely more likely to be correct than will those of hate, hypocrisy, and self-seeking," he seems consistent with his relational universal and his practical certainty remarks. Why? The phrase "infinitely more likely" affirms a highly probable, not absolute, outcome and implies widespread applicability. This claim illustrates his idea that when consequences in a particular case are unclear, deference should be given to the tendency of dispositions or habits "in the long run" (MW 14, 37). In Maria's silent deliberations about whether to talk with Molly Greenwood about her reactions to Irene Sebastian's moan or yelp or both, Dewey, theoretically speaking, might advise her to consider how her prior experience with similar situations and pertinent research may inform her thinking. But her experience and knowledge of research may be insufficient. What does she do then? Codes of professional ethics may or may not be unhelpful. Data regarding educators who have lost their professional licenses may or may not be useful. The advice of valued colleagues may be suitable. School policies may be useful. Maria's search for answers will not always reach the level of practical certainty. Her best choice may be to test her own informed judgment: advising Molly now may be helpful ("Think about it."), but reaching an evaluative conclusion of Molly's behavior may be ill-advised (e.g., "Why do you think two other people described Irene's sounds so differently?").

Conclusion

Many teachers and administrators, like Maria, may wish to know more about relational universals or practical certainties. They may also desire to learn more about principles that should not be "lightly discarded" (LW 7, 330). Desiring to know more often merits a collaborative exploration that leads to a study of what is being thought, researched, and practiced in other schools, cities, and countries – and in fields or disciplines that throw light on the work of schools, e.g., social work, psychiatry, neuroscience, cultural anthropology, social psychology, ethics, and law. Dewey's orientation toward using ethical principles, in general, suggests the importance of each educator enjoying a breadth of personal knowledge, plus, personal responsibility in a cooperative school community where everyone works with others "to discover *what* principles *are* relevant to . . . [their] own social [or school] estate" (LW 7, 283; emphasis original). This idea – that each educator should collaborate in order to deliberate more insightfully – is warranted because ethical recipes and panaceas do not appear to exist, and schools are obligated to have regard for – care for – the well-being of their children and adults. Hence, each person needs to think for herself, welcome others into the forum of her mind, and act empathetically in the interest of others (LW 8, 125–39). In many schools and districts, this probably means teams of teachers and administrators working together to pinpoint and promote specific ethical principles and emphases. In particular, districts and schools probably need to build climates, cultures, and communities

that encourage a reflective flexibility while considering the developmental
levels of students and the uniqueness of each problematic ethical
situation.

Working collaboratively, thinking empathetically, deciding deliberatively, and acting reflectively, however, do not lead to a simplistic
relativistic ethic. In fact, Dewey strongly objects to any kind of relativism
that stymies thinking by automatically implying that everything is relative to and determined by one's personal preferences or cultural practices.
Here Dewey argues that if the statement "everything is relative" is the
unvarying answer to most ethical questions, it may take the form of an
absolute principle and, probably, a discussion inhibitor or "logic stopper"
(Gribble 1969, 35). Rather than stimulating discussions (e.g., about how
acts are indeed relative to specific intentions, facts, conditions, people,
principles, virtues, context, and consequences), a one-dimensional personal and cultural relativism often impedes inquiry, deliberation, and
research. In this form, Dewey thinks the practical meaning of ethical
relativism is that "all moral principles are so relative to a particular state
of society that they have no binding force in any social condition"
(LW 7, 283).

Positively, Dewey asserts that quests for the clarification of values and
principles may be aided by "social forces" that "create and reinforce
searches for the principles which are truly relevant in our own day"
(LW 7, 283). Among influences in recent decades, it may be argued that
social forces have helped schools and societies understand that the
principles of equal respect and regard for all persons, not just people
who are admired, appreciated, or wealthy, are meaningful universal
claims. Perhaps, although it may be too early to say, more individuals
and societies are also recognizing that the consequences of war include
both horrendous processes and outcomes, including the destruction of
lives, cultures, and basic civil rights (Pinker 2011). Conceivably, too,
societies are learning that wars are increasingly intolerable and catastrophic ways of addressing local, regional, and international disputes
(LW 7, 366–71). But peace education is, if not rare, long overdue in
many parts of the world (Noddings 2011). Similarly, many ethical,
social, and political forces seem to be revolutionizing the way some
women, poor, vulnerable, and abandoned, are being treated (Manne
2018). Arguably, ethical awakenings that ignore those who are deemed
culturally, politically, and economically expendable are biased and lack a
genuine interest in the full implications of personal fairness, social
justice, and mutual regard and respect.

Accordingly, it seems that teachers and administrators should not think and work in isolation – from one another or from those in other districts, cities, and countries – but should collaboratively address ethical issues that affect students and societies. To repeat, as Garrison, Neubert, and Reich (2012, 103) suggest, the reconstruction and utilization of ethical principles is a multigenerational, multi-entity, and multinational endeavor. Hence, history – including critically evaluated laws, policies, and practices of generations of schools and boards – is a type of "moral telescope" that can inform educators and students (LW 17, 318). An intentional study of the history of K–12 education, especially, can offer telescopic insights into ethical ways of organizing schools and addressing ethical quandaries (Button and Provenzo, Jr. 1983; Warren 1985). What, educators seem well-advised to ask, does the history of children, women, the poor, and other disrespected groups have to say about our current structures, policies, and practices?

While Dewey's thoughts about virtues and vices could easily be extended, the ones already noted – honesty, justice, equity, impartiality, concern for the good of others, kindness, and fairness – are suggestive of principles that may be thoughtfully considered for use in particular situations today. Dewey's rejection of the vices of "hate, hypocrisy, and self-seeking" – not to mention others – are also instructive as educators seek to establish relatively secure and stable ethical communities in schools (LW 7, 242). While rejecting the temptation to "surrender to chance, to caprice, to prejudice," is appropriate, Dewey argues that it is desirable to use warranted principles to help establish democratic cultures in schools (320). To foster reflective, ethical cultures, Dewey claims that these concepts and their meanings need to be reexamined, reinterpreted, and, if merited, reutilized in the light of particular school situations as other variables are also considered, e.g., intentions, desires, agency, and responsibility (320). Furthermore, he stresses the importance of making qualitative judgments about an experience or "situation as a whole" (LW 5, 259), apprehending the "nature of any act" by its consequences (LW 7, 252) and thinking that is "regulated by qualitative consider-ations" (243). Pappas (1997a, 536) rightly stresses that "the situation is not simply where deliberation takes place; it is a context constituted by a pervasive quality that guides and renders meaningful the discriminations and steps taken in deliberation." Immediate apprehension, persistent inquiry, and sustained reflection, obviously, are complementary activities and crucial companions in Deweyan-informed ethical decision-making (Kestenbaum 1996).

Discussion Questions

1.　Now that we are deeper into Maria De La Garza's thinking about ethical issues, how would you describe her approach?

2.　How would you describe the ethical forum of your own mind? Which cultural traditions and fields of inquiry and creativity most influence your thinking?

3.　Do you know of prospective visitors who need an invitation to your forum? A critic of Dewey? What do they have to offer that is underappreciated by Dewey?

4.　Illustrate a way in which Dewey's explanation of ethical principles is useful. Explain how the idea could impact school and classroom discussions.

5.　If asked, how do you think Dewey might explain further how society can have secure or stable ethical values if it does not have any traditional absolute or universal ethical values?

RELATED READINGS

Biesta, G. 2015. "How Does a Competent Teacher Become a Good Teacher?" *Philosophical Perspectives on Teacher Education*, 1–22.

Biesta's article identifies sound judgment as the quality that otherwise competent teachers must acquire before they can become ethically good teachers. The process of developing judgment is seen as an important part of employing ethical principles and making decisions.

Dewey, John, and J. Tufts. 1932. *Ethics*. Vol. 7 of *John Dewey: The Later Works, 1925–1953*, edited by Jo Ann Boydston, 1–512. Carbondale and Edwardsville: Southern Illinois University Press, 1985.

Chapter 14, "Moral Judgment and Knowledge" ("The Nature and Office on Principles," 275–83), provides insight into why Dewey rejects nonexperimental ethical theories. Special attention is paid to his view of the instrumental and interpretative roles of principles.

Noddings, Nel. 1998. "Thoughts on John Dewey's 'Ethical Principles Underlying Education'." *The Elementary School Journal*, no. 5, 479–88.

Noddings responds both appreciatively and critically to Dewey's article "Ethical Principles Underlying Education" (EW 5, 54–83). She focuses on his claim that moral education includes both the way education is conducted and the kinds of moral citizens developed thereby.

Stengel, Barbara S. 2009. "More than 'Mere Ideas': Deweyan Tools for the Contemporary Philosopher." *Education and Culture* 25 (2): 89–100.

Stengel identifies three ideas that determine how Dewey's ethic may enhance one's ethical reflections and, thereby, actions: (a) entertaining the perspective of "the other" in ethical conversations, (b) recognizing the continuity of ethical thought and practice, and (c) understanding how *what is* informs what can and should be.

Simpson, Douglas J., and D. Mike Sacken. 2016. "Ethical Principles and School Challenges: A Deweyan Analysis." *Education and Culture* 32 (1): 63–86.

This article clarifies Dewey's approach to arriving at secure knowledge and practical certainty while rejecting absolute theoretical certainty. An extensive application of Dewey's ethical approach is embedded in an analysis of a high school testing scandal and a related personnel problem.

Strike, Kenneth A. 1988. "The Ethics of Teaching." *The Phi Delta Kappan* 70, no. 2 (October): 156–8.

Strike illustrates how a deontologist and, largely, nonconsequentialist ethicist may use ethical principles to address or solve issues. He demonstrates his position by using the principles of equal respect of persons and benefit maximization as he examines problematic school scenarios.

Case Study: Controversial Research Issues

On one of Maria's Observational Walks through the Academy's middle school, Novella Arnott trotted up to her to say that she and next year's sixth-grade social studies class had decided to submit a research proposal about the long-closed Morton Tire Company. The students wanted to examine employment practices, demographic staffing patterns, and salary and benefits policies and practices during the last five years of the company's operation. She wanted Maria to see the first draft of the proposal before she revises and submits it to the District Research Review Committee (DRRC). Novella mentioned having made an appointment via Kenseisha Jackson, Maria's administrative assistant, to discuss the first draft with her. Maria noted that the DRRC guidelines only apply to teachers and high school students but maybe the grade-level requirement could be waived. She noted that Novella's reputation as a second-year teacher and researcher and the Academy's emphasis on students doing research on civic and leadership concerns might ease the way for a tweaking of the guidelines.

After Novella discussed the proposal with Maria, she met with the DRRC. She learned that the DRRC had the same observations about the Morton study that Maria mentioned. The first observation they raised concerned the age and experience of the middle school students: they had little if any experience as researchers, might jeopardize confidentiality interests because of their developmental levels, and might spread rumors and facts about former and current citizens of the town. The second observation focused on Novella's request for a revision to the DRRC guidelines to include all Academy students or at least middle and high school students. The stated observations were twofold: (a) there was no precedent for granting exceptions to the DRRC guidelines and (b) the process for revising the DRRC guidelines includes both district faculty and board approval. The grapevine provided other possible objections, especially if one rumor was true: the manager who oversaw the closing of the Morton factory was believed to have assaulted several female employees, favored others with higher salaries, and, on occasion, promoted others outside of normal channels. While he had died fifteen years earlier, he still had two adult granddaughters, both respected Harbor educators, and several grandchildren in the area.

Of course, Novella and the students were open to pursuing information wherever it led, whether to confirming or disconfirming any relevant question. But their focus and time was very limited. Their main interest was in learning to do research and, secondly, learning more about their community. But doubts by local residents, school staff, and students also raised questions about the possibility of exposing assaulted women to the public. Most critics were confident that Novella and her students could do different kinds of research that would not scandalize the company employees and embarrass relatives and their families. Assertive community opponents contested the history project and protested to Maria, the superintendent, and the board. A number of faculty and community supporters of the planned project and of Novella's guidance of the study recommended that the class and Novella respond in writing to the objections before submitting two proposals, one for an expansion of the research guidelines to include middle school students and the other for approval of a research proposal by Novella's class. Simultaneously, the two ideas were developed into proposals. Concurrent with their development were several rumors: (a) Novella was an uncompromising critical race theorist who wanted to use her students to promote her Marxian ideas, and (b) Maria undermined Novella's efforts by not preparing her adequately for the two controversies and not taking a leadership role in either controversy. In response to the rumors, Maria, Novella, and Matthew Webb, assistant principal, prepared a low-key but clear response. Together and separately but somewhat casually they noted pertinent details of Maria and Novella's conversation and Maria's early small group leadership support for the two proposals.

A year later, Maria and Superintendent Roosevelt were extremely pleased when the Harbour School Board, with one abstention, supported both the revised research guidelines and the adjusted history research project. Previously, nearly everyone interested had studied and discussed the modified research proposal, the expanded research guidelines, the board's attorney's report, and the recommendations by two independent consultants. One consultant's closing remarks floated through the district and community: "The desire to protect the students, the teacher, the school, and the relatives of the deceased employees from distress is admirable; the desire to protect and promote open inquiry, responsible citizenship, and historical understanding is likewise commendable. The project is judiciously and reflectively crafted."

QUESTIONS

1. If you were Superintendent Roosevelt, what concerns would you want clarified in the research project and the district guidelines? What prescriptions and prohibitions, if any, would give you pause?
2. If you were a parent of sixth-graders, what concerns might you want addressed in the research guidelines? Or would you never vote for middle school students doing research?
3. How would you describe the conflict of ethical principles or values in this case study?
4. If you were an adult child of the late tire company manager or one of his alleged sexually assaulted company employees, would you speak publicly about the proposed research?
5. What do you think of Novella's statement, "I would not approve class research questions that violate the district's guidelines for discussing controversial topics. Doing this kind of research is also teaching"?

CHAPTER 4

What Does Regard for People Imply?

> The ultimate significance of this appeal [to "sympathy and benevolent regard for others"] is, however, to make us realize the fact that regard for self and regard for others are both of them secondary phases of a more normal and complete interest: regard for the welfare and integrity of the social groups of which we form a part.
>
> —John Dewey, *Ethics* (LW 7, 299)

Introduction

The epigraph draws attention to one of Dewey's primary ethical principles: regard for self, others, social groups, and more. Along with other theoretical implications, the principle provides a glance on how one should examine different ethical problems and situations. In addition, the principle appears to suggest his "unifying thread" of ethical thinking: that is, *"moral conceptions and processes grow naturally out of the very conditions of human life"* or social interactions (LW 7, 308; emphasis original). Ethical interests are not unusual or strange; they are a typical feature of life. Likewise, the principle, when informed by moral science, suggests broader, more inclusive ethical dimensions, embracing both local and global concerns for "any possible neighbor" (MW 8, 82), the "social whole" (LW 7, 300), and national and international well-being (LW 7, 366–71). Consequentially, this principle is embedded in Dewey's fourfold description of the good or moral self, including faithfulness or trustworthiness in recognizing the claims embedded in human relationships (LW 7, 285; see also Chapter 6).

In context, Dewey indicates that an ethic that deals exclusively with either individualistic or altruistic concerns is inadequate because it fails to deal thoughtfully with the need for individuals to contribute to their own welfare, the welfare of other individuals, the well-being of groups, and the common good. An underlying emphasis is that the welfare and ethical viability of a society, group, and individuals are interdependent, not separable. The well-being of billions, millions, dozens, and the one is linked, e.g., acting to ensure the health of the planet and, thereby, its inhabitants influences every individual. Thus, a person's social, economic, emotional, spiritual, physical, intellectual, and political good is entwined with the good of others and vice versa. Dewey rejects, therefore, both traditional selfless and selfish ethics. Rather than each person having either "an exclusive regard for his [or her] own profit" or for the well-being of others (LW 7, 299), they should be involved in mutually regarding relationships that nurture everyone's satisfaction, happiness, and flourishing. His reconstructed view of happiness, while not dismissing these activities, is not focused on parties, celebrations, and festivities; he sees happiness largely as a byproduct of developing and sustaining a balanced life and interest in one's self, others, relevant groups, and the common good. This view of happiness is sprinkled throughout the following discussion of regard for people and, later, in his discussions of good schools (see Chapter 7).

For educators qua educators, this orientation suggests at least an interest in themselves as individual selves, as professionals, and as colleagues. While the local situation is Dewey's ethical focus, he claims that "the greater good of all must be extended" across domestic borders to transnational settings (LW 7, 371). For him, a moral science is essential to extending respect and regard for any group or person in "the wide stretches of time and space" (MW 8, 82). The need for schools to foster local, regional, and international mindedness in ethics, therefore, is manifest. Figure 4.1 portrays this multidirectional aspect of ethical concern and suggests some of its complexities, e.g., competing virtues and goods. As a multifaceted concept, moral mindedness focuses and refocuses as appropriate on relationships with individuals and groups. Much like moving from one problematic ethical situation to another, there is an ebb and flow of the focus of ethical relationships and interests in schools and societies. In Figure 4.1, the broken lines indicate the interconnectedness of the identified dimensions in Dewey's thought.

Our chapter title – "What Does Regard for People Imply?" – is related to developing the ability to sympathize with those for whom we ought to have concern or compassion, regardless of whether they are family members, recent immigrants, people of different or no faiths, inheritors of dissimilar cultures, or advocates of diverse grand narratives or worldviews. Noddings (1984, 24) adds that "To care [for people] is to act not by fixed rule but by affection and regard." Affection and regard are ethical game

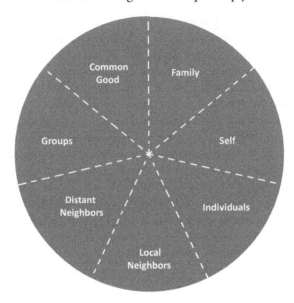

Figure 4.1   Multidimensional moral mindedness

changers. Facts, data, principles, theories, and reflection alone are insufficient. Attempting to understand the minds and affections of peoples from
diverse locales or schools, therefore, is somewhat like endeavoring to
understand the peoples of the world. In fact, many local realities mirror,
in significant ways, elements of global ones. In schools, educators become
or serve as local cultural workers or guides who help welcome and initiate
students and others into multiple diversities and realities (Freire 1998;
Ruitenberg 2016).

Relevant Contextual Variables

Before examining more specifics of Dewey's approach to ethics under the
headings of Regard for People, Consequences and the Common Good,
and Accountability and Responsibility, another aspect of Maria's story
merits attention. We identify this part of her story – and that of others' –
simply as Relevant Contextual Variables. Maria's present situation is one
of the most challenging faced by educators and is aggravated in settings
where people lack sufficient knowledge of one another and are inexperi-
enced in dialogical sensitivities. But hardly anyone is sufficiently well-
prepared to interact wisely, intelligently, sensitively, and courageously in

every ethical situation. Moreover, as Derrida observes, language and one's knowledge is regularly inadequate when individuals and groups seek to communicate their affections and reflections (see Ruitenberg 2016, 8–15). Thus, a teacher as a hospitality worker may abandon their teacher's role of power and seek to focus on the student as a guest, visitor, and questioner. Responsibilities, in part, are negotiated between the student and teacher. Of course, the degree to which this hospitality ideal is practiced in schools is a function of contexts, policies, and personalities (Ruitenberg 2016, 107–15). The Academy family, in hindsight, might have avoided a tragedy when Nocona Parker was a newcomer.

Maria's immediate challenge is how a person or colleagues might discuss and address equal respect and regard for others in the context of charges of racism and colonialism. Or, much worse, in the midst of the realities of racism and unrecognized present-day oppression. Maria's present context includes the following: for the better part of a decade, some district personnel, including a portion of the personnel of the now existing Academy, have intermittently heard fragments of charges of district racism and discrimination. Neither the conveyors of the rumors nor district leaders, however, requested an investigation of the rumors. Some suggest that leaders are apprehensive about making the rumors more salient by openly recognizing them. But allowing apprehension to stymie action is usually a counterproductive approach to real and imagined problems. Of course, at least some conveyors of the rumors may have been fearful of reprisals if the status quo supporters retain their district alliances and powers. Fears, unfortunately, probably undermine many would-be discussions about a variety of sociocultural challenges. Whatever the case, the hypothesis that fear causes some people to remain silent about reported racial prejudices and inequities probably indicates that the district is not a sufficiently safe place to discuss some of the world's most pressing social issues. Regardless of the reasons for the inaction, the concern about a racially unbalanced employment pattern seems to have escalated from just a few teachers whispering in a corner to semi-open discussions by some school and district personnel. The growth of whispering in hallways to episodic chats nearly anywhere on the Academy campus is a noticeable development, especially when personnel vacancies are being advertised and filled.

Maria is sure she understands personally and theoretically many issues of discrimination, the desire for a harmonious work environment, and the stress of open and fruitful discussions. On the other hand, she does not consider herself an expert facilitator of highly controversial discussions, much less a problem-solver of complex racial and legal problems. She understands, however, that the most pressing social and school problems are usually solved by groups, not individuals. Individuals, she has tentatively concluded, seldom think comprehensively, reflectively, and empathetically about the many complexities of oppression. But, at least, being a member of groups that have been oppressed and her years of living in culturally and demographically diverse and charged settings has led her to think that ignoring rumors provides, at a minimum, an opportunity for misinformation and malfeasance to grow. And, she concludes, there is a high probability that accurate information is being ignored as half-truths spread. Besides, she asks herself, does ignoring important concerns demonstrate authentic respect or regard for those who are experiencing the consequences of bias? Why not at least investigate what are deemed discriminatory decisions, practices, and structures? Her sensitive-discussions maxim – "Making myself and colleagues uncomfortable in the pursuit of justice, freedom, and happiness might be undesirable, but the failure to pursue justice, freedom, and happiness for all is unacceptable" – is a reminder of why both respect and regard for others is imperative.

Nevertheless, Maria's thinking seems sound even though she has other pressing priorities. The Academy is on the cusp of reaching important academic, sport, and social service benchmarks. She needs to focus time and energy on student, staff, parental, and programmatic matters. With a somewhat divided mind, she concludes, however, that the anecdotes of prejudicial employment practices and racial insensitivity require attention now. She knows too that school gossip and ad hoc complaints are difficult to address, seemingly a special form of human quagmire (Enomoto and Kramer 2007). Plus, the reported stories are not about just any matter. Addressing the overlapping issues will probably entail painful, prickly, and, possibly, divisive discussions. Likely, it will require employing a consultant to work with staff on perceptions and realities of unfairness and insensitivities, which could create mayhem with interpersonal relationships, teaching and learning, and, perhaps, career trajectories. But not doing anything now seems to have similar and more serious risks, she concludes.

A basic reason for resisting exploration of these issues, she admits, is that she wants to avoid an allegation that is directed at her. She is almost certain that she is the focus of a circulating tale: preferential employment. Still, she recognizes that an intentional injection of Academy disequilibrium could facilitate new opportunities for problem-solving, growth, and fairness – educative moments for staff that carry over into classrooms. Could she and the rest of the Academy's leadership team and lead teachers reasonably guide discussions and actions despite the disequilibrium that may be triggered? Recalling her position – the principal of the Academy for Civic Responsibility – was a little embarrassing. If she would not support an open discussion of equal regard for people, how could she expect the Academy staff, students, parents, and guardians to discuss these concerns?

Happiness, she remembers hearing, is not always experienced in the process or the immediate outcomes of doing what is ethically required but often occurs as positive outcomes are fostered by ethical means and ends. Dewey avers too that happiness is cultivated when one's interests involve and result in character development. Specifically, when one's concerns involve "alert, sincere, enduring interests" in publicly shareable matters, one's satisfaction develops (LW 7, 302). Or a person is happiest when there is an animated, continuous interest in others, including their lifelong needs and development (302–3). Personal interest in others "brings happiness because it fulfills the self," expresses "the kind of self which a person desires" (302), and contributes to "the enrichment of the lives" of others (302–3). True interest in people is accompanied by "a *will* to know" which specific conditions affect "the general good" (281; emphasis original), including one's life (281–2). Thus, in democratic settings, both the comprehensiveness and the content of the common good should be collaboratively determined (280–3).

Maria's first inclination – aside from the desire to avoid the issue of her appointment – is to take what she considers a measured-but-not-slow approach: to talk with a recently retired principal, Amarjit Nigam, to find out what he knows about the rumors. This approach would provide time to think through issues and a safe place to have open conversations. She also knows that Jit will candidly but kindly raise probing questions. She would also have time to reconsider the situation if he thinks matters are more challenging than she expects. Her first meeting with Jit, her favorite middle school retiree, proves sobering, even unsettling. She learns she is at the center of two, not just one, scenarios. In fact, there are three scenarios but neither Maria nor Jit was aware of the third at this juncture. In the first scenario, she is deemed an improperly promoted assistant principal. The principal position, according to a rumor, should have gone to a better qualified, more experienced senior assistant principal in the district and not to Maria. The main criticism, for some, is that her Academy position should have been given to one of her district colleagues. The second criticism identifies her as a person who uses her newfound power to play favorites or hire friends or friends of friends.

That Jit is a sympathetic elder statesperson partly redeems the conversation, for his warm openness causes her less pain than she would have otherwise experienced. Believing that the suspicions of some were, perhaps, largely based on decontextualized information, false perceptions, embellished stories, and empathetic feelings for the other finalist, Jit suggests that Maria contemplate moving forward with her plans to have dialogues about diversity and fairness at the Academy if Superintendent Kennedy concurs and its timing is carefully considered. He cautions, nevertheless, that she should expect some unknowns. The unknowns might include facts that are interpreted correctly by critics; a sizable district frequently has strands of bias and insensitivity about economic, racial, ethnic, gender, cultural, and religious diversity. The arrival of new populations, mixture of long separated groups, decreasing fiscal resources, and growing professional desires frequently cause people to scrutinize correctly, but sometimes excessively, personnel choices.

Thinking back on her conversation with Jit, Maria realizes that she had been right and wrong. She rightly thought Jorge Muñoz, the assistant superintendent of personnel, was one of the most visible leaders accused of unethical hiring practices. But the discriminatory-hiring story also includes the superintendent, Peter Kennedy. Some consider Peter primarily responsible for Maria's believed unmerited appointment to the Academy's principalship and the loss of a longtime staff member who did not receive the appointment. The other staff member's move to another district seemed to stamp Maria's appointment with a seal of disapproval.

When Maria and Jorge talked about the rumors, they decided to meet soon with Superintendent Kennedy to discuss some tentative ideas. Unfortunately, in multiple ways, Kennedy suffered a hemorrhagic stroke that evening and died of complications from brain swelling three days later. As Maria and Jorge waited for their appointment with Deborah Roosevelt, the newly appointed interim superintendent, they continued to discuss alternatives or hypothetical ways of approaching the rumors and realities, e.g., observing that the problem could be deferred but informally monitored unless additional information soon arose to indicate another option was merited, addressed in part by studying and reissuing demographic data on all district employees and schools for the last decade, examined by Jorge who would report back to Interim Superintendent Deborah Roosevelt, studied by Jorge at the district level and by principals at the site level, before reporting back to Deborah, making recommendations as appropriate, and studied by a widely respected district leader or external consultant who would report back to Roosevelt. Maria and Jorge, then, mulled over another option that might be possible if they became casualties or collateral damage in the controversies: seek district assignments that are low profile but comparable in responsibilities. They liked the district and its success in educating nearly every child and attending to the interests of every family, biological and foster. They also wondered, among themselves about when, if ever, they should start searching for positions in other districts. But they wanted to avoid premature decisions.

Stop and Think

What issues, if any, do you see in Maria's and Jorge's plans? Are there better options or hypotheses to consider?

Regard for People

To better understand the phrase regard for – and Maria and Jorge's immediate situation – it is helpful to observe that Dewey (LW 7, 297; emphasis original) thinks the phrase has a double meaning: "[a] that action as a matter of fact contributes to the good of others, or ... [b] that the *thought* of others' good enters as a determining factor into...[one's] conscious aim." In the first sense – "as a matter of fact contributes to the good of others" – the implications include the idea that central office personnel and principals need to understand how critical school and district, not just student and staff, evaluation is in determining if intentions, policies, and actions are in reality effective, educative, and equitable. The second meaning – "the *thought* of others' good enters as a determining factor into the conscious aim" – may be especially useful when interventions are undergoing evaluation – but could become a formalistic or coercive cliché, e.g., when someone judgmentally insists, "My recommended changes are absolutely essential if we're really interested in students!" Efforts to reproach and manipulate aside, sincere and conscious attempts at meeting the needs of children and staff are essential.

Dewey also explains that a more typical and encompassing interest than regard for one's self and others is being invested in "the welfare and integrity" of one's familial, social, and professional groups (LW 7, 299). Notice that the welfare of every person as well as of each group is linked to integrity, trustworthiness, reliability, authenticity, and consistency. Notably, Dewey encourages personal and group ethical identities, which are formed by reflectively developing ideals (e.g., freedom, fairness, equity) and habits (e.g., inquiry, deliberation, experimentation). With the possession of personal and group integrity, he implies that ethical challenges can be more readily and correctly addressed with fewer counterproductive discussions and consequences. Without ethical integrity in groups and among leaders (including classes of students), a thick ethical school culture and community appears largely unachievable.

The phrase regard for – and expressions such as concern for and consideration of – may serve as an umbrella-like concept that indicates both the focus and scope of Dewey's ethical ideals. Ideals, growing out of legitimate desires, can become "forces" that lead one to "*think* of objects and consequences" that might otherwise be overlooked (LW 7, 300; emphasis original). This panoramic lens, however, provokes many questions: Regard for whom and which objects? Are there specific domains that have higher priority and require continued attention in a situation? How will regard for diverse peoples be demonstrated in complex situations where conflicting ideals and goods frequently exist? Or better: Since each person is diverse from every other person, how do we learn to embrace our legitimate differences as we collaborate and cooperate in pursuit of mutual interests and the common good? In part, Dewey's interest in these and other questions emerge as the responsibilities of groups and individuals and the consequences of decisions and actions are deliberated. For Dewey, these elements constitute a mosaic of interpenetrating concerns. They can only be addressed as situations are discussed and unfold and as particular questions are implied or articulated and addressed.

Dewey observes, too, that the principle of regard for identifies a number of interconnecting emphases and that each clarifies that his ethic has a relational dimension. First, he includes the importance of demonstrating regard for what may be labeled personal matters of students and staff: desires, interests, rights, individuality, purposes, intelligence, identity, and personality. Figure 4.2 draws attention to aspects or qualities of a student, counselor, or teacher that may need attention episodically or regularly.

Second, Dewey suggests that having regard for people includes attending to environmental dynamics or the "social whole" (LW 7, 300): peace, injustice, freedom, kindliness, friction, collegiality, oppression, satisfaction, engagement, withdrawal, and belongingness. Third, inquiry itself is both an environmental and personal matter. That is, inquiry ought to be both (a) a sustained district and school activity that is regarded highly, and (b) a means for identifying and deliberating about problems and interests. Maria's story vividly demonstrates the need for inquiry, i.e., "caring for . . . looking after, paying attention" to the details of problematic situations

Figure 4.2   Illustrative spheres of regard for individuals and groups

(LW 16, 247). Without an emphasis on a community of inquiry and teachers as investigators that pursue collaborative research and action (LW 5, 23; Johnston 2006), Maria's and others' stories at the Academy may be ignored and, thereby, foster additional problems. Moreover, the habit of students, teachers, and visitors sharing their stories is an effective way of moving from cognitive understanding to affective-cognitive understanding. Figure 4.3 highlights some types of individuals and groups in an educator's fluctuating spheres of regard. The figure should be seen as malleable, providing room for the inclusion of people who are beyond one's local setting but still in one's sphere of interest, e.g., students in an exchange program, attendees at an international environmental conference, refugees in tent cities, and former students and friends working in different parts of the world.

Dewey's idea of regard for people and groups is further clarified by his use of the words *respect, equal respect,* and *mutual respect.* The two concepts of regarding and respecting people, for Dewey, share similarities yet have differences. For starters, it is evident that neither respect nor regard is an arid or abstract intellectual trait that is devoid of affection. Second, each is or becomes, if Dewey is right, a virtue and, ideally, is embedded in an interpenetrating web of desirable qualities where affections form an organic unity. This fusing of virtues constitutes "integrity of character," a central

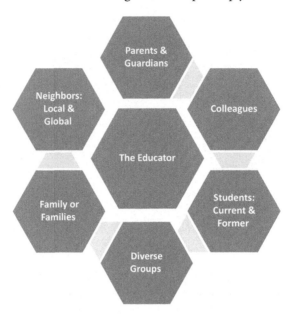

Figure 4.3   Regard for people: an educator's variable matrix

interest for anyone concerned with social, emotional, and moral health and development (LW 7, 257). Importantly, he does not think that personal integrity is a discrete product of character but, instead, emerges in a complex of affections and habits. Group integrity, as well, is a quality of socially or professionally linked people, persons who possess affections, dispositions, and habits of regard and respect for each other. Moreover, both respect and regard connect to sympathy and benevolence: they help keep virtues from becoming sentimentalized and, in turn, they help inform and energize both regard and respect (MW 14, 136; LW 7, 299).

Are there shades of meaning that differentiate respect from regard? Dewey seems to differentiate the concepts at times. For example, the word *respect* may be preferred when he discusses obligations, duties, and law; when he implies a slightly richer cognitive quality; and when descriptors such as deepest (EW 3, 101), tremendous (LW 3, 362), and profound (LW 15, 177) are found. He may have a preference for *regard for*, at least on occasions, when concentrating on people and human betterment; when indicating a moderately warmer concept; and when using prefixes such as affectionate (MW 7, 394), sympathetic (LW 7, 156), benevolent (LW 7, 299), consideration of (MW 14, 39), and caring for (LW 16, 246–8).

On one occasion, he brings together the two words to convey greater feeling and significance: he alleges that the peoples of the world, religious or not, need "mutual respect and regard which constitute charity as the inspiration of peace and good will" (LW 15, 183). Speaking of love, peace, and good will, Dewey may appear to be a romantic, but he clearly is not (Pappas 2008, 153–5, 280–3). He is a meliorist who is interested in using the numerous social forces and extensive capacities of people to develop richer, deeper, and wider lives.

A caution, nevertheless, is merited, for Dewey's word choice may not be as finely honed as described or may be, on occasion, more nuanced than implied. He speaks, for example, of the *"emotions* of curiosity, caution, respect for the freedom of others" (MW 14, 136; emphasis added). Interestingly, Dillon (1992) observes – overlapping with Dewey's notion of fusing qualities and having "sympathy and benevolent regard for others" (LW 7, 299) – that respect and care are unifiable virtues. She (Dillon 1992) speaks of a "care respect," a respect that is evident in a colleague who may organize extraordinary support for school families who lose almost everything in disasters, e.g., fires, floods, earthquakes, tornadoes, and hurricanes. Dillon's notion of care respect might be episodically manifested while Dewey's benevolent regard for seems to be desirable on a regular basis. Both orientations seem to facilitate the construction of humane and democratic school cultures that are suffused with reflective emotions. These cultivated emotions serve school communities well as they move beyond a largely rational or intuitive ethic to an intelligent, flexible, and demonstrative ethic that inspires, forms, and informs relationships and projects.

Even though Dewey includes the affective dimension in ethical reflection and action, he recognizes that the further removed a person is from her usual face-to-face interactions, the greater the possibility of the dilution of affections (LW 7, 257). This dilution underlines the importance of developing sympathy for anyone within an individual's sphere of responsibility (Simpson and Sacken 2014). Conversely, shallow or thin affections are a challenge for some educators and students even in everyday face-to-face interactions. Think back through earlier segments of Maria's story to consider actions that may signal a lack of regard for at least certain individuals, maybe even exacerbating stressful personal circumstances. On the other hand, there are distortions of the principle of regard for people, e.g., an excessive emotional regard that shows favoritism to familial, social, racial, religious, political, and professional groups at the expense of those outside of these circles (LW 7, 295). Dewey warns too of the

dangers of turning regard for people into pity and sentimentality, manip-
ulating the concept for personal advantage and developing an overly
"intense emotional regard for others" (295). Additionally, one should
recognize the difference between one having an ethical respect for everyone
as a result of their being persons and one having respect for a person only
because he or she is a gifted researcher, dancer, or friend. These and other
distinctions, e.g., cultural and philosophical, may be critical when clarifying ethical concerns (Chan 2006; Dillon 2003).

Presently, Maria's deep regard for others prompts self-interrogation. She
wonders if she has made several moment-by-moment imprudent decisions
and speculates about the Academy teachers who may be upset by several of
her employment recommendations. She recoils at her own questions: Do
I have too much regard for some staff and not enough for others? Have
I shown favoritism when making some appointments? Have I undervalued
the interests of some? Have I taken it for granted that I sympathize with
everyone appropriately? Am I undermining the well-being and integrity of
the Academy?

Stop and Think

Envision yourself as Maria as you make plans to populate afresh the forum of
your mind with two of the following people: a community person who is a
close friend, a new faculty member, a central office supporter, an aggrieved
former colleague. Which two people would you add to the forum of your
mind to help you think differently and richly about your ethical
situations? Why?

Prejudices, Consequences, and the Common Good

While one's intentions (e.g., malicious, benign, generous) are important
ethical considerations, alone they do not necessarily resolve problems or
justify actions. Plus, one may have good intentions and horrible consequences. Intentions too can be extremely difficult if not impossible to
identify, personally and socially. Suspicions, of course, do not constitute
public evidence. Dewey's emphases, therefore, are more inclusive and place
significant weight on the consequences of decisions and actions. His aims
are many, including the development of (a) people who are open-minded,
imaginative, honest, caring, and courageous; (b) groups that are committed to forethought, deliberation, justice, freedom, and peace; and
(c) societies and nations that are guided by ideals that include

collaboration, inclusion, compassion, transparency, and the common good. In part, he sees families and schools and agencies as instruments that ideally nurture the previously mentioned qualities and habits and that underscore that "everyplace in which men [women, and children] habitually meet, shop, club, factory, saloon, church, political caucus, is perforce a school house" (MW 7, 304). The consequences of perforce educational endeavors, of course, need to be evaluated in ways that consider their outcomes, not just their professed missions or goals. Perforce schools should be reasonably accountable for their consequences. Like schools and districts that have an ethical obligation to evaluate themselves to determine both their academic consequences (e.g., in mathematics, literacy, social studies, art, and science) and their social consequences (e.g., emotional, ethical, material, and political), Dewey thinks that perforce schools have an obligation to serve all segments of society well, not just the people who can presently access their resources and corporate leaders and investors.

As prospective and actual consequences of actions are evaluated, the common and individual good regularly need to be foregrounded. In fact, both kinds of good are complementary and intertwined. Hence, Dewey identifies a general method for the study of desired and actual consequences (MW 5, 278–304; MW 14, 132–45). For desired consequences, he argues that proposed actions as well as their probable consequences be studied. When the consequences of a prospective decision or act are in doubt, he (MW 14, 37) claims that potential outcomes should be evaluated by the probable effects of a particular tendency of dispositions or habits, not by an individual act: "In cases of doubt, there is no recourse save to stick to 'tendency,' that is, to the probable effect in the long run." In research efforts, he observes that reflective inquiry ought to be "regulated by qualitative considerations" or by the "concerns and issues of living" (LW 5, 243).

In the midst of research endeavors, Dewey's (LW 5, 397) concern about "the prevalence of prejudice" is manifest. For him, the tendency to judge others and their abilities by irrelevant factors and stereotypes (e.g., physical features, linguistic differences, cultural backgrounds, sexual affinities, geographical identities, educational achievements, political beliefs, religious commitments, class preferences) is "the fault of civilization" and should be "the cause of civilization" (LW 5, 397). That is, racial prejudice or bigotry is rooted, at least in significant ways, in the values and cultures of people. He contends that prejudices can be effectively addressed only by developing a common understanding (but not by forcing unanimity of explanations) of the nature of prejudice and miseducation, which have common roots. That is, schools and societies often simultaneously (a) nourish prejudices by ignoring or affirming them; (b) slight the development of virtues and, thereby, promote the growth of vices; and (c) impede pedagogically effective ways of both addressing prejudices and nurturing virtues.

Maria's largely inherited situation at the Academy, for example, appears to illustrate the neglect of virtue and the nourishment of prejudice in, at least, the district and the community. Harbor School District has largely discouraged open and effective teaching and learning about diversity and inclusion. Traditional ways of discussing virtues and vices have dominated the district's pedagogy. But a pedagogy of explanation and condemnation of racism is a largely ineffective way of diminishing vices and fostering virtues. Consequently, pedagogy needs to include more than explanation. Pedagogy needs sharing personal, community, school, and national stories and research that can affect the whole student. Activities need to include inquiry, collaboration, discussions, and storytelling. But even if schools should have scientifically warranted and relatively effective school programs, the challenge of perforce school and society learning can be left largely untouched. Harbor and Academy personnel, but not everyone, seem to have generally ignored indicators of prejudice. Thus, the district has frequently failed to cultivate desirable virtues that Dewey sometimes calls "a common mind, a common outlook" that includes seeing and feeling "the same [general] way" about the ethics of personal and professional relationships (LW 5, 396). Dewey encourages an understanding built on the habit of "coming together" for enduring discussions that lead to a process of "agreement" building regarding basic needs, interests, rights, and responsibilities (396). What does he suggest as worthwhile outcomes of conversations? At a minimum, he encourages respect, fairness, equity, harmony, disagreement, understanding, reasonableness, and sympathy (396–7). But he also notes that social, recreational, and personal relationships (LW 7, 285) are critical aspects of developing people who are characterized by "independence of judgment, personal insight, integrity and initiative" (300). Ethics, therefore, is not a means of producing school or societal uniformity. Instead, inquiry, reflection, imagination, and creativity are intrinsic to the nature of ethical dialogue.

As observed earlier, Dewey's (LW 5, 397) concern about "the prevalence of prejudice" grew beyond a superficial approach to social, political, economic, and pedagogical considerations. For him, prejudice is both "the fault" and should be "the cause" of societies (LW 5, 397). That is to say, societies have inadequately identified the causes and the effective treatments of prejudice: the two problems need to be approached as natural challenges and studied scientifically (MW 13, 242–3). In short, adequate interventions for prejudice need to address organismic factors or humankind's "impulses, fears, jealousies, and dislikes" (LW 5, 397) and, as Mill claims (LW 7, 244), the internal cultures or emotional development of people. External cultures and practices too need careful examination, for they are typically the expressions of internal values. In addition, Dewey highlights the fact that people are not born fully developed and fair-minded and each person has "to learn to be human" and develop into "an individually distinctive member of a community" (LW 2, 332). Humanizing people, therefore, should begin shortly after birth and continue until death. On occasion, however, he passionately employs his early New England Christian vocabulary to identify egregious behavior: he claims that depriving children of a reflective and dialogical education indicates that the "old Adam, the unregenerate element in human nature, persists [in society and schools]. It shows itself wherever ... [there is] attaining results by use of force instead of by ... communication and enlightenment" (LW 2, 332). When employing his later Darwinian lenses, he notes that prejudice, including anti-Semitism, reveals that "the struggle of civilization against prejudice is the struggle of civilization against barbarism, ... [that] still exists" in each person (LW 5, 397). The stubbornness of prejudice, he claims, demands a comprehensive education that is community-wide and that attends to the whole person. The peoples of the world and in each locale need to understand prejudice as an unending responsibility, not as a problem that can be readily extinguished (LW 5, 397).

Since Dewey thinks that the sources of prejudice are not simply cultural-ideological-economic influences but are also blended with human impulses and emotions, they need to be addressed by a wide range of effective interventions designed to nourish virtues and convert impulses into commendable desires and emotions as well as into ethically warranted purposes, plans, and actions (LW 13, 43–7). Dewey's reference to "sub-human" impulses (LW 5, 396–7) is an outmoded one that may sound repulsive to many contemporary ears. But Pinker (2011, 2016) observes, although not referencing Dewey's terminology, that even children and youth who appear least likely to entertain hostile or antagonistic feelings toward others, such as very young children and well-educated youth, are regularly known to possess such feelings. If he is correct, denying these early human feelings appears counterproductive. Dewey (MW 13, 243) also mentions research that supports the claim that there is an "instinctive aversion" of people to "what is new and unusual, to whatever is different from what [they] . . . are used to, and which thus shocks . . . customary habits." Xenophobic behavior, therefore, seems at least partially predictable. If so, should educators prepare future educators to help students for probable shocks so they can ethically handle the experiences? Likewise, if the human brain offers valuable information regarding prejudicial development, should present and future educators not study relevant aspects of the neurosciences (Hauser 2006; Pinker 2002, 2011)?

Of course, many well-prepared teachers and leaders are adept at addressing numerous challenges and making decisions instantaneously on the bases of their existing knowledge, including situational facts, legal rulings, relevant codes, and collegial deliberations. When considering the aforementioned goods, which promote the common good, three emphases appear paramount. To begin, Dewey indicates that schools need to foster the common good in and among school groups (LW 7). To continue, he notes that manifesting a respect and regard for people who are outside of one's affinity groups is obligatory. If not, discrimination is likely present, especially if there are other novel elements in a problematic situation. Third, in order to think reflectively and act ethically as individuals and groups, he reasons that there is a need to democratize units of power and authority. The "remaking of the social environment, economic, political, and international" (260), he contends, is critical to providing both external and internal school and social conditions that facilitate the development of a robust ethical regard for students and educators. Thus, any society that supports the democratization of its schools, perforce schools and communities, by means of policies and practices that foster a healthy regard for every individual and group, likely promotes the common good of people.

Yet, Dewey cautions that student satisfaction and happiness differ for individuals and groups; for "no two concrete cases of happiness" are the same in substantive details (LW 7, 247). But they are comparable in that they are examples of the satisfaction that comes from fulfilling desires (247). He argues, moreover, that happiness is more than personal or individual realization, for life is a social experience prompting answers to the question: "Do they [social conditions] tend to lead members of the community to find their happiness in the objects and purposes which bring happiness to others" (243)? Nor is happiness a chance or short-lived moment. To the contrary, it "is a stable condition" that is maintained by "the self" or the whole person. The self, one's "qualities of mind and heart," that interacts with others should be nurtured to construct a happiness that is secure and stable yet open to differentiated forms (198).

He reasons, however, that the common good cannot always be deter-mined precisely "in advance" (LW 7, 281) of making many decisions, for learning what is good involves evaluating particular decisions and iden-tifying their consequences (281–3, 345). Predictably, he claims the common good involves both stable and dynamic elements as a shared stream of values that are constructed and modified. Thus, collaborative engagements – conversations, deliberations, decision-making, and undertakings – should be ongoing (345–7); for "without active cooper-ation," – or repeated engagements – Dewey explains, "both in forming aims and in carrying them out there is no possibility of a common good" (347). Insofar as Dewey is correct, a cooperative sharing of human resources and opportunities, political and social powers, and institutional and district leadership is not just a nicety. Instead, these means are essential to a common well-being (347). Indeed, the common or general good "demands the full development of individuals in their distinctive individuality," not sacrificing them to greater goods (348). Individuals should be "free to develop, to contribute and to share ... as social conditions break down walls of privilege and of monopolistic possession" (348).

In order to clarify that a mutual regard and commitment of people to one another is a need rather than a preference, Dewey highlights what he means by having an interest in others. First, he connects interest in people to regard or concern for others: "Interest *is* regard, concern, solicitude, for an object [e.g., person, activity or end]; if it [an interest] is not manifested in action it is unreal" (LW 7, 291; emphasis original). This provocative claim means a person – educator, student, custodian – who professes an interest in or regard for someone *is moved to act* on her or his behalf. Stated similarly, an interest, for Dewey, is "the dominant direction of [one's] activity, and in this activity desire is united with an object to be furthered" (290). Without "impulse and desire ... enlisted, one has no heart for a course of conduct" (290). If, for instance, there is no passion for working with a particular student, group, or school, fewer interactive engagements between teachers and students will likely exist. In such cases, the teacher's so-called interest is actually bogus (291). Similarly, politicians, policymakers, and business leaders who profess an interest in communities and schools but create and support policies that enhance the well-being of only a portion of the public are less than attentive and, probably, disingenuous.

When educators have what Dewey indicates is a genuine interest, their impulses and desires coalesce, and they develop an informed "heart for"

(LW 7, 290) nourishing parental and student growth as they fulfill their responsibilities. Genuine interest, then, means a teacher "*cares* for" staff and administrators as they care for students and parents (290; emphasis original). Dewey concludes that this interest involves the whole person – "intellectual and practical, as well as emotional" (MW 4, 274) – and stems from joining "benevolent impulse and intelligent reflection" (LW 7, 298). This caring interest in and regard for students makes it much more likely that educators will act responsibly and work effectively on students' behalf. Even so, interest in and regard for people are not educational panaceas. They appear essential but not sufficient to do the work of educators. Other resources and overlapping educator qualities are required, too, e.g., a vibrant passion for learning, a keen interest in one's teaching fields, and a love for teaching itself are essential (LW 13, 342–5; Simpson and Jackson 1998).

Returning to Maria's current problem, it seems clear that she has talked recently with her longtime friend, Zoe Jackson, an educational leadership professor. Among the topics they discussed are what current research appears to suggest about how to create or restore a vibrant ethical community that is characterized by empathy and respect and regard for people, how to analyze and teach about controversial issues in conflictual times, and how to work with colleagues to navigate sensitive social and political discussions with students so that these endeavors become enjoyable educative experiences. Maria visited Zoe because she knows that whether she remains at the Academy or goes elsewhere, she must learn how to better discuss delicate matters and enable others to talk together about such topics. She understands how even a single word or glance can virtually extinguish student and staff interactions. Yet, she knows that many discussions seem stymied because of real and pseudo fears of offending someone by asking a taboo question, losing a friend by introducing an unpopular idea, and experiencing group denunciation by clumsily using a term or making a dated counterargument.

Hence, educators, especially, and students too need to become experts at engaging in productive conversations about contentious issues. For example, classes could carefully identify terms, phrases, arguments, and narratives that should be avoided in class discussion – even if some are allowable in an ideal world – because the discussions themselves ideally indicate that classmates respect one another and care about each other's interests. Other conversational aids may be added before or during discussions, including what it means to resolve conflicts (Gelfand and Brett 2004; Thompson, Neale, and Sinaceur 2004) and forgive others (Stewart 2012).

Stop and Think

Suppose you have a colleague who regularly ignores certain responsibilities and several of her students. Should you be disappointed with yourself if you only mention the colleague's behavior to a mutual friend? Would you, by Dewey's standard, be interested in your colleague and her students if you do nothing more?

Accountability and Responsibility

Few people are thrilled with the idea of being personally liable, accountable, and responsible. But, ethically speaking, the three ideas can be powerful impetuses for educative action and growth. Dewey, therefore, ties together these concepts in a meaningful way: "Liability is the beginning of responsibility. We are held accountable by others for the consequences of our acts" (MW 14, 217). His interpretation of these concepts is empowered by his directing attention to the future, not exclusively to past actions and present situations: "The individual is held accountable for what [she or] he *has* done in order that [she or] he may be responsive in what [she or] he is *going* to do" (217; emphasis original). The aim of accountability and responsibility, therefore, is primarily forward looking and educative: "Intelligence becomes ours in the degree in which we use it and accept responsibility for consequences" (MW 14, 216).

Educators, Dewey thinks, should underscore the fact that we possess intelligence to the extent that our understanding and habits are used for good ends and to the degree that learning from the consequences of life affects future desirable habit formation and action. Responsibility, he (LW 8, 137–8) contends, entails that individuals and groups are accountable for evaluating their intellectual conclusions and their potential outcomes and the actual consequences that "follow reasonably from" (137–8) their own thinking. An anticipated step, he argues (138), entails taking intellectual responsibility for likely outcomes as much as a completed step requires responsibility for actual outcomes. Being reasonable, therefore, means reflecting on potential "consequences before acting" (LW 16, 312). In a word, reflective pre-consideration or rehearsal of issues informs decision-makers of potential undesirable consequences (e.g., school restrictions and in-school suspensions) as well as potential desirable consequences (e.g., satisfactions and accomplishments). But his argument should not be applied unreflectively. For example, there is a difference between a student intentionally using a sexist term to enflame a class discussion and an English as a second or third language student innocently using the same word. Both may be educative moments; neither is desirable, but the former is done with intent and, perhaps, malice. The second is actually a *different situation* because of the new intention. In the future, there may be occasions when neuropsychologists will provide information about one's intentions (Pinker 2011, 531).

Stop and Think

In your school, is sufficient attention given to the idea of being responsible for the consequences that "follow reasonably from" public and political language? Which types of consequences are important to consider as an educator?

Considering consequences, Dewey (MW 14, 155–70) acknowledges, is a complicated undertaking. The process entails district and school leaders understanding that they are partially responsible for nurturing environments that support desirable consequences and for treating people with regard even when colleagues' behavior falls short of expectations. Also, as indicated above, Dewey's goal was to maintain regard for one's self, others, groups, and the common good of classes, clubs, teams, and schools. As a result, responsibility involves both the individual and common good. But Dewey went beyond the district, school, and community to note other entities and forces in society that are responsible: business, politics/government, and education/law. In the business sphere, he (LW 7, 299) maintains that "the test of an industry is whether it serves the community as a whole, satisfying ... needs effectively and fairly ... providing the means of livelihood and personal development to the individuals who carry it on." For the political realm, he (MW 9, 129) asserts that democracy's moral ideal is measured by its participatory outcomes: that "a social return ... [is] demanded of all and that opportunity for development of distinct capacities be afforded all." From a legal and educational perspective, Dewey (LW 7) argues that the ultimate test of laws and institutions, is "what they do to awaken curiosity and inquiry ... render men and women more sensitive to beauty and truth; more disposed to act in creative ways; more skilled in voluntary cooperation" (364). Dewey warns here that a lack of widespread and skilled "voluntary cooperation" (364) in creating and reconstructing laws and educational institutions is a hallmark of anti-democratic social, political, and economic forces.

Conclusion

That Dewey considers having a regard for people a crucial element in developing personal and social ethical robustness is clear. But this specific clarification does not lead to the conclusion that being ethically healthy is a simple and easily achieved undertaking. The development of knowledge and understanding, although immensely challenging at times, is much more easily achieved than is the formation of attitudes, affections, dispositions, and habits. This complexity exists, in part, because organismic and environmental inheritances are powerful forces and counterforces in one's life and in school and social interactions. A spouse, new baby, tiny apartment, and tight budget can challenge nearly anyone. If a chronic depressive disorder is a factor, regard for nearly anyone can be a staggering undertaking. The stress of caring for elderly parents or grandparents adds to one's challenges. Regard for the folks in one's school community – educators, students, staff, parents, guardians, and volunteers – may make one wonder if Dewey was naïve. When one is attuned to the interests of others, the common good of communities, peoples, and nations, life, broadly speaking, can be exceedingly complicated, even grueling. But life is frequently more balanced than described and is enhanced when one shares life with caring friends, family, and colleagues. In an interesting way, Dewey's emphasis on "the local" situation (LW 2, 368–9) may be comforting, even if confounding, given his emphasis on global ethical problems (LW 7, 314–71). But the fluidity of world events, expansion of diverse ideas (MW 9, 92), and the "physical annihilation of space" (92) makes it clear why "the local" situation is so important (LW 2, 368–9): it is the practical center of most people's lives and work and, therefore, influence. Yet, broader concerns are regularly injecting themselves into local school situations.

Given the above, Dewey's (MW 7, 278–83) conclusion that people sometimes exhibit malformed ethical attitudes and habits, even as they wish to be constructive, is not unexpected. If, for instance, some educators are unkind, even acerbic, when making decisions and evaluative judgments, their personal situations may include childhood abuse, emotional exhaustion, physical challenges, nutritional deprivation, clinical depression, or constitutional faultfinding. Ultimately, if their off-putting propensities and habits remain unchanged, however, they may discredit educational ideas and their own professions. They may also negatively reflect on their supervisors who may seem disinterested in the well-being of both staff and students. Thus, superintendents who do not address the mistreatment of students and staff by central office and site-based leaders undermine their own ethical interests. Educators who allow or demonstrate an ethic of harshness, therefore, will lack rapport with many if not most colleagues and students. On the other hand, Dewey hints at a qualified happiness that can bring administrators, teachers, and students closer together in an atmosphere of mutual regard as they transcend, in some measure, their individual constitutional, cultural, and developmental worlds. Of course, his thoughts about happiness are not designed to be a substitute for needed mental health care although the topics overlap sometimes.

The immediate aspect of happiness that concerns Dewey is an outgrowth of our desire for experiences and things that bring personal satisfaction involving human relationships, social goods, aesthetic pleasures, and sensual fulfilments (MW 7, 281–3). Of course, he expects educational institutions, including schools, to help "create an interest in all persons in furthering the general good, so that they will find their own happiness realized in what they can do to improve the conditions of others" (LW 7, 243). In these experiences, a person achieves a happiness that is approved – or found approvable – in a threefold way. First, the happiness approves itself to the individual (248). That is, the person's happiness confirms to them its worthwhileness. Hence, one's enriched quality of life is deemed "invaluable" (248). Second, the happiness that one nurtures and experiences is approved by others who have mutual desires and interests and profit from common concerns (248). Third, as justification expands, reflective morality, including the contributions of moral science (178–80, 306–9), comes to "demand that what is approvable ... [become] an end" (246). Hence, happiness that is approved in this threefold manner is characterized by both ethical means and warranted ends (248). Dewey adds that a threefold procedural pattern of development is necessary. Thus, the purposeful choices made by someone enable them to select objects and interests that lead to personal satisfaction and others' good, the selected ends are suggested by the reconstructed desires that are "in agreement with needs of social relations," and achieved happiness is "harmonious with the happiness of others" (248).

Throughout life, therefore, personal happiness should be woven into a balanced life, one wherein what a person "gets from living with others balances with what he [or she] contributes" to others' lives (MW 9, 369). The getting and the giving is not focused on "external possessions, but a widening and deepening of conscious life – a more intense, disciplined, and expanding realization of meanings. What he [or she] *materially* receives and gives is at most opportunities and means for the evolution of conscious life" (369; emphasis original). One condition of happiness is recognizing that "conscious life is a continual beginning afresh," ensuring unending new starts, fresh experiences, and open landscapes (370). Maria appears to intuitively grasp Dewey's idea that personal beliefs, Academy practices, and social arrangements that regularly deny new starts to youth, parents, and staff do serious damage to everyone.

On the other hand, Dewey's ethical emphasis on happiness does not encourage a constant and direct pursuit of happiness; for it is understood largely as an offshoot of a life that pursues the well-being of one's self and others: reflecting and deliberating with others, sympathizing with them, maximizing a caring regard for them, and enjoying, and encouraging others to enjoy, a life that includes multiple and diverse pleasures and excellences. While happiness is interruptible, it can be found "in the midst of annoyances; ... [and] in spite of a succession of disagreeable experiences" if one keeps developing and exercising both courage and composure (LW 7, 198). Pinker's (2009, 393) cautionary message is that it is not, as a whole, the "rich, privileged, robust, or good looking who are happy; it is those who have spouses, friends, religion and challenging, meaningful work."

Discussion Questions

1. How do Dewey's thoughts about the principle of regard for people help identify professional education responsibilities? How can the important details of having regard for people be foregrounded in personal interactions and embedded in school contexts and cultures?
2. What might Dewey mean by his statement that "regard for self and regard for others" are phrases of "a more normal and complete interest" in "the welfare and integrity of the social groups of which we form a part" (LW 7, 299)?
3. What understandings and qualities does a person need to consider in order to address successfully complex ethical and pedagogical challenges?
4. If you were assigned the task of evaluating a particular state's, province's, or district's economic enterprises, political engagements, and laws/schools using Dewey's criteria, how would you go about rating the three domains – business, politics/government, and education/law – that Dewey mentions? How would you nuance your conclusions to ensure that you fairly capture the multiplicities of the entity's realities?
5. Is Dewey correct about the attainment of happiness? Does it really include devoting a portion of one's life to others, groups, and the common good? To growing intellectually, emotionally, aesthetically, and socially?

RELATED READINGS

Dewey, John, and J. Tufts. 1932. *Ethics*. Vol. 7 of *John Dewey: The Later Works, 1925–1953*, edited by Jo Ann Boydston, 1–512. Carbondale and Edwardsville: Southern Illinois University Press, 1985.

Chapter 15 "The Moral Self Responsibility and Freedom" (303–8) is Dewey's discussion of the unique role of responsibility in ethical development and personal freedom. He provided a glimpse of a growing, liberated person who is characterized by responsibility, freedom, and more.

Dillon, Robin S. 1992. "Respect and Care: Toward Moral Integration." *Canadian Journal of Philosophy* 22, no. 1 (March): 105–32.

Dillon proposes that respect, care, and care respect are ideas that can be placed on a continuum. She places Kantian respect as a minimal and inadequate level of respect from a moral perspective and identifies care respect as an optimal level in certain situations.

Noddings, Nel. 1988. "An Ethic of Caring and Its Implications for Instructional Arrangements." *American Journal of Education* 96, no. 2 (February): 215–30.

Noddings provides an overview of important details of her relational theory or ethic of care. She summarizes her interest in promoting a moral life by moral means via schools.

Pappas, Gregory Fernando. 1993. "Dewey and Feminism: The Affective Domain and Relationships in Dewey's Ethics." *Hypatia* 8 (2): 78–95.

Pappas argues that an ethical decision-maker should be characterized by a variety of characteristics, including, but not limited to, affective qualities, reflective dispositions, and personal relationships. In doing so, he helps identify Dewey's ethical decision-maker as a sensitive, fully engaged person.

Simpson, Douglas J., and D. Mike Sacken. 2015. "The Ethical Principle of Regard for People: Using Dewey's Ideas in Schools." *International Journal of Progressive Education* 11 (1): 41–58.

Simpson and Sacken describe Dewey's principle of benevolent regard for people as a pivotal part of his ethical method of analyzing problematic ethical situations. The work highlights the concepts of a mutual respect of people and warm regard for one's self, others, associated groups, and the common good. The case study captures the value of being a people-regarding teacher and administrator.

Case Study: Regard for Others – Multiple Parties and Conflicting Demands

Maria always thought that matching students and teachers was a critical aspect of increasing school performance. However, it was not always an easy task, as the needs of a teacher could mesh poorly with the needs of students. She always told prospective teachers that many principals most seek and admire adaptability in teachers. If Maria were being truthful, she would say adaptability was what teachers and administrators most admired in students, too. Her image of an excellent teacher was built on one who could manage whatever class he or she got without complaining or asking for much

---

assistance. There were teachers that did really well with certain subgroups of students but were unable to adapt to meet needs of other types of students. Maria did not consider those excellent teachers – competent maybe, but nothing more. She preferred teachers that closed their classroom door when school began and produced the expected outcomes with little or no drama. Unfortunately, too many teachers wanted the same autonomy but could not produce the needed student achievement consistently. She felt some knew they were not cutting it and just wanted solitude so others could not see their flaws.

Because a school was not filled with adaptive and competent teachers or students, matching students and teachers often seemed like a zero-sum game. By ensuring some students and/or teachers got their needs met, Maria left others in an unfortunate situation where some students would underperform or remain stuck in their lack of success. Maria believed she had a better-than-average faculty and student body, especially in terms of the district as a whole. Like a lot of magnet or specialty schools, she had a lot of teachers and parents that chose to attend her school versus being sent there due to geography. Parents had to apply for admission and some students came from rather distant parts of town. Some were escaping their students' assigned schools. Maria initially had a chance to staff her school with teachers applying within district, and thereafter to add teachers as needed for the most part. Some teachers also took refuge in the Academy, and overall, Maria believed she could build and maintain a good faculty there. Her best teachers by and large came because the new ideas and structures appealed to them, and they anticipated an interesting student and faculty mix.

Nonetheless, she had plenty of complex students with a mix of learning and social issues. And her teachers were a mix as well, with some really excellent teachers who embraced the challenges and changes of the Academy, and others who wanted a safe classroom and few responsibilities beyond teaching curriculum. Some of those left quickly, but others dug in and passively resisted the demands of the school. It goes without saying, Maria thought, that the school was a poor fit for some students for generic or specific reasons. The Academy did a lot of things beyond the classroom and school, and students were often in new situations, performing service and representing the Academy in public. Students had to learn to embrace such roles and be collaborative learners through a variety of experiences.

Maria also tried to perform pedagogic duties as much as she could. She worked with students and teachers on projects, taught classes when she could, sponsored at least one student organization each year, and mentored a small group of students that was struggling in some ways. It was hard to fit these tasks in, but without them, she would not feel as though she were an educator anymore, just a manager. Oddly, doing these things helped Maria build and maintain relationships with some teachers, while others seemed to resent her for continuing her role as an educator, as though Maria was competing with them. She did these things for strategic reasons, to be more a "we" than solely a "they," but mostly because the connections with students kept her sane.

One difficulty in remaining an educator, was that Maria formed relationships with students and knew about the complexities in their lives. She personally connected with them. That was her strength as a teacher and always had been; she treated her students like individuals, like patients maybe, and advocated for their best interests. The Academy certainly had such teachers who connected with students and thereafter sought to promote their interests even after the students moved on to another grade. Those teachers were essential and annoying at the same time. They acted like relatives, even surrogate parents for "their students." Usually those special students were a subset of those they taught, but some seemed to feel connected to any student that passed through their lives. These were the teachers that most often used the word *love*; they had an expansive sense of duty.

So, here Maria was as the year wound down and the prospective teacher-student mixes began to be an issue of planning and advocacy. There were always teachers, students, and parents who seemed indifferent to these critical decisions and just focused on the daily tasks. She could anticipate which teachers would intervene in some way, trying to guide the pathway for students, positively or negatively, and some parents establish immediately a pattern of seeking whatever seemed the best for their children. At any school, the most important resource for students was teacher excellence or competence. Not everyone got that, however. But data was pretty clear that as early as kindergarten, some teachers were optimal for students. And vice versa, some students were sought and gladly received in any classroom and others were received with emotions varying from reluctance to terror by most teachers, due to the student, the parents, or both.

Maria's job was to allocate resources to students and teachers alike. She had to establish a "perilous equilibrium" and then find accommodations as needed when the equilibrium collapsed. She had to find resolutions for panicked and outraged teachers and parents alike. The equilibrium was like a fragile boat held together but subject to becoming swamped or even sinking if too many people believed their needs were not her priority or that their situation was intolerable. The individual storms could not be always anticipated, but the fragility of some people or settings was sometimes apparent. Maria saw herself as a good strategist and problem-solver generally, but she knew she had been the type of teacher she now described as excellent: adaptive and self-managing. After a few years, she had rarely ever sought administrative help as a teacher. She had her group of peers with similar tendencies and she used them as sounding boards and collaborators. She found herself wishing that needy teachers, who seemed forever getting overwhelmed, would find more appropriate careers. She saw them as undermining children's education.

Ms. Doughty, a middle school language arts teacher at the Academy, confused Maria. She was an experienced, organized, and driven teacher who collaborated well with most of her team. Her students did as well or better than other students generally, and she rarely asked Maria or other administrators for help in matters like classroom management. She did not expect or appeal for only high-performing students; in fact, she preferred a mix of students academically. She did not draw many parent or student complaints either. Not all students shone in her room, but those who struggled or performed poorly usually were having problems in other or all classes and had struggled for a good while. Maria had always viewed Ms. Doughty as competent, sometimes excellent. Some students and parents were grateful to and praising of her. In a nutshell, she was not a problem teacher.

Maria knew one of Ms. Doughty's struggling students this year quite well. John Verhoven had been mediocre academically during elementary, but since about fifth grade, he had done more poorly academically and behaviorally each year. He was not qualified for special education or other interventions. He scraped by and was generally disliked by peers and teachers alike. He was a loner but argumentative and got in some fights with other students. He was sarcastic to peers and teachers. His parents, when asked to help, said they had no ideas how to help improve his work or behavior. His work was not that horrible (he was able to get mostly Cs, a few low Bs, and he did acceptable work on standardized tests, so it was not a crisis), but he just had always been an unhappy child. He had increased absences from classes and school during the last two years and those teachers who were aware of him saw him as a likely drop-out by early upper school. He was the sort of student that no one really missed if absent because things were more placid.

Maria knew him because she volunteered to mentor him last year and had met with him many times although always by her initiation. He had come to talk a bit more and even about a few personal matters. She knew his parents lived apart and, in his view, neither seemed to want him. He spent his free time primarily playing video games. He did not participate in any school club or activity. He was much more often passive aggressive than not but could erupt or be harsh to others.

Maria did not feel successful with John. They had made some progress. He had fewer absences than the previous year, because if he missed a class or day, he had to come see and talk with her. He said once that it was the worst punishment she could give him. A lot of times he just sat stolidly and listened to her, answering her questions if at all with a single word or phrase. He was rarely overtly angry or rude to her anymore, unlike peers and some teachers, but he seemed disengaged. She tried to get him to talk about what he liked, but he did not say much, even about video games.

She had spoken with his teachers about him, asking for suggestions based on their experience with him. Most found him not particularly disruptive but a profoundly negative impact on the class. He made his young sixth-grade teacher cry because he made her feel inept, and she found him disagreeable, which made her feel worse to admit that about a student.

He was academically surviving in Ms. Doughty's class, but they did not get along and Maria felt that Ms. Doughty had given up on him apart from getting him to pass and move on. He was often by himself at a desk in the corner for inappropriate remarks he made to her or a peer. He did not seem to mind being there, Maria felt, because he could be ignored and ignore others. If pushed to join in or participate, he almost always said something that left him in the corner or otherwise ignored. Maria thought of it as a détente between teacher and student: if she left him alone, he would do marginal work and leave others alone.

Maria knew John would have done better in John Schmidt's language arts class, as Mr. Schmidt was amazing with difficult students and relentlessly tried to connect with them. He was probably the best teacher in middle school when it came to working with students that exhibited behavioral challenges. But he already had more than his share of challenging students. Maria remembered an elementary teacher she knew in graduate school that was like Mr. Schmidt who eventually moved into administration because he always got the toughest students and more than his share. He told her it wore him down, but every year he ended up carrying more than his load, so he decided to leave the classroom. Maria had experienced a similar situation some years, but not continuously and understood how overwhelming being "the-difficult-student teacher" could be. Nonetheless, she knew if she had known John better at the beginning of the year, she would have slipped him into Schmidt's class, maybe by trading out another difficult student to Ms. Doughty. She intended to do that next year: match John to the best set of teachers for him.

She knew that some teachers and parents would be doing the same thing, meaning those students with no advocates would be sorted randomly, with star and difficult students being sorted in various ways as teachers, parents, and whoever try to leverage students into or out of different classrooms, in a mix of motives from "doing what is best for this student" to "I already have more than my share," and more. Maria simply did not know what to do to make this selection process more equitable and educationally reasoned. She knew some teachers and parents could make her life miserable if she did not give them what they wanted. She also knew that helping struggling students could lead her to overload a few teachers unfairly. This situation was complicated by students who had special education classifications, of course, but there was a process ostensibly to individualize their programs to meet their needs, although it too was influenced by parent behaviors and teacher needs and wishes. Maria believed the allocation of students was the ultimate sausage factory of the school, where negotiating students' educational experiences was a sub rosa process where legitimate and illegitimate factors played a part even when the actors were doing the best they could. What she could try to do was see that no student got only the best of things and people and no one got only the worst. But was that enough? John was the epitome of a student who gets less or the least because no one wanted him, and few would prioritize him. He was a lost cause best left more or less alone to slide through school until he left or barely finished. She might be able to shift his experience by intervening, but how many others like John were among the legion of lost students?

QUESTIONS

1. What are the major problems you see in the situation?
2. If you were Maria, how would you attempt to improve matters for the upcoming school year?
3. From a policy point of view, what does Harbor School District need to do to address the systemic problem Maria identifies?
4. Should Maria ask two or more teachers to work with John Verhoven in the upcoming year? Why or why not?
5. Will it help the Academy if its teachers discuss the challenges Maria sees? Why or why not?

CHAPTER 5

What Is a Problematic Ethical Situation?

> An integral part of moral action ... is the element of uncertainty and of conflict in any situation ... The conventional attitude sees in the situation only a conflict of good and of evil; in such a conflict, it is asserted, there should not be any uncertainty ... [Yet] the more conscientious the agent is and the more care [she or] he expends on the moral quality of [her or] his acts, the more he [or she] is aware of the complexity of this problem of discovering what is good; [she or] he hesitates among ends, all of which are good in some measure, among duties which obligate [her or] him for some reason. Only after the event, and then by chance, does one of the alternatives seem simply good morally or bad morally.
> —John Dewey, "Three Independent Factors in Morals" (LW 5, 279)

Introduction

In Chapter 1, we briefly consider the question, What is a problematic ethical situation? In that chapter, we give attention to the relationship of diverse expectations in reflective inquiry, including seeking to resolve or solve ethical problems. In a related vignette, we note that Irene Sebastian, a third-grade Academy teacher, had been reported for screaming at her students. From that chapter, a person could say that an ethical situation involves making a practical decision about what should or should not be done (LW 7, 9), e.g., What needs to be investigated to clarify what Irene had done, and how should Maria and Academy colleagues respond to the situation? For Dewey, a problematic situation involves these kinds of ought questions and more, including complexities that may not be readily apparent. While tackling this subject, he notes how his views differ on occasion from others' conclusions. For example, in *Ethics*, one of his interests is to explain that moral situations entail doubts and perplexities brought about when "different desires promise opposed goods" (164). In such situations, each good is "an undoubted good in its place," but each

94

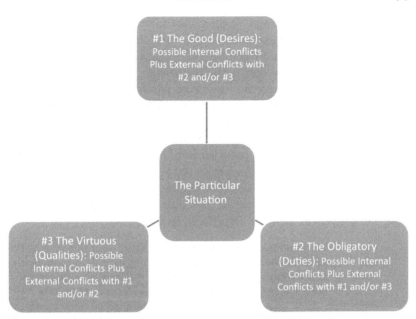

Figure 5.1   Dewey's three-factor theory of moral conflict and deliberation: the good, the obligatory, the virtuous

good can conflict with another undoubted value (165). Thus, ethical issues often emerge between well-meaning people who differ about the importance or priority of competing goods. In each situation, a query that could arise is: How do caring and fair-minded people settle disputes and conflicts about diverse desires and priorities?

Ethical deliberation, Dewey continues, may involve analyzing conflicts with a single factor or with two or three factors: i.e., "the good, the obligatory, the virtuous" (LW 5, 279). Figure 5.1 depicts these three factors, but it probably exaggerates their so-called independence, as do Dewey's own words "independent variables" (279). Dewey finds importance in the fact that all three factors may be present in any ethical situation rather than just one of them (496–503). Hence, as Pappas (2008, 2) observes, with Dewey's ethical approach educators are not forced to choose "between deontology, virtue ethics, and consequentialism." Dewey's ethic incorporates elements of these three theories as well as others and attempts to avoid misguided forced choices between them.

If Raymond Boisvert's (1998, 152) observations are warranted, one may conclude that the good represents Dewey's "highest ideal." Hence, his

apparent heightened attention to the good and desires explains in part why
he is sometimes considered an informed desire theorist (Anderson 2010).
From a developmental perspective, Anderson says it is worth observing
that Dewey differs from most desire theorists in at least two respects: he
rejects the notion that a person has a fixed set of virtues or character, and
he argues that a desire should not be approved unless it has been evaluated
by people who are deemed sympathetic persons. The second point about
evaluation includes asking both what the desire, if acted upon, would
contribute to one's character and what would change throughout one's life
if continually acted upon (Anderson 2010). This joint evaluation, for
Dewey (LW 1, 157), involves communication that is "the greatest of
human experiences." Why does he give such high praise for communication? He answers in, perhaps, hyperbolic fashion,

> Of all affairs, communication is the most wonderful. That things should be
> able to pass from the plane of external pushing and pulling to that of
> revealing themselves to ... [people]; and that the fruit of communication
> should be participation, sharing, is a wonder by the side of which transub-
> stantiation pales. When communication occurs, all natural events are
> subject to reconsideration and revision; they are re-adapted to meet the
> requirements of conversation, whether it be public discourse or that
> preliminary discourse termed thinking. (LW 1, 132)

Thus, shared experience, involving joint communication, is not only a
pedagogical essential but also a problem-addressing and problem-solving
necessity. Otherwise, problematic situations are misconstrued and un-
addressable. Alluding back to the issue of racism, then, means that genuine
communication is the gateway to sharing and participating together in the
pursuit of answers and actions.

Dewey's emphasis on the desirable or the good is a critical theoretical
and practical point. Succinctly, he asserts that

> the task of moral theory is ... to frame a theory of Good as the end or
> objective of desire, and also to frame a theory of the true as distinct from
> specious, good. In effect this latter need signifies the discovery of ends
> which will meet the demands of impartial and far-sighted thought as well as
> satisfy the urgencies of desire. (LW 7, 191)

Parenthetically, the purchase of this kind of moral theory is dependent on,
in part, "rational insight, or moral *wisdom*," and experimental inquiry
(191; emphasis original).

In *Ethics*, Dewey also explains that his immediate interest is both
focused and limited: he does not plan to address how a person might

overcome a desire when they are already "convinced [an attitude or act] is wrong" (LW 7, 164). Thus, he does not discuss how an educator could address his antipathy for a colleague and overcome his desire to spread misinformation about her. In other works, however, Dewey delves deeply into the realms of moral development and education. When discussing ethical growth, for instance, he describes how moral learning should be integrated into everyday school experiences, not separated into a distinct curriculum. Schools, also, should foster an understanding of ethical ideas and habit formation and a comprehensive development of each person that is concerned, broadly speaking, by nurturing a conscious, refreshing, and satisfying life (MW 9, 331–70; Simpson 2017).

In our work, we employ Dewey's analytic approach of examining problems in a twofold way. First, his method is employed to address ethical dilemmas that involve undoubted goods in particular situations. The search to understand the common and conflicting goods that students and colleagues affirm is a powerful way to cultivate educationally effective, ethically thoughtful, culturally sensitive, and democratically oriented schools. For Dewey, the ability to understand another's view of the good often occurs concurrently with one's growth as a sympathetic person. Second, Dewey's method is used to address ethical conflicts and controversies that concurrently involve, at least for some, goods and evils. Employing his method this way is beneficial for several reasons. To begin, while Dewey's analytic process is an integral part of his pragmatic philosophy, it is also a method that may be employed profitably by educators who are not philosophical pragmatists, for inquiry is – or ought to be – a central part of addressing ethical problems. Furthermore, broadening the applicability of his method beyond undoubted goods (e.g., choosing between requiring a music or an art course) allows inquirers to learn in the process of investigating a problem whether they actually know – or have grounds that warrant the conclusion – that only undoubted goods are involved in an ethical case. For example, was the choice of a sport between soccer and USA-style football at the Academy simply one between two undoubted goods (LW 7, 165)? If so, how does a faculty or committee determine that each is an undoubted good? How would the district, Academy, and parents decide? What questions and issues should they raise? What information or data should they explore? Who should serve on and chair the evaluation committee? Similar questions arise about a plethora of curricular, service, pedagogical, disciplinary, purposive, organizational, and structural choices.

As Dewey also notes, often it is "after the event, and then by chance, [that] ... one of the alternatives seem[s] simply good morally or bad morally" (LW 5, 279). Dewey's method, therefore, is useful when some think there appears to be a choice between good and evil as well as when there appears to others to be a conflict between undoubted goods. In addition, Dewey thinks that certain controversies – e.g., administrative, fiscal, personnel – are frequently more complex than assumed and less resolvable than expected. The intensity of a dispute about an elective course versus a required sport course, for instance, may reveal complexity, uncertainty, and undoubted goods but may also suggest intentions and desires rooted in less than admirable reasons, e.g., a dogmatic preference for a sport that one played, or a sport that an offspring plays, and a game that has the potential for greater sales at a family sport goods store. Disclosures regarding conflicts of interest are needed. The teasing out of the desired, the desirable, the undesirable, and the good is required.

Notice, too, that Dewey (LW 5, 279) goes beyond desires and goods to obligations or duties: a person "hesitates ... among duties which obligate him [or her] for some reason." Duty considerations are tied to the ethical person or educator in Chapter 6 when human relationships, trust, and faithfulness are discussed. For example, the Academy staff often feel conflicted about keeping a healthy balance between their personal and professional lives. Unfortunately, they probably tend to sacrifice their personal lives – and families – to their professional responsibilities. Maria, especially, seems to be skewed toward the professional dimension but is realizing that a good or flourishing life does not solely consist in work, even rewarding work. She intellectually understands the importance of concerts, vacations, political activities, the theater, friendships, spiritual development, and physical activity (see Higgins 2011, 145–75). But she has not yet sustained the equilibrium she wants and needs. She understands too the interactive relationships of a good life to being a good person and leader and the lack thereof to being a shriveling person and burned-out educator.

Obviously, Dewey's approach has multiple advantages. To begin, attempting to identify conflicting goods can help participants better understand one another, contribute to the development of regard for each other, and enhance the well-being of individuals and the common or school and district good. In time, working in communities on problems can contribute to the construction of a thick democratic culture. Parents and teachers, therefore, who want more resources to better serve students with autistic challenges have goods in mind just as do parents and teachers who seek more resources to serve English as a second language students well. Looking for the desired and desirable goods of others can open the door to understanding Dewey's phrase "good in some measure" (LW 5, 279). That is, unquestioned goods, when evaluated by their consequences, contributions, and costs, are not always of equal value in every context. They usually are not as-if absolutes; they are contextual goods. Hence, understanding the desires and goods of others is a helpful step toward resolving conflicting desires and interests among educators and partners. Dewey's method, therefore, may be especially useful in stagnant, polarizing situations, e.g., board meetings, political discussions, religious dialogues, and healthcare controversies. Often people should step back from their passionate assertions and, later, discuss the merits of their conflicting desires and goods (and duties and obligations because they sometimes conflict with educators' desires). Plus, they might need to ask themselves how their contentious interactions are shaping themselves – their disposi-tions and character. This approach to disagreements about goods also applies to disagreements about virtues and duties. To illustrate, how should districts, schools, and teachers prioritize – when such is fiscally necessary – social, emotional, intellectual, aesthetic, ethical, and physical objectives?

In passing, we acknowledge that Dewey's view of good and evil is sometimes considered underdeveloped and believed incapable of addres-sing "the capacity of human beings ... to commit heinous crimes" (McDermott 1991, xxxii). While this assertion is a compelling question in particular disagreements (Boisvert 1998, 167–8), it is basically beyond the scope of this work. Instead, we turn to his understanding of contexts, cultures, and environments to discuss concepts basic to his view of prob-lematic ethical situations. Our discussion begins with contexts, cultures, and environments; continues with an analysis of conditions, continuities, interactions, transactions, experiences, and education; and concludes by focusing on a problematic ethical situation. Inescapably, these concepts overlap and commingle, making it difficult to discuss one idea without referencing others. Per practice heretofore, Maria De La Garza's story illustrates aspects of Dewey's thinking.

Context, Culture, and Environment

To think in a Dewey-informed manner about ethical issues and decisions is, in part, to reflect on relevant contextual, cultural, environmental factors, data, and experiences. Without an understanding of the importance of these ethical constructs, the chances of drawing ethically warranted conclusions are compromised. These concepts are distinguished below.

Context

In Dewey's theoretical framework, each of the divisional concepts suggests a relatively broad yet differentiated aspect of ethical situations. Collectively, they identify fertile realms of information about schools, educators, students, communities, societies, and nations. As this conceptual triumvirate is examined, note that in his treatise *Context and Thought*, Dewey underlines the idea that "Context is *incorporated in* what is said and forms *the arbiter of* the value of every utterance" (LW 6, 6; emphasis added). The contexts that arbitrate the meanings of communication are windows into who students are and what they find significant (6). Stated similarly, contextually nourished beliefs and values are invariably embedded in each person's thoughts, affections, behaviors, and practices. Thus, the claim that contextual factors nourish, continue nurturing and forming one's beliefs and emotions, and govern the meaning and significance of every utterance, is not a random statement (6). Collectively, these thoughts clarify why Dewey decided that "the most pervasive fallacy of philosophic [and thereby ethical] thinking goes back to neglect of context" (5). This idea, even though a relatively predictable claim today, is still sobering: *the most common mistake of ethical thinking is ignoring the sources of a person's ethical thinking.* This claim is also helpful when educators think about their own and students' ethical thinking: self and other understanding are required. Educators should not misjudge the contexts of one another and their students.

In view of the above, it is not surprising, if sometimes disingenuous, to hear people who are accused of making offensive remarks counter by claiming: "My words were taken out of context." If the accused person is correct about his words being decontextualized, the decontextualizing person may need to reconsider his remarks and, perhaps, acknowledge his error, e.g.: "Sorry. Please clarify what you mean." Conversely, if a person who is accused of being offensive attempts to shield herself from legitimate criticism by claiming her comments were decontextualized, she compounds the situation; she attempts to deflect responsibility for her offensive comments to a listener's implied misinterpretation. In any case, if the context of a speaker's comment is the arbiter of one's meaning, extraneous matters – like a contrarian's appalling prior experiences – should not be a stealth arbiter of the person's comments. Claims of knowing more about what a speaker herself intends to say than she does are often questionable too, if not off-putting and silencing. Even so, the opportunity to address the vicious mistreatment of an audience member is worth pausing to address, e.g., a woman who alludes to her sexual and physical abuse merits both empathy and attention.

A person who interacts regularly with others, as educators do, is obligated to avoid known offensive words, phrases, and illustrations. Given cultural, regional, and national sensitivities, educators – not to neglect students – need to stay current in their understanding of offensive language. In addition, a careful analysis of the different uses of the concept offensive is helpful. That is to say, there are different kinds and degrees of offensiveness, some legitimate, some unfortunate, and others suicidal (Callan 2016; Fernald 1995; Galupo 2009).

Further, Dewey argues that context is composed of "three deepening levels or three expanding spheres" that focus on particular ideas and entities (LW 6, 20–1). Our analysis begins with his first, "narrowest," or personal, sphere, and then moves to his third, "widest," or experiential, sphere, before looking at the second, or cultural, sphere (20–1). The first, individual or personal sphere, identifies "the range and vitality of the experience" of a particular person (20). This sphere throws light on both uniqueness and stereotyping. The personal experiences of a student, say, and the influence of them on him, when examined, offer fresh perspectives into his individuality and why he thinks, feels, values, and acts as he does. How widely and deeply was he touched or scarred by the attention he received? Does the personal experience still have the power to alter the course of his future experience? Experiences also enable the individual educator to employ specific influences to better sympathize with students and to evaluate their prior and continuing learning. This knowledge is enormously helpful, for no matter how broad or limited one's experience (20), this knowledge enables each teacher to employ their understandings and appreciations to contribute to others' learning. In turn, educators can enhance every student's introduction to a broadening world, i.e., supplementing their "limitations" and diminishing their "biases" (20–1). Any supplementation or modification of personal experience, of course, should be artistically, not clumsily or arrogantly, undertaken (20–1). As Callan (2016) and Freire ([1970] 2003) emphasize, neither a pedagogy nor a dialogue of denigration has a place in schools.

Educators better understand and appreciate their own and others' thinking when they reflect on specific experiences and their "range and vitality" (LW 6, 20). Maria and her context, for instance, are much more deeply appreciated when her childhood in Jalisco and Alberta, youth in California, her nursing studies in Texas, and military deployment in Germany and Afghanistan are understood. The latter especially clarifies her passion for addressing the unique and common needs of diverse people, even those who appear – and, unfortunately, may be in some way – adversaries. Her time as a nurse in Kabul tested and accentuated her beliefs about equitable treatment of people as she cared for injured Afghan and coalition soldiers, Taliban and Al-Qaeda fighters, and, momentarily, a surviving child suicide bomber. Understanding why her convalescing fiancée ended her life in Germany and how such impacted Maria's psyche, not to mention life trajectory, may make a profound difference in understanding the meaning of her decisions at the Academy. Obviously, Maria did not suddenly emerge as Principal De La Garza. Neither does any child, parent, or colleague emerge amorphously. So, ignoring the personal experiences or stories of Academy personnel and students eliminates them as persons, thwarting attempts to understand, teach, and learn with them.

Dewey's third, "widest and deepest," or experiential, sphere, examines ordinary experience, human nature, and philosophical thinking (LW 6, 20–1). This sphere constitutes an examination of "the make-up of experience itself," potentially including the "multiplicity" of human interactions and the common form or "structure of . . . all experience" (21). Dewey admits that this domain – "that inclusive and pervasive context of experience in which philosophical thinking . . . takes place" – can be challenging. But it need not be overwhelming, he concludes, if experience is appraised during one's ordinary experiences, not just during formal schooling. Thus, ordinary experiences plus formal educational ones are not just helpful but fundamental to understanding and appraising the nature experience (21). The flow and integration of these experiences help raise life to a more conscious and fertile level, from miseducative and noneducative to educative ones.

Given the connection Dewey makes to broad experiences and philosophical thinking, his concepts of philosophical attitude, disposition, method, inquiry, and task are worth a foregrounding. He asserts that the philosophical attitude is "averse to taking anything as isolated" and, therefore, the philosophically oriented educator should attempt "to place an act in its context" to ensure its meaning is clear (MW 9, 335–6). Consequently, one's attitude when analyzing problems should be "as unified, consistent, and complete" as feasible (334). Moreover, having a philosophical disposition entails being "sensitive to new perceptions, and [recognizing one's] responsibility ... [for] connecting them" with existing ones (335). In turn, being open to new perceptions suggests the ability to add to, revise, and, as warranted, move beyond one's present self to a different one. Similarly, being open-minded includes discovering meaning in context, not forcing one's own meaning into it. The educator, therefore, is concerned with "general and enduring" components and patterns in class, school, and neighborhood contexts (Deen 2012, 334). She may ask, for instance, what general and recurring themes and values are present in the Academy. When pursuing their pedagogical tasks, do faculty also attend to the relationship of facts and values and to the "inclusiveness" of their topic (LW 16, 358)? Finally, the philosophic task of the Academy personnel – and increasingly of students – is to ensure that an inclusive "temporal-spatial context" composed of "special topics, propositions, conclusions" contribute to understanding the uniqueness of school experiences and situations (Deen 2012, 334). Collectively, these philosophical inclinations form philosophical mindedness.

Philosophical thinking, therefore, takes place as educators and students locate problems in their contexts and recognize that they arose out of earlier exchanges and will contribute to succeeding interactions and problem-solving (Deen 2012, 334). In each ethical situation, therefore, one figuratively reexamines past videos to cull relevant information for understanding a particular situation and its potential future courses (MW 14, 132–8). Educators' and students' reflective and imaginative work seeks to penetrate the future in order to examine probable consequences of possible choices. Entering the future is accomplished by means of dramatic rehearsal, deliberation, and empathy that enable one or a group to see on "the screen of imagination" the likely consequences of hypothetical ways of addressing a problem (MW 14, 133). In a sense, dramatic rehearsal resembles a live theatrical performance with multiple possible endings that stimulate a teacher and/or class to select an ethical ending that most adequately explains the data and influences the well-being of the affected.

For Maria, Dewey's concept of context has been particularly helpful, especially in the personal sphere: "the range and vitality" of her and others' individual experiences (LW 6, 20). In particular, she thinks of interactions that shaped her thinking and life in immeasurable ways. She later decided that the scope and strength of her experience had been considered both under- and over-evaluated. Significant adults and classmates told her, in different ways, that her ideas were trivial; her – and others' – immediate ideas were at "the narrowest and the most superficial" level (LW 6, 20). Unfortunately, only a few, other than her family, told her everyone begins at this personal level and later moves to wider spheres and deeper levels. But some also told her that her early experiences shaped her in important ways, too. In response to the disrespect she heard in her early life experiences, Maria recalls her grandmother's unforgettable words, "Palabras estúpidas. Señor perdóname."

Much later when Maria was an assistant principal, one of the school's first-year teachers was noticeably different. Indeed, he could not be ignored. He had the qualities for an effective teacher plus other admirable characteristics. Moreover, he was loved by his students and their parents; his social skills were superbly crafted. His energy was demonstrated by his volunteer services; his natural leadership abilities were manifest too. Plus, he engaged in community and civic activities. He was, if not absolutely perfect, close, especially if one were unattached. Having no attraction, Maria envisioned her love dancing along the road from Würzburg to Füssen. Later, as Academy principal, she offered Matthew an assistant principalship and learned more about what Dewey meant by the phrase "disrespect for experience" (LW 6, 21).

Culture

External and internal cultures, Dewey's second contextual domain, include systemic, structural, procedural, material, and value elements that constitute people's or an individual's culture (LW 6, 21). Hence, he claims "the cultural-environmental conditions" (Deen 2012, 344), the "context of culture" (LW 6, 3), and the "complex of [situational] conditions" are summarized by "the word Culture" (LW 13, 67; emphasis original). He stresses too the fact that "the moral factor is an intrinsic part of the complex of social forces called culture" (MW 13, 71), indicating that the moral overlays and seeps into cultural and social fabrics. Furthermore, he argues that cultural moral factors are integral parts of a system "of beliefs about value (together with all the processes by which these beliefs are formed and maintained) and social organization" (Deen 2012, 290–1).

Importantly, his concept of culture suggests a closer, warmer atmosphere than context that, while encompassing culture, gives more attention to cognitive, theoretical, spatial, and temporal elements. Understanding this domain leads back to the personal sphere or "the range and vitality" of each individual's experience (LW 6, 20) as well as to a person's unique

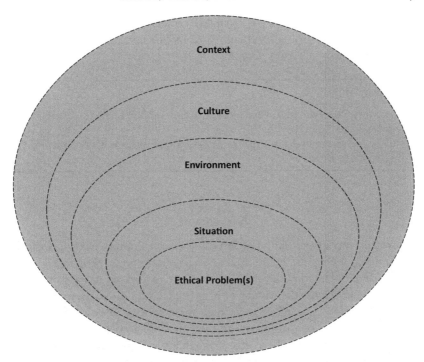

Figure 5.2   The context, culture, and environment

"culture of mind and spirit" (LW 7, 320). Moving gradually toward an insider's view of a local Islamic external culture is only a beginning when it comes to understanding a specific Muslim student. Understanding each Muslim's unique reconstruction of his historical and local external cultures as well as his distinct mind and spirit is an aid when personalizing curricula (see Ghobash 2016). In short, a Muslim child is, like a member of any other group, somewhat like millions to billions of other people, but is also uniquely himself. This unique child is, without a doubt, no one else and is the person insightful teachers work diligently to understand and teach. His tutoring his teachers about who he is is a lovely possibility. Yet, he cannot be expected to articulate with a comprehensive clarity the mature faith and philosophy of his parents and community.

A context, ultimately, is both the whole and its subparts as suggested in Figure 5.2. Yet the context is not a summation of the measurable parts of a classroom or school. Instead, thought, including scientific and ethical inquiry, "never gets far away from qualitative existence" (LW 5, 261–2);

for, thinking is "regulated by qualitative considerations," such as "the concerns and issues of [the] living" and "actions and ... consequences" of "enjoyment or suffering" (243).

Stop and Think

How might Dewey's ideas of external and internal cultures help teachers better understand a specific Jewish, Hindu, Christian, Buddhist, or nonreligious student and their affinity groups? How does a teacher learn about students' internal cultures?

Environment

Of course, the spatial-temporal setting – e.g., a Primary School Spanish Laboratory, 9:00 a.m. February 21, 2040, Edinburgh, Scotland – of a particular problematic ethical situation is embedded in an environment. Figure 5.2 represents the surface of deep-rooted and interwoven phenomena. In addition, it suggests that these three spheres of context, culture, and environment constitute the immediate and deeper conditions of a problematic situation. The concentric circles indicate how elements are contained within one or more larger, more comprehensive spheres. The broken spherical borders suggest the porous nature of the components and point to how ideas and values flow into and out of one another. To identify these spheres and their influence on a problematic situation may be seen as a normative responsibility when addressing complex problems.

The Academy's environment, like any school, is composed of numerous elements. In *Experience and Education*, the social element is revealed in Dewey's claim that "whatever conditions interact with personal needs, desires, purposes, and capacities to create the [desired and desirable] experience" are part of an environment (LW 13, 25). Drilling down, he adds that the "most important" environmental element is "the total *social* set-up of the situations" (LW 13, 26; emphasis original) in which people interact. Since people interact continuously, "the total social set-up" – including openness, friendliness, inclusiveness – needs priority attention. Staff, unconsciously and consciously, regulate many of "the objective conditions" of the Academy and constantly shape the social fabric that facilitates or inhibits the desires, dispositions, and habits of everyone (LW 13, 24). Remembering, however, that "the environment ... is never twice alike" (MW 14, 105) and that acts occur in and are a part of "specific surrounding conditions" points out the need for ongoing environmental analyses, evaluations, and reconstructions (107).

Objective conditions, for Dewey, are those that are outside a person. Thus, observing, selecting, regulating, constructing, and episodically removing objective conditions is a responsibility of educators but one that can be shared fruitfully with students, volunteers, and parents. The immediate aim of regulating objective conditions is to ensure that they facilitate productive interactions and transactions with students' internal conditions so that new "internal states [e.g., enjoyment, reflection, appreciation]" are produced (LW 13, 24). The "internal conditions" of each person (e.g., the impulses, desires, purposes) must interact with the "objective conditions" of the environment – e.g., the physical and social conditions – in order for educative experiences to occur (23–4). Hence, educators should evaluate classroom and school processes and activities in the light of the principles of continuity and interaction (31): Do new experiences connect and integrate with prior learning (continuity), and do students engage with one another and their environments in educative ways (interaction)? Are new "internal states" also demonstrated (24)? Is there enjoyment? Is there intellectual, moral, physical, aesthetic, and emotional growth? Do belongingness and community emerge?

For Dewey, student interactions should be woven into at least two intersecting sets of activities: the educative and the aesthetic. The first set – the educative-noneducative-miseducative triad – is based on Dewey's widely employed term, *education*, and refers to interactions. Educative experiences promote intellectual, emotional, and social growth in the present and the potential for future growth. Noneducative experiences involve little or no growth. They are largely meaningless. Miseducative learning involves misinformation, misunderstanding, and misinterpretation, e.g., developing national, social class, religious, and gender stereotypes and prejudices (LW 13, 17–38). In the second or aesthetic triad, three kinds of linked experiences are distinguished too: experience, *an* experience (Dewey italicized *an*), and aesthetic experience. He thought it also essential to minimize two kinds of pseudo experiences, i.e., anesthetic and nonaesthetic. These pseudo experiences include haphazard activities, monotonous repetitions, mis-enculturation, and disconnected explorations (LW 10, 42, 62–3).

Meaningful endeavors occur throughout the aesthetic experiential continuum: experience, *an* experience, and aesthetic experience. In the initial type, called simply experience, there are starting points, connections, and conclusions but often with limited coherence and continuity.

Interruptions in experience and periods of stagnation may occur too. Yet, students engage and grow with one another, interact with their environments, and receive feedback during their interactions (LW 10, 41–3; LW 13, 31). In *an* experience, there are enhancements that are marked by sustained interest, enjoyment, continuities, meaning, fulfillment, and wholeness (LW 10, 41–2). The most rewarding, but often less frequent, learning experience is an aesthetic experience that contains all of the positive qualities of experience and *an* experience plus a heightened pleasure in the creative processes of doing, making, and perceiving and in the satisfying, nourishing, and consummating moments. Aesthetic experiences are decidedly rewarding, memorable, and transformative (LW 10, 33–4). At the Academy, staff consciously raise questions about how educative experiences can be enhanced and elevated to *an* experience and, at least often, to an aesthetic experience.

The spatial and temporal features of planned environments are necessarily vital elements. The spatially identifiable environments that may be employed include homes, parks, laboratories, classrooms, athletic facilities, learning centers, museums, and buses – or particular places and sites, such as St. John's, Kolkata, Mecca, Seoul, Sydney, Puerto Rico, Orkney, and Shanghai (LW 13, 22–4). But regardless of the spatial setting, the contexts, cultures, and environments of a person and a school bleed into one another. This mixing of elements means that a school environment is actually "many, not one" (MW 14, 38) and, thus, "not all of one piece" (39). Obviously, deeply understanding the "conditions of the local community, physical, historical, economic, occupational ... [is crucial to utilizing] them as educational resources" (LW 13, 23). In *The Public and Its Problems*, Dewey draws a curricular conclusion that is more important than often understood: "the local is the ultimate universal, and as near an absolute as exists" (LW 2, 369). For him, educators should excavate the local context of each learning and ethical situation, regardless of whether the local environment is immediate or remote and singular or multiple. When the local is well understood, invisible pathways that connect the student with their past, present, and future are uncovered and can be utilized in ethical development.

Temporal and spatial elements are frequently joined, resulting in a mixture of the past, present, and contingent future and the local and the global. So, the "environing conditions" of an internet site, a book, an historical artifact, a chemistry experiment, a writing laboratory, or a bus ride home can offer captivating information. Intellectually entering "Greece," "an imaginary region," or interacting "with the objects which [a student] . . . constructs in fancy" (LW 13, 25) are important aspects of a stimulating environment even if remote (25). Regularly, then, realities that "are remote in space and time" may "form [one's] . . . environment even more truly than some of the things close" (MW 9, 15). "The things" that vary or differ – interests, worries, abilities, ordeals, tastes – for a student are their "genuine environment" even if outside classrooms and schools (15). Recognizing the learning opportunities offered by the "great diversity of [school] populations, of varying languages, religions, moral codes, and traditions," Dewey encourages pedagogical innovation and ethical imagination when accessing these resources (MW 9, 87).

Like Dewey, many today rightly conclude that school diversity is an invaluable part of the often unseen environment of students (MW 9, 87). The cultures, languages, values, tastes, arts, philosophies, religions, and talents in a classroom offer innumerable curricular opportunities. Why, then, an Indian, Irish, Caribbean, or Indigenous student acts in both similar and diverse ways from others is important. His acts are ethically meaningful when interpreted via a specific local situation and a unique person. But a student is seldom if ever largely understood by using convenient terms as primary windows of interpretation, e.g., national, ethnic, religious, or areligious. Equally, avoiding stereotypes of groups is crucial. In this area, keeping in mind the personal sphere of context – "the range and vitality" of each person's experience (LW 6, 20) – helps avoid typecasting. No two people have matching experiential ranges, exact emotional attachments, or identical intellectual interests. Considering complex environments, unique students, and the challenges of teaching and learning, there is no reason to wonder why Dewey likened the gifted teacher to "a great orchestral conductor" who constructs, reconstructs, and utilizes environments "to [meet] the developing needs of a group of learners who are thoroughly understood" (LW 11, 544).

Almost needless to say, the human element of the environment penetrates and infuses the worlds of students and educators. In these interwoven worlds, the emotional growth of students is at least as crucial as the intellectual. Dewey, therefore, correctly expresses apprehension about students in stressful, even chaotic, families and schools. He argues that the pressures of moving in, among, and out of expanding and contracting environments and their emotional climates can contribute to developmental problems, especially if the "unworthy features" of schools – e.g., loneliness, ostracism, intimidation – are pronounced (MW 9, 24). Contemporary researchers (e.g., DeWall 2013; Williams, Forgas, and Hippel 2005) indicate that unrelieved or forced social isolation is among the most destructive of social forces children encounter. Strike (2010, 17–37) adds that the concept of alienation best describes why many urban students are disengaged and that building strong school communities is essential to serving them and others well. Ruitenberg (2016) goes further to argue that many students need to find hospitable teachers.

For multiple reasons, Dewey draws the conclusion that schools should magnify the importance of students learning and employing life-enhancing continuities – skills, understandings, and dispositions – that are instruments of "dealing effectively with situations" in their school and post-school years (LW 13, 25–7). Learning to use intellectual and social skill sets and school services to handle present and future challenges can be developmentally liberating (25–7). Yet, a troubled student attending an underprepared school – whether in London, Cairo, Buenos Aires, or Puebla – is likely to experience an alienating, "a divided world, a world whose parts . . . do not hang together . . . [and therefore create] a divided personality" (26). Everything considered, one can argue that schools appear ethically obligated to develop conditions that counter social and school forces that promote harmful student exclusions and, alternatively, seek to foster healthy personalities through integrated school-community-family services, including helping students build "a world of related objects" (26). Dewey implies that stressful school conditions ought to be understood, monitored, reduced, and, when possible, eliminated (Deen 2012, 327). Staff, also, need to be prepared to identify and serve well students who manifest signs of alienation (Strike 2010) as well as students who show symptoms of unaddressed mental health challenges (Carsley and Heath 2015).

No doubt, schools should remove counterproductive conditions and foster interactions that incorporate the desirable – not merely the desired – features of an "objective environment" (MW 14, 38). These "objective conditions" can then interact with the "internal condition[s]" of students so that learning occurs and students can foster new "internal [reflective and healthy] states" (LW 13, 24). That the "objective conditions" of an environment – e.g., the physical, social, and aesthetic circumstances – must interact with the "internal conditions" of each student (e.g., the impulses, feelings, abilities, and ideas) is critical (LW 13, 23–4). When there are interactions and transactions between the objective and internal conditions, both the student and the environment "undergo change," and "connective relations" are made (LW 16, 242). Transactions, of course, should be "enmeshed in a body of activities" that are socially and emotionally healthy (LW 16, 42–3). This "togetherness of human and non-human" elements facilitates making both fruitful learning and healthy schooling possible (LW 16, 43). Consciously or not, Academy educators are, at least informally, mental health support personnel.

Stop and Think

Which kinds of classroom and school conditions are often the most influential determinants of students' belongingness and social inclusion? What does recent research suggest about the kinds of people or students who are likely to be excluded from mainstream social groups?

The Problematic Ethical Situation

Given the above analyses, Dewey has a detailed answer to the question, What is a problematic ethical situation? But, in short, a problematic ethical situation involves a practical problem that is characterized by the presence of "conflicts," "sincere doubts," "moral perplexities," "undoubted goods" (LW 7, 164–5), and, for some, good and evil (LW 5, 279). Importantly, however, a problematic ethical situation, if it is addressed, entails inquiry as students, teachers, parents, and administrators deliberate about certain goods, qualities, ends, and duties (LW 5, 279). In *Human Nature and Conduct*, Dewey notes too that since "situations are continuous" there is "a continuous modification of habits" by students and educators and that it is this "mutual modification of habits" that enables those concerned "to define the [precise] nature of the moral situation" (MW 14, 30). That is, decisions to modify behavior suggest there may be a potential or actual ethical issue in a situation. In *Unmodern Philosophy and Modern Philosophy*, sets of activities – inquiries, deliberations, interactions, transactions, and modifications – involve people who appreciate varying practices, beliefs, and behaviors. Thus, change includes both qualitative and quantitative modifications (Deen 2012, 335).

At this juncture, it is interesting to note Dewey clarifies two additional considerations that "limit and define a moral situation" (MW 14, 34). The first, he emphasizes, "is that consequences fix the moral quality of an act" (34), and the second "is that upon the whole ... consequences are what they are because of desire and disposition" (34). Two ideas ensue. First, the consequences of choices or acts – the worthwhile, detrimental, and indifferent – establish whether they are ethical, unethical, or neutral. While other considerations merit attention, the immediate and evolving outcomes – student learning, equitable opportunities, freedom of thought, employment fairness, mental health, and personal meanderings – reveal the quality of an act, policy, tradition, or law. Second, in *Freedom and Culture*, Dewey highlights the fact that individual and group desires for freedom, equality, respect, rights, inclusion, friendship, security, independence, and community are important to recognize (MW 13, 65–106). Desires, while potentially productive, can become counterproductive as they are distorted by impulsive, immature, narcissistic, and dogmatic agendas. Thus, the identification of desires that have both social and antisocial potential can help educators assist students in reaching their goals in fruitful and people-regarding ways. Finally, Dewey also thought it essential to understand that an ethical situation is characterized by participants' "voluntary activity" (MW 5, 187). Coerced behavior, obviously, raises a set of inquiry flags, e.g., Are educators ever justified in using coercion? If so, when and why? What are the detectable consequences of using coercion with students? But, of course, students can coerce one another, too. Exposing coercion for what it frequently is – a misguided and, perhaps, destructive mistreatment of another individual for one's personal satisfaction – is a potentially rewarding way to begin developing a mutual caring respect in schools.

Dewey (Deen 2012, 335–6; emphasis original) probes further into the importance of "spatial and temporal *togetherness*" – which includes student and faculty "connections and relations, and interconnections and relationships," continuities and discontinuities, and equilibria and disequilibria – and, while often perplexing, it can facilitate rewarding change (335–6). Dewey also identified three kinds of general qualities – "*epistemic, practical,* and *esthetic*" – of situations that are interpretively valuable (336; emphasis original). This trio of qualities, while separately identifiable, often fuse as student experiences and interactions with one another and educators nurture class and school understanding and "*togetherness*" (336; emphasis original). When Dewey uses the term *epistemic,* he deliberately rejects the historical baggage of the word *epistemological* (e.g., one's being engrossed in the problems of knowing but failing to give adequate attention to the problems of people). Epistemic, for him, suggests a "search for truth" or well-supported knowledge claims that, in turn, serve as instruments for learning more and solving everyday problems (345). Hence, doing ethics in schools – and elsewhere – involves searches for warranted claims that lead to more student and educator knowledge and to an understanding of how to address practical problems.

Dewey also reconstructs many ideas, including the idea of the practical, associating it with the "qualitative aspects of a situation" (Deen 2012, 338). Explicitly, he argues that the practical "is nothing more nor less than the whole conduct of life" (218). While conducting their lives at school, both teachers and students, therefore, are involved in determining how to identify and appreciate when statements are warranted in fields of inquiry, creativity, and practice. Since no one – the textbook editor, software specialist, website owner, publisher, professor, educator, or student – has a "virgin mind" (LW 8, 214), schools are also places where warranted, less warranted, and unwarranted opinions are evaluated (214). If not, the miseducative forces of societies and individuals will have a profound – and, time and again, determinative – influence on the development and discussion of ideas and practices in schools and elsewhere.

The aesthetic experience, at least for Dewey, involves understanding, appreciating, and creating art, music, and literature in places where one lives, works, and recreates. Cumulatively, it involves "the net outcome" of "the course of living" one's life "as a rhythm of interactions that are balanced and unified and interactions that are in a state of imbalance and tension" (Deen 2012, 327). Educationally, the aesthetic experience is an intrinsic part of teaching and learning, inquiring and concluding, deliberating and deciding, imagining and creating, and envisioning and producing. Sensitivity to the "rhythm of interactions" (327) of individual and class engagements characterize these aesthetic experiences as surely as do students' studying and enjoying the great works that are displayed in museums and performed in concert halls. Moreover, participating in situations that display the creation and demonstration of courage, compassion, inclusion, friendship, togetherness, and reflection in classrooms, schools, and neighborhoods can be simultaneously ethical and artistic works.

The Whole Situation

In view of the above claims, it is apparent that, for Dewey, problematic ethical situations occur in particular yet dynamic contexts, cultures, and environments and are differentiated by unique people, conditions, continuities, interactions, transactions, and deliberations. In addition, a whole ethical situation includes doubts, conflicting goods (LW 7, 164–5), and judgments about right and wrong (LW 7, 280). Furthermore, a problematic ethical situation is distinguished by inquiry as participants deliberate goods, ends, and duties (LW 5, 279). As Figure 5.1 suggests, there are also spheres of tension and harmony, not just one or the other in ethical situations. In these situations, there is often "a mutual modification of habits" by participants (MW 14, 30) as their collaborations, dialogues, and reflections lead them to reconstruct linguistic, cognitive, affective, and social inclinations and habits. Moreover, Dewey states that two factors – consequences and desires – establish both the limits and meaning of "a moral situation" (MW 14, 34). That is, limits and meaning are revealed in "the moral quality" of acts (MW 14, 34), and the consequences are "what they are because of [participants'] desire[s] and disposition[s]" (34). In problematic situations, it is not rare for unplanned communications to promote "collateral" learning (LW 13, 29) and "attendant" or connected ethical development (LW 5, 32). As these unplanned learnings are noticed, educators are well-advised to ask: "what *other* things" are being learned by students along with the intended curriculum (LW 5, 35)? Is there, intentionally or otherwise, a hidden curriculum?

Another noteworthy, if sometimes confusing, comment by Dewey is that right and wrong are "determined by the situation in its entirety" (LW 7, 280). What, however, is an entire situation? Contrary to some, Dewey does not think that right and wrong are decided completely in a detached situation or by each person's preferences alone while in a particular situation. Moreover, he does think it is acceptable – even necessary – for one's own and others' reflections to be evaluated. Plus, he argues that a similar ethical situation could be considered along with the current one. Nor does he imply that attitudes, intentions, principles, goods, obligations, virtues, and consequences are irrelevant to a whole situation. Quite the reverse, he claims that ethical judgments should be determined by everything ethically relevant in "the [entire] situation" (MW 7, 280). What, however, is *in an entire situation*? What is ethically relevant? The unique configurations of participants' individualities, personalities, and knowledge bases are in a situation. The entire situation, therefore, is a uniquely rich cultural and intellectual setting, not a nearly empty sphere that stands apart from the rest of reality.

Dewey's specific comments are, as they should be, invaluable. In the immediate context in *Ethics* (LW 7), he argues against the idea that an ethical principle by itself determines an act's rightness or wrongness. Instead, right and wrong are determined with the help of vetted and reflectively employed ethical principles, appraised virtues, analyzed goods, and many other factors in the "whole situation" (LW 7, 291). Ethical principles are tools to help one think about attitudes, acts, and consequences, but the acts are judged right or wrong by principles plus other situational variables (e.g., participants' intentions, desires, and goods), present ethical continuities (e.g., long-standing but conflicting goods, duties, and ends), and prospective consequences (e.g., sympathy for some but antipathy for others) that inform ethical judgment.

Moreover, much like fair-minded judges and jurors, educators are challenged to determine if a person's involvement in an ethical situation was a clear choice (or a coerced one), an action (or a reaction), an intention (or an accident), a typical behavior (or an atypical deed), and so forth (LW 5, 187). Was the person's decision based on a dismissal of a pertinent ethical principle or a capitulation in an overpowering quandary? Did one react without thinking of the seriousness of the situation? Was there "a mitigating circumstance" (MW 14, 75)? Thus, a whole situation could include nearly anything that participants are or bring with them as social beings.

A second way that "the situation in its entirety" (LW 7, 280) may be understood is from a qualitative perspective (LW 5, 243–62). In this case, "the [regulative] quality of a situation as a whole" reveals "an intellectual connection" (257) to those who possess "sensitiveness to [its] pervasive quality" (259). Much like art connoisseurs and students who have heightened appreciation for aesthetic qualities, students and teachers who are sensitive to fairness, kindliness, and conscientiousness may have an intensified appreciation for these qualities, especially when school examinations, student promotions, and individual honors are being decided. When unfairness appears to be the pervasive quality of a situation as a whole, the details of the situation should be studied to determine if related facts support one's immediate perception. To have a sensitivity to qualities without intemperance is a decided plus, but as usual, Dewey cautions that the results of further analysis and reflection "may confirm or may lead to rejection" of an original opinion (259).

Certainly, thinking, including reflections on ethical situations, "never gets far away from qualitative existence" (LW 5, 261–2). In fact, Maria's present concern regarding fairness in employment practices demonstrates how a perception of bias may indicate the need for inquiry and, among other changes, realignment of policies and practices. Stated positively, the desire for racial, gender, religious, identity, and ethnic equity in employment practices opens the door for strengthening and elevating the ethical architecture of the Academy's culture (Wagner and Simpson 2009, 119–32). Recall, too, Maria's inquiry into Irene's reported screaming at her students. Molly, a school psychology intern, reported the incident to several other teachers, but Irene's students understood the sound, not as a scream, but as a muffled moan. They were not really frightened by but rather concerned for

Irene. What, then, Maria wondered at the time, accounts for the discrepancy between the children's perceptions and Molly's?

Someone could claim that since every factor in a situation is unique (which Dewey affirms), the individual teacher or group involved has to decide for oneself or themselves (which Dewey affirms with qualifications). For manifold reasons, Dewey thinks that ultimately Academy educators and students have to decide for themselves what should or should not be done in ethical situations. Even so, he clarifies that they should not habitually decide alone as individuals, without consulting the reflective thinking of others, professional standards, relevant laws, district regulations, and applicable research. Students, as minors, should be disposed to interact with their guardians or parents too. The common good, therefore, involves learning what others think is good for them and others, not each person making isolated or arbitrary decisions about the well-being of others.

For Maria – or any individual Academy educator or student – to decide what is right or wrong entirely alone would be comparable to attempting to make a warranted decision without any input from familial values, cultural beliefs, educative experiences, district guidelines, professional obligations, moral development research, and legal responsibilities – or without the influence of context, culture, and environment. Clearly, such action is impossible. Everyone learns from past and present people, circumstances, and experiences. Plus, Academy educators and students should inquire and make decisions with one another; for, doing ethics is a social and collaborative as well as a personal activity and obligation (Peters 1966, 8). Figure 5.3 captures some of the complexities of Maria's entire ethical situation. The more Maria and her colleagues understand Academy students and relevant social events, the greater their potential contributions are to the school's and, thereby, the district's well-being.

Assuming Dewey is correct, each person – student and educator – needs to interact with others as well as in the forum of their mind, a mind that is continually being constructed. An individualistic approach, when based on ignoring relevant information or a flawed view of personal responsibility, is, according to Dewey, a horrific imposition that exceeds the cruelty of forcing an unexamined code of ethics or set of cultural mores on others (MW 14, 74). Why? Because the fully individualistic or the you-alone-decide paradigm throws the entire problem and "responsibility for judging each case" on each student or educator, "imposing" on each, ultimately, "the burden of discovery [of pertinent theories, ideas, data] and adaptation [of one's action to the specific situation]" (MW 14, 74). For Dewey, accessing the minds of others – the reflective ideas of knowledgeable people, relevant laws, professional standards, students, parents, and colleagues – adds to the richness of

Figure 5.3   The entire ethical situation: participants, contexts, problems, and phenomena

the forum of one's mind and community. Working toward a better under-standing of an entire situation and "learning to *act* with and for others" while also learning "to *think* and to judge for" one's self is a collaborative, community-oriented, and deliberative pattern worth cultivating, Dewey claims (MW 6, 98; emphasis original).

Obviously, reflection and deliberation create conflict as well as consen-sus. But the tension among some Harbor District staff regarding believed discriminatory employment practices may be caused by having too few facts, ill-informed discussions, secrecy, and fear. Consequently, problems and conflicts, at times, are caused by a lack of collaborative reflection and deliberation. In such situations, Dewey's "consensualism" – nurturing agreement, equilibrium, satisfaction, and harmony by Maria and others – is a good that may not be possible (Murphey 1988, xxii). Of course, Dewey resisted a consensualism that was based on sacrificing either ethical or epistemic integrity. Even with dialogue, solutions are not guaranteed.

Discussion thus far has largely occurred among several teachers and among Maria, Jorge, Deborah, and Stephen Weinberg, the director of district data collection. Weinberg, however, has held open forums and private conversations with staff, parents, and others while updating district data collection goals. Due in part to Weinberg's in-depth research and discussion sessions with staff, the four – Maria, Jorge, Deborah, and Stephen – think that data indicate diversity goals are largely but not completely being met by each school and that district policies and procedures are almost sufficiently clear, operationalized, and monitored. These two clarifications alone were worth the study. But several claims of prejudice and insensitivity were also identified. One district-level claim indicates that Cecilia, Jorge's daughter, had been hired for a central office position even though she did not appear as well-qualified as two other applicants. A school-level claim about Maria suggested that she tolerated derogatory remarks about Indigenous people and discriminated against people of Cuban heritage. In later discussions, Superintendent Roosevelt and Weinberg clarified that Cecilia had never been a Harbor employee and is employed by a nearby school district. That district's board made an independent decision about her employment.

Infrequent rumors regarding Maria tolerating derogatory remarks by Mirana Cabello about an Indigenous family and Maria being biased against Cuban immigrants were found principally at the Academy. The two claims seemed connected and found mostly among a teacher friendship group. Maria, as expected, was distressed when she heard the accusations. Yet, she admitted that she had contributed inadvertently to both problems. She appeared to tolerate a disparaging remark on one occasion, although she had later said publicly that she regretted her inability to correct the impression immediately. The context of her remark, she continued, was at the end of a substitute teachers' orientation session and immediately before lunch. After the group session had concluded, a substitute teacher candidate asked how teachers could motivate Indigenous students to learn since their families might be indifferent to education. Caught off-guard by the questioner, a former full-time teacher, and simultaneously her administrative assistant's handheld sign ("See Superintendent ASAP!"), Maria paused, making vague comments about respecting others, getting to know parents, and learning about Indigenous people's various educational interests.

As Maria thought back to the situation, she concluded that her problem had multiple aspects. First, she was surprised that Mirana, a friend and former colleague, crossed the line of typecasting Indigenous people. From everything she knew about Mirana, she was an unbiased supporter of all peoples. Second, Maria had wanted at the time to clarify – and did in her afternoon orientation session – that having open dialogue did not imply that it was appropriate to speak derogatorily of groups. But, third, she quickly wondered how she could publicly counter the derogatory comment given Mirana's presence and fragile mental health. While Mirana's residential treatment for depression and anxiety disorders was no secret, it was still professionally confidential. At the time, she wondered if an open response to Mirana would hinder her recovery. Fourth, she talked openly, but in private, with Mirana. Fifth, she realized that she had to decide shortly what her responsibilities to the district and Mirana were: Should she advise Mirana to delay her plans to return to teaching and inform the personnel department about potential problems with Mirana's desire to return to work at this time? Her first step after seeing Superintendent Roosevelt and having lunch was to refocus on the upcoming session and to add some pertinent clarifications to her upcoming presentation.

When Maria talked with Mirana, Mirana thanked Maria for helping her understand that her earlier language had been pejorative. Mirana had added that she could not recall exactly how to express her thoughts at the time. Her medicines, she continued, were still interfering with her thinking. After later discussions with Mirana, Maria concluded that Mirana did not appear prepared to deal with everyday classroom responsibilities. Her ultimate recommendation to the personnel department was evidently interpreted by someone as prejudicial against Mirana and, by extension, Cuban immigrants.

Stop and Think

If you were Deborah Roosevelt, how would you identify the primary quality of Maria's situation? Should she expect a principal to always be prepared to respond immediately and publicly to typecasting?

The Ethical Problem

The problem in an ethical situation is, for many, typically clear and its solution straightforward if responsible parties admit their roles and modify their conduct. Contexts, complexities, conditions, and perspectives may seem essentially clear. The precise problem is evident, the initiators are known, and the consequences are obvious. The solution is a matter of determining and applying equitable and effective treatments. Dewey, however, notes that straightforward situations are not always as they appear. He observes that careful analysis and inquiry are demanded before and, often, after decision-making:

> A moral situation is one in which judgment and choice are required antecedently [or prior] to overt action. The practical meaning of the situation – that is to say the action needed to satisfy it – is not self-evident. It has to be searched for. There are conflicting desires and apparent alternative goods. What is needed is to find the right course of action, the right good. (MW 12, 173)

Dewey's comment, however, may not seem to align with the kind of problematic situation that arose in Maria's substitute teacher orientation session. In her situation, she had almost no opportunity to inquire into or to determine what would satisfy the immediate problem. Given Maria's divided attention to her administrative assistant's message, her audience leaving the session for lunch, and Mirana's fragile mental health and her comment, the situation appears different in kind, one that seems to demand an almost instantaneous reply to several matters. But she failed to live up to her own and professional expectations and had experienced guilt for nearly two years thereafter. Shortly after the incident, Maria might have thought that "the right good" was in reality a series of "right goods," e.g., the goods of demonstrating respect for Indigenous peoples, protecting Mirana's delicate pursuit of recovery and reemployment, and illustrating to aspiring substitute teachers how a leader should respond instantly to multiple challenges.

Dewey's advice, nevertheless, is considerably more helpful for external evaluators, or appraisers who are not immediate participants in a problematic situation, e.g., Deborah Roosevelt. She did not attend the orientation session. In fact, Dewey argues that a set of steps is often warranted by ethical decision-makers in Roosevelt's situation and means that

> inquiry is [to be] exacted: observation of the detailed makeup of the situation; analysis, into its diverse factors; clarification of what is obscure; discounting of the more insistent and vivid traits; tracing the consequences of the various modes of action that suggest themselves; regarding the decision reached as hypothetical and tentative until the anticipated or supposed consequences which led to its adoption have been squared with actual consequences. (MW 12, 173)

Examining an ethical problem as an external evaluator, therefore, can be tangibly different from responding reflectively to a situation as an internal evaluator. If Maria had been an external evaluator, she could have accessed her knowledge and understanding, listened to her colleagues, and identified, scrutinized, and addressed, if not solved, the problematic situation. In the process of addressing the problem, an Academy teacher or an assistant principal could assist Maria as they focused specifically on a unique problem, a particular situation, a local context, a specific person or group, a set of variables ("the good, the obligatory, the virtuous" [LW 5, 279]), the ethical maturation of participants, and so forth. Collaboratively, Maria and others could draw on their broad knowledge, experience, sensitivities, perceptions, skills, and insights to examine and address the whole situation.

But, for problems that involve in-situation decision-makers, like the one that occurred on Maria's staff development day, Dewey appears to expect an alternative approach. Maria, like others, has to rely primarily on her current moral self (LW 7, 285–92) – her thoughts, emotions, and habits; attitudes, dispositions, and sympathies; goods, obligations, and virtues; and knowledge, perceptions, and intuitions – and it must guide her, at least until inquiry is possible. Maria making millisecond qualitative judgments of the whole situation (LW 5, 259), capturing the meaning of the moment (252), and acting on her bodies of knowledge and commitments inform her. And, occasionally, at least, she must respond immediately even in the midst of multiple distractions. Hence, her everyday ethical development and decision-making are tremendously important: they continuously shape her attitudes and inform habits – her self – to guide her in emergencies as well as at other times. "The most important instrumentalities for morality, *the cardinal virtues*, are," argues Pappas (2008, 302; emphasis added), "the traits of character ... that assist us in determining what morality requires here and now" (302). But like Maria during her emergency, a person may need to revise her opinion later (LW 5, 259). As a result, it is important to understand that immediate apprehension, persistent inquiry, sustained reflection, and moral qualities are complementary ethical forces. Moreover, imagination and creativity are important in every aspect of ethical thinking and decision-making.

Dewey argues that one of the qualities of a good person is that she or he is a careful and generous, not a caustic or harsh, critic when making evaluations of others (LW 7, 268–72; see Chapter 6) – another relevant feature of Deweyan ethics. He also argues that each person should recognize the limits of one's knowledge, admitting that everyone frequently lacks apposite details of a situation. In Maria's situation, for example, hardly any prospective substitute teacher in the orientation session knew of Mirana's mental health challenges and Maria's impending recommendation regarding her employment, and how the two matters interrupt what seems like an easy issue for her to address. Even fewer who learned of the incident during coming days were probably told that, yes, Maria did respond, but ineffectively, with a vague comment about teachers respecting families and getting to know parents. For nearly anyone to say anything about the situation would likely be sharing partial information or easily misconstrued facts. These kinds of experiences happen in life and cannot be avoided completely. But being careful and generous with one another's reputations and careers remains important.

The other ethical challenges that Harbor School District discovered through their review fell into three areas: the district's failure to provide additional academic support for district athletes, many of whom are students of color; the failure of the district to enable their current staff employees to prepare to become classroom teachers; and the insufficient support the district provides for current teachers who could enrich the leadership diversity pool. These matters led to the appointment of a study committee and, eventually, a recommendation to reassign a central office administrator. Related changes included constructing a more open, safe, and welcoming environment and structure for the discussion of the board, district, and school challenges.

Conclusion

Dewey's emphasis on addressing problematic ethical situations, from both an external and internal perspective, provides light but not perfect clarity for educators. Instead of offering definitive answers from either perspective, he offers insight with which to approach-respond, analyze-perceive, and address-resolve problematic situations. The agenda he proposes includes an ongoing (a) preparation of staff, students, and parents/guardians to address ethical challenges; (b) utilization of school and classroom conditions to maximize desirable interactions; and (c) institutionalization of democratic communities of inquiry. As well, the agenda he proposes involves being sensitive to situations without being overconfident about one's knowledge base and conclusions. Being overconfident about conclusions is detrimental in a variety of ways, especially if combined with harsh judgment of one's colleagues, students, and parents who are involved in complexities that cannot always be shared with others. Educational administrators and leaders, in particular, are often in no-win or lose-lose situations. They cannot openly share confidential information and, much of the time, cannot clearly explain and justify the specific grounds for their decisions because of confidentiality concerns. They are virtually silenced and dare not rejoin rumors, except, perhaps, by sharing nonconfidential facts, such as the policies and procedures for addressing such matters. Plus, they dare not insult people by saying, "Trust me." Leaders can, however, speak and act wisely as they authentically share what is well-advised during a crisis and withhold that which is confidential. They can also communicate every day by the way they manifest the qualities of a good leader in community activities, budget discussions, school service projects, celebratory occasions, and ordinary operational activities.

These observations lead to Dewey's next insights, those that are embedded in his concept of a good self or person. One might say that his proposal regarding good people is that they become more consciously, broadly, and deeply ethical. In his opinion, the selection of the means and the ends of fostering good people is many-sided, e.g., private and public, individual and social, and personal and institutional. With his emphasis on democratic means and ends, it is manifest that a part of becoming good people or selves lies in cultivating good communities and societies. Schools and districts are obligated to nourish the growth of ethical people while avoiding coercive practices and privatized efforts to define *the* good person. Furthermore, individuals – whether board members, superintendents, principals, central office personnel, teachers, volunteers, students, or parents/guardians – are not entitled ethically to foist their private, individual desires or preferences on districts, schools, and classes. Keeping in mind that a reflective, dynamic, open, public, personal, and ethical cultivation of good selves, schools, and societies is challenging, in part, because of the twin dangers of neglecting one's own personal growth and of imposing ethical particularities on others.

Discussion Questions

1. When you think about Maria's current situation, how do the good, the obligatory, and the virtuous commingle and conflict? What steps did she take to address them?

2. Which questions would you expect Deborah to raise at her next breakfast with Maria and Jorge? If you were she, what tentative decisions would you want to confirm or disconfirm?

3. Of the three topics of context, culture, and environment, which ones appear most important to a teacher or a principal? Illustrate your thoughts.

4. When, if ever, are educators obligated to address offensive or insulting statements they hear? If a teacher is quick to correct students' choices of words and explanations, what are the probable consequences? If a teacher does not draw attention to others' use of particular terms and phrases, is she facilitating miseducation?

5. What can districts do, if anything, to encourage students and educators to decelerate their making ethical judgments until more information is available and accelerate their seeking supporting information before expressing their opinions?

RELATED READINGS

Anderson, E. 2010. "Dewey's Moral Philosophy." *Stanford Encyclopedia of Philosophy*. Last revised January 12, 2013. http://plato.standford.du/entries/dewey-moral/.

Anderson provides an overview of many of Dewey's ethical emphases, including discussions of impulse, habits, intelligent conduct, practical judgment, aesthetics, and social ethics.

Dewey, John. 1929–30. "Qualitative Thought." In *Essays, The Sources of Education, Individualism, Old and New, and Construction and Criticism*, 243–62. Vol. 5 of *John Dewey: The Later Works, 1925–1953*, edited by Jo Ann Boydston. Carbondale and Edwardsville: Southern Illinois University Press, 1984.

This article is a brief account of Dewey's logic of qualitative thinking. He addresses issues in the sciences, mathematics, ethics, and aesthetics.

Dewey, John. 1942–8. "Valuation Judgments and Immediate Quality." In *Essays, Reviews, and Miscellany*, 63–72. Vol. 15 of *John Dewey: The Later Works, 1925–1953*, edited by Jo Ann Boydston. Carbondale and Edwardsville: Southern Illinois University Press, 1989.

Dewey's article clarifies his view of the nature of qualities. He discusses environmental and organic conditions, the qualities that define certain events and complete situations.

Kieffer, C. C. 2013. "Rumors and Gossip as Forms of Bullying: Sticks and Stones?" *Psychoanalytic Inquiry* 33 (2): 90–104.

Written from a psychoanalytic perspective, Kieffer discusses rumor and gossip as a form of power and bullying that can be found among nearly all populations, including students, parents, educators, and board members.

Loughran, J. John. 2002. "Effective Reflective Practice: In Search of Meaning in Learning about Teaching." *Journal of Teacher Education* 53, no. 1 (January/February): 33–43.

Loughran's exploration of how an educator's assumptions affect their attempts to make sense of teaching and learning situations is applicable to ethical discussions as well as other teacher activities. The accuracy of one's assumptions, therefore, should be carefully interrogated.

Case Study: The Reverend

As the administrative assistant shepherded Maria into the office, she was greeted by a handsome man, about her age, who extended his hand with a broad smile. "Principal De La Garza, it's a pleasure to meet you! I'm Reverend John Michael Smith, but everyone here calls me Rev. Jay. It seems like we should have met some time ago. Would you like anything to drink? Tea? Coffee?"

"Nothing, thank you, Reverend Smith. I appreciate your taking the time to speak with me. Your church is lovely."

"As is your school in a traditional way that fits our community so well. I feel like we are twin pillars of this community, so close and connected by community members. It seems we share a common purpose of providing essential resources to families and children. Tell me, how can I help you?"

"Your church has grown so much during the years I've been at the Academy, both in facilities and membership. Your presence and impact are very clear here. In fact, I was talking to one of my lower school teachers, Ms. Abalos, and she mentioned the impact you and your church have on the Academy. I felt rather embarrassed as I was not aware of any direct impact you had."

Reverend Smith took a deep breath and sat back. "You're quite direct, Ms. De La Garza. There's a back story here I need to share. I was raised in a relatively small town in Utah. Like most folks there, I was a Mormon. I learned there the power of community. In our town, every child had enough to eat and whatever they needed for school, like shoes and a coat, supplies, and if necessary, academic help. And parents were not permitted to completely flounder either. We helped each other through hard times. But the town was often seen as a mini-theocracy. The school board, superintendent, city council, mayor, almost everyone of influence was Mormon. And if you were not, you might feel left out of decision-making that shaped the town. I had friends who were not Mormon, and they said they often felt on the periphery of things.

"I ultimately found the situation a bit oppressive, so after completing my mission, I came here to attend the state university. I studied history and political science and became convinced one of the most important clauses in the Constitution was the Establishment Clause. It created what the Supreme Court described as a wall of separation between church and state. I think your school and my church have important roles in this community, but an explicit, public partnership is dangerous – and there are other churches here and some private schools. The Academy should be nonsectarian and open to any member of the community. I love the Academy's focus on developing informed and actively engaged people."

"I think our school properly integrates the primary purposes for which public schools were created and extended to all children in this country. I am very proud of the balance we have forged and the breadth of education we provide."

"I agree. My older children attend your school. Ruth is in the fourth grade and Peter is in second. Ms. Abalos is his teacher this year."

"Again, I feel awkward. Although I know about your children, I did not know they were *your* children."

"Well, there is a good reason for that. My wife Alexandra does most of the school contacts. I met Alexandra at university; she is a huge part of my church being here. She was born and raised here. She was not from an affluent family but was an extraordinary student and became the first in her family to attend university. She is a pediatrician and has a clinic near here, The Community Clinic. I had decided to go to seminary after undergraduate studies and she was headed to medical school. She always intended to return home to serve this community. We both believe we were guided by God to this city, this community, and plan to do our life's work here. We were so excited when the district established the Academy as it seemed the perfect place for children to be educated."

"You never considered a sectarian school for your children?"

"Never. We did not want our children to grow up in a religious bubble. We wanted them to experience fully the diverseness of our community. And we are both deeply grateful to you because the Academy is an ideal setting for them. You ensure they get a full awareness of our country and world. I admire the work you have done in forging a school that mixes children from all over the city and at the same time involves students in this community for service. I will say our church is remarkably diverse too, which I would love for you to experience if you and your spouse would ever choose to visit our services."

"Maybe not. My now-deceased fiancée was a woman."

"You would be surprised how many families associated with the LBGTQ+ community are members at the church. We are a church that is open to all who seek a spiritual community that nurtures all who seek God."

"Thank you. What do you see as the connection between your church and the Academy? Am I correct to assume Ms. Abalos and her family are members of the church?"

"Yes, Dorothy and her family joined us five years ago. I should tell you that six, no seven, teachers and some staff members have joined our church."

"Well, okay. That's a cord between us?"

"Let me get back to the fuller description of that connection. I would estimate that 35 percent of your student body attends my church. We provide a preschool program with scaled fees so any family can use it, as well as after-school programs in sports and the arts, and free tutoring. When our families seek advice about where to school their children, the Academy is always our first suggestion. We began sending lots of families to you when we were both new in the community and, as we have grown, we have been so pleased to have the Academy as an option for our families."

"I would say your church is represented well in the Academy."

"I agree and attribute a lot of that to your leadership and the collective hard work of your faculty and staff."

"Do you work with other schools?"

"We thought about it, but those schools – and leaders – are not nearly equals of the Academy and that would mean my church family was scattered about. We have been able to keep our students close. I have tried intentionally to stay off the radar screen, however. Unlike some ministers, I think school curricula should teach about the role of religion but never instruct in matters of faith. The separation is healthy for both institutions."

"Okay, I think we are on the same page so far. Are there other ways your church is connected?"

"Here are some of the ways my church touches your school: We make sure every child of the church has new shoes and a jacket when the time comes, school supplies and a backpack, and access to free tutoring. My church decided that having *any* child come to the Academy without these resources was unacceptable. So the group of businesses that approached you several years ago to offer to provide for any student school supplies as needed were from my church. And the Women's Group that provides shoes and jackets? My people too. And your PTO [Parent-Teacher Organization]? A majority of active members are my congregants and the presidents, as an example, have been from my church for the past seven years. We are engaged in the community, but the Academy is a special service for us."

"I feel somewhat invaded. How was I kept out of knowing this, I wonder?"

"We remind the congregation and those acting on behalf of the church to keep the church's name out of their efforts."

"I'd guess you are completely and immediately aware of everything happening at the school then?"

"In truth, I'd say yes. But I'm committed to avoid interfering with the operations of the Academy. I do not want to appear too closely connected. Other churches and the district itself probably would be very uneasy."

"I am not sure how I feel yet, but I appreciate your attention to the importance of separation. I am not sure where the boundary should be on every matter, but I am sure boundaries are important protections."

"I would guess you may want to think about all I have said. Perhaps we can talk again. I think I have honored the meaning and spirit of the Establishment Clause, but if you know the case law, you know how muddled these issues are. I feel like a dam has broken for me, because I do not like being surreptitious. And I need to tell you two more things so I feel I have been fully open with you. The school board member for this part of the district is not your friend. She dislikes the school because she believes it is cherry-picking the best students and leaving the general attendance schools with fewer good students. She has been trying to build a coalition to review whether the Academy should continue its existence. The superintendent knows this and, while she strongly supports the Academy, she may be vulnerable, like many of us. I doubt she can withstand the pressure if a majority of the board turned on her. Our board member will have an opponent when she runs again next year, and he will be on the right side of this issue. He is a member of my church and we have already begun to plan his campaign. He will be a serious candidate. Moreover, the current board member has created some issues in her life that would hurt her. We are contemplating when to bring those issues into the campaign."

"I knew the politics of the Academy were complicated, but this is much more subtle and complex than I expected."

"Urban politics are always a blood sport. I will try to gather other ministers to support the challenger but stay in the background. One more thing about this: Your assistant principal is a mole the board member placed to gather information against the Academy and, regretfully, you.

"Now, the second issue. Ms. Abalos told me, and I need to tell you – I hope you will not disclose that this information came from me. As you know better than I, experienced teachers tend to believe they have earned the right to teach the better students, like a privilege of continuous experience. A few of your teachers are actually trying to forge an alliance with some parents from more affluent parts of the city who bring their children to the Academy. They tell the parents their children will not get the same quality of education if the classrooms are mingled with all sorts of students. Since elementary, particularly, does not have pre-AP [Advanced Placement] and AP classes to sort out students and create classes for more advanced learners, students are just thrown together irrespective of learning backgrounds. If this were to progress to where our board member hears and seeks to get involved to support the affluent parents, it could trouble all we have discussed. My wife and I, as well as most of the parents from our community, would hate to see grouping of students to limit diversity, as I'm sure you would."

"Thanks for that information. I was aware of the issue, but this seems a different matter perhaps. I will look into it. Let me ask you a question. If I were removed from the Academy, what would you do as a parent and pastor?"

"I would have to see who replaces you, of course. Before that, I would use whatever influence I could to protect you. If the Academy became no more than the average school, as a parent I'd have a difficult decision. The children of the community deserve more than mediocrity."

"Thank you for your openness with me. I have a lot to ponder. I hope as long as the Academy is here, both it and the church will be inspirations for the children."

"Thank you, I am confident we share a commitment that will shape a quiet but genuine partnership."

As Maria walked out of the church, she stopped and looked down the long aisle to the three-story crucifix. She shook her head and smiled slightly, murmuring, "Well, God, what have you gotten me into? And what shall I do?"

QUESTIONS

1. How would you feel if you were Maria? Do you trust your feelings?
2. What legal rulings and case law are relevant?
3. Is Maria close to becoming a poker chip for Reverend Smith's church? What dangers is she likely to face?
4. Given the Harbor District's commitment to educating all students, is the interest of some teachers in teaching students from wealthier families defensible? Do you see any relevant ethical principles?
5. Is the confidential relationship Maria now seems to have with Reverend Smith problematic? If so, how?

CHAPTER 6

What Are the Qualities of an Ethical Educator?

The good self "should be *wise* or prudent, looking to an inclusive satisfaction and hence subordinating the satisfaction of an immediately urgent single appetite; it should be *faithful* in acknowledgement of the claims involved in its relations with others; it should be solicitous, *thoughtful*, in the award of praise and blame, use of approbation and disapprobation, and, finally, should be *conscientious* and have the active will to discover new values and to revise former notions."

—John Dewey, *Ethics* (MW 7, 285; emphasis original)

Introduction

Much has been written about the qualities of a good leader and teacher, especially if good is loosely employed as a synonym for competent or successful (Darling-Hammond 1996; Zhao 2010). Of course, an educator's being good or ethical overlaps with being competent, but the two interests, even when intersecting, are distinguishable (Biesta 2015). Our interest largely focuses on traits (e.g., attitudes, dispositions, habits) and behaviors (e.g., acts, conduct, endeavors) that help describe a person as good regardless of whether they are a cashier, principal, parent, politician, or social worker. Obviously, the roles one accepts – familial, civic, career, government – affect some, if not many, manifestations of one's character. Considering the complexities of an individual's personality, life, and culture, Dewey thought that behavioral expressions of qualities are multifaceted, being variable yet stable, personal yet situational, organismic yet contextual, and predictable yet unforeseen. For him, these factors and more influence how a person comes to be described as a good or ethical educator.

Reasons, nonetheless, exist for objecting to the label "good person" (EW 3, 363). The concept, for some, may suggest an unquestioning or passive individual. For instance, some parents and educators may think a good child is one who is largely quiet, obedient, and responsible. In certain political circles, a good person may be a resident who respects authority, obeys laws, pays taxes, votes, and supports a political party's or ideological entity's agenda. In addition, family and friends may describe a spouse as a good person if the spouse is employed, amicable, cares for their children, and uses reason rather than intimidation or violence to settle disputes. Dewey also mentions "a pathology of goodness as well as of evil" (MW 14, 6), such as when one's ethical foci are mainly on negative matters, e.g., controlling desires and avoiding vices (6). In these types of "drab morality," Dewey said that "the mark of goodness" may be little more than the "absence of social blame" (6). An even more repulsive moral turn may be suggested when a person becomes "so good" he is "priggish," "too good for this world" (6). If a judgmental attitude emerges, a prude may become a moral pedant too, categorizing vices and virtues that everyone should avoid or display. This type of person may adopt a meticulously itemized and highly classified system of goods and evils – prescriptions and prohibitions – that, when imposed, deprives many people of their "freedom and spontaneity" and enjoyment of life (LW 7, 278). These flavors of illusory goodness, Dewey suggests, are why many prefer "to be good fellows [or folk] rather than to be good men [and women]" and choose "polite vice" to "eccentricity" (MW 14, 6). "The Puritan," Dewey concludes, "is never popular, not even in a society of Puritans" (MW 14, 6). Consequently, the so-called "thoroughly good [person] . . . can do more harm than a number of bad men [or women]" (EW 3, 363).

On the other hand, there are legitimate reasons for describing a person as good or ethical – or otherwise. Dewey's approach to describing a good person is multidimensional as the epigraph intimates. The quotation highlights his beliefs that an ethical person is wise (prudential) in life and takes a broad approach to personal satisfaction, including understanding what it means to enjoy a good and meaningful life; faithful in human relationships and acknowledges the legitimate claims of others; thoughtful in evaluative judgments, expressing carefully approval and disapproval of others; and conscientious in moral deliberations, while acquiring new values as well as refining existing ones. But before proceeding to Dewey's fourfold description of a good person, three caveats need attention. These caveats contextualize Dewey's fourfold depiction of a good self.

The Concept of Ethical Growth

Growth is a widely recognized Deweyan concept but a particularly impish one to define in a way that satisfies many people. Some philosophers (e.g.,

Callan 1982), for example, are concerned about conceptual ambiguities, and those (e.g., Edmondson III 2006) who want permanent aims find his dynamic claims off-putting. Hook (1959, 1013; emphasis original), however, captures Dewey's sense of growth when he claims: it "is an inclusive and not single exclusive end. It embraces *all* the positive intellectual, emotional, and moral ends which appear in everybody's easy schedule of the good life and the good education – growth in skills and powers, knowledge and appreciation, value and thought." Johnston (2006, 106–8, 110–12) draws these dimensions of growth together to discuss social growth or development of the whole person. Cumulatively, Johnston notes that growth is identified with one's ongoing, not occasional, development, tying the idea into the concept of "growth-as-continuity" (109), one of Dewey's two major emphases regarding educative experiences in *Experience and Education* (MW 13). Growth entails evaluative learning that clarifies experiences and leads to greater satisfaction in life and to one's flourishing in community with other socially minded people (Johnston 2006, 111–12). Growth, ethically speaking, may entail various kinds of experiences – e.g., educative, aesthetic, intellectual, spiritual, social, emotional – and interactions with people as one becomes progressively "wise ... faithful ... thoughtful ... *conscientious*" (LW 7, 285; emphasis original). Growth is tied to increasing one's intellectual, aesthetic, emotional, and ethical sophistication. In addition, an educative growth experience, for Dewey, is two-dimensional in that it occurs in the present and enables continuing growth in the future.

Dewey's concept of moral growth is also illuminated by examining his three qualifying assertions about (a) the imperfectability of agents, (b) the impermanence of growth, and (c) the interpenetration of human traits. These three concepts are distinguished as well as blended at times below.

The Imperfectability of Agents

First, note Dewey's claim about the imperfectability of people: there is "no good person in an absolute sense" (LW 7, 272). Despite contrarian beliefs, everyone has at least a "speckled" character (MW 14, 36). For educators, implications abound, e.g., they should not think of themselves, their colleagues, or their students as capable of becoming ethically finished no matter how well they live in current circumstances (LW 7, 306). This point, however, does not imply that educators should expect little ethical development in school communities or be suspicious of one another, e.g., expect colleagues to be exposed for deviating from ethical expectations.

But it should lead to a rejection of an either absolute good or bad classification of students and faculty. Human nature is too complex for this type of simplistic classification.

On the other hand, patience with imperfect children and adults is a virtue worth advancing. People are at times insincere, unkind, and self-centered. Remembering that character development ought to be a life-long personal-family-community-group undertaking is especially beneficial. Being ethical is not, therefore, always easily pursued and seems improbable, if not impossible, to achieve as an isolated individual. Moreover, ethical growth is an encompassing kind of growth, influencing one's total person and life, not merely how one advances in one's thinking about ethical theory or controversies. Being ethical, then, involves a progressive development of the whole person. Thus, it is clear that Dewey (Pappas 1997b, 447–68) reworks ethical claims that are proposed by some virtue ethicists (character-centered ethics), deontologists (principle or act-centered ethics), and consequentialists (outcome-centered ethics). Their strengths, as interpreted by Dewey, are incorporated into his holistic view of the self and ethics: character, actions, conduct, and consequences are all important in the growth of ethical educators and students.

While ethical perfection is impossible, ongoing moral learning and maturation are both possible and desirable. Of course, people can stagnate and become unethical too. An ethical educator may sadly, semiconsciously, begin thinking that she or he is morally superior to others and undercut her or his own development. An outcome of ethical arrogance, stagnation, or inertia may mean one "rests on his [or her] oars ... [and] permits himself [or herself] to be propelled simply by the momentum of his [or her] attained right habits, loses alertness; he [or she] ceases to be on the lookout. Without ethical alertness, his [or her] goodness drops away from him [or her]" (LW 7, 272). Of course, more than personal goodness is at stake when an educator stops growing ethically: the welfare of students and schools, and, indirectly, society may be compromised. This is because each self influences other selves: "only that self is good which wants and strives energetically for good consequences; that is, those consequences which promote the well-being of those affected by the act" (LW 7, 288).

Consider how Dewey's claims may contribute to school activities. Olivia, one of Maria's favorite teachers, is believed to have jettisoned her own well-being and that of Robert's, a twelfth-grade admirer, when she and he, after becoming sexually active, disappeared one weekend. In this kind of situation, Dewey – seemingly creating his own good-bad dichot-omy – claims that one goes from good to bad "as soon as he [or she] fails to respond to the demands for growth" (LW 7, 307). Apparently, earlier demands for growth could have empowered Olivia and Robert to subor-dinate their developing interests to their and their school's overall well-being (285). If ethically alert, wise, and maturing, it appears that Olivia could have controlled the desires and events leading up to her and Robert's passionate involvement and, thereby, avoided the decision to raise their yet-to-be-born child in another community. Dewey asserts, too, that "it is in the *quality* of [a person's] becoming that [her or his] virtue resides"; and it is the direction of her growth, not the level of her attainment, that is most important (306). Virtue, then, does not reside in the number of worthwhile activities Olivia pursues. If she had been becoming a qualita-tively different or an "enlarging, liberated" person, she could have met the "new demands" of her teaching position (307). Governing her sexual attraction to Robert seems plausible. But the reconstruction and redirec-tion of her desires after her affections budded would have been more challenging. Perhaps, however, their romantic interest developed in a flash. Moreover, Olivia may not have already learned that she needed to be attentive to sudden impulses (258). Plus, an unconfirmed rumor adds a thread to Olivia's and Robert's story that, if true, is distressing.

As noted above, Dewey (LW 7, 307) speaks in *Ethics* of a "growing, enlarging, liberated" person who is continuingly being transformed; in *Experience and Education*, he writes that converting impulses into intelli-gent desires and purposes is a necessary part of being liberated (LW 13, 39–47); and, in *Freedom and Culture*, he notes the need for a democratic culture that offers liberating social and political conditions for everyone (LW 13, 63–188). In consequence, fostering and sustaining liberated people appears to be a personal, familial, social, economic, institutional, and political obligation. Virtually no one is exempted from contributing to the liberation of those around them.

In Olivia's situation, Maria's turbulent feelings were unclear to most: few know that she is Olivia's godmother and one of her former teachers. Olivia's life flashed before Maria as she struggled with the idea that Olivia had, in Dewey's description, become bad although "acting upon a rela-tively high plane of attainment" (LW 7, 307). Maria's knowledge of Olivia's actions challenges her belief that she is an outstanding teacher. Why, Maria wonders, had she been oblivious to Olivia's resting "on . . . [her] oars," permitting herself "to be propelled" by her previous ethical development and ceasing to notice that her good was fading (LW 7, 272)?

Indeed, Maria wonders, how had Olivia become unmindful of her own development and her waning interest in others?

Stop and Think

If everyone has imperfections, when do they become career and life altering? Why are some imperfections so significant? Which kinds of flaws seem tolerable? What influence do context and situation have on one's answer?

The Impermanence of Growth

Dewey also asserts that the habit of making "wholesale judgments" about a person is counterproductive (MW 14, 36). Instead of defining or labeling students and colleagues either good or bad, districts are better advised to focus on enhancing their ethical judgment, cultivating a set of habits, and identifying a cluster of inclinations that should be nurtured (MW 14, 36). When building school communities and cultures, therefore, the desired and, ideally, desirable character of a person should be fostered by identifying the tendencies to be nurtured and selecting school conditions that foster the desirable tendencies and, thereby, character. But attempting to produce replicas of a person who exhibits an admirable set of virtues may deteriorate into unreflective outcomes. Imaginatively, reflectively, and, as Hansen (2001, 107–9) notes, indirectly fostering ethical maturation may be more likely to enable a person to develop traits that interpenetrate his or her other habits than relying primarily on an obvious and intentional teaching of virtuous behavior (MW 14, 29; LW 7, 255–60).

Upon reflection, Dewey's advice against wholesale judgments of a person being either good or bad and interpreting Olivia as, first, a good and, second, a bad person may seem to need more work. If Olivia's interest in Robert, for example, was speckled (MW 14, 36) and she became bad when her interest was converted into a passionate attraction and then sexual involvement, she might be viewed as changing gradually and significantly over time. If so, is this a wholesale judgment of Olivia as a person? To Robert's family and others, the answer may immediately be that Olivia is indeed a disgusting person. An across-the-board judgment, they might contend, is appropriate for her: she is a self-centered, out-of-control predator. Otherwise, how could she exploit a seventeen-year-old boy, an outstanding student, and a regular contributor to his community?

For her to conceal her scheme and virtually abduct Robert is unforgiveable. He is scarred and his future is endangered.

But Robert's family and friends may wonder if Olivia's actions are even more sickening than they originally concluded: Are her actions better described as "conduct" – which, for Dewey, implies "purpose, motive, intention" – and was she consciously pursuing a particular outcome (Eames 1969, xxxiii)? If her behavior is considered a series of planned actions or conduct that developed over weeks and months, her decisions may be viewed with less generosity. Still, how can Olivia be considered devoid of moral sensitivity since she voluntarily returned Robert to his parents' home and went immediately to local authorities? Would she have planned to help raise her child with Robert if she had been morally meritless? Does the Academy, whatever its present conclusions, seem well-advised to recall that life is – or should be – "a continual beginning again" (MW 9, 370)? Likewise, should districts – and parents – remember that they are in the people-building business and leave the delivery of scarlet letters to the inhabitants of Hawthorne's Boston?

The Interpenetration of Human Traits

Turning to Dewey's concept of the interpenetration of "virtuous traits" (LW 7, 257), it is noteworthy that he emphasizes that "unity" or "integrity of character" progressively enables a person to act in a holistic manner (257–8). Notwithstanding, individual qualities of character are still recognizable. For example, when the virtues of persistence, courage, impartiality, equity, self-control, trustworthiness, and wisdom (257–8) are fused elements of a person's character, individual qualities are periodically discernible. In Dewey's words, the interpenetration of virtues means that:

> At one time persistence and endurance in the face of obstacles is the most prominent feature; then the attitude is the excellence called courage. At another time, the trait of impartiality and equity is uppermost, and we call it justice. At other times, the necessity for subordinating immediate satisfaction of a strong appetite or desire to a comprehensive good is the conspicuous feature. Then, the disposition is denominated temperance, self-control. When the prominent phase is the need for thoughtfulness, for consecutive and persistent attention, in order that these other qualities may function, the interest receives the name of moral wisdom, insight, conscientiousness. In each case the difference is one of emphasis only. (LW 7, 257–8)

Olivia, but definitely not overlooking Robert, seemingly lacked sufficient self-interest or regard for herself – and others – to subordinate her immediate desire to her own "comprehensive good" (LW 7, 258). Or perhaps she had failed to attend sufficiently to her comprehensive good, one that was personally relevant, richly diverse, and consistently foregrounded in timely ways. Or the strength of her "inclusive and enduring satisfaction: wisdom" (LW 7, 308) was lacking when compared with her immediate desires. Dewey (170–3) looks at the situation from the angle of habit formation too: "our actions not only lead up to actions which follow as their effects but they also leave an enduring impress on the one who performs them, strengthening and weakening permanent tendencies to act" (170). He (171; emphasis original) asserts, therefore, that

> If one surrenders to a momentary impulse, the significant thing is not the particular act which follows, but the strengthening of the power of that impulse – this strengthening is the reality of that which we call habit. In giving way, the person in so far commits himself not just to *that* isolated act but to a *course* of action, to a *line* of behavior.

Olivia's course of action may have included nearly unconscious decisions to mislead her colleagues, the discarding of some professional responsibilities, the undermining of respect for the Academy, and the devastating of her students and Robert's friends. But the course of her action extends beyond these possible acts and consequences. Her action flows into the future, making it easier for her to disregard her prior values and habits to be transparent, responsible, honest, and trustworthy. If Dewey has these changes and consequences in mind, his conclusion that one may change from good to bad rapidly appears more reasonable. His seeming dichotomous use of good and bad in this situation may not necessarily contradict his rejection of its use when seeing everyone as good or bad.

An upside to an integrated approach to disposition development, if Dewey's theorizing is sustainable, is that "self-control" should no longer be viewed as a separate possession or a forced decision but as a constituent part of "an interpenetrated whole" (LW 7, 258). When virtues are developed as habits or fused qualities, "the very structure of the self . . . signifies a building up and solidifying of certain desires; an increased sensitiveness and responsiveness to certain stimuli [are] . . . confirmed . . . [and the] capacity to attend to and think about certain things [is enhanced]" (MW 7, 171). In the process, students develop capacities to make appropriate choices by both reducing the strength of their unreflective habits and building up their intelligent habits (MW 14, 55).

Dewey also maintains that qualities, dispositions, and habits are dynamic, and, through their interactions, they experience mutual development

(MW 14, 30). Concrete consequences of their interaction include students developing into the kind of people they are already becoming by means of established customs, habits, and conditions (26, 33–4). As a result, some develop "weak, unstable, vacillating character"; others create "strength, solidarity" as they mature (30). Still others may develop habits in particular social, economic, and educational conditions that tend to "make all habits more or less bad. For . . . [that which] makes a habit bad is enslavement to old ruts" (48). From this viewpoint, the real challenge everyone faces is not between "reason and habit but between routine, unintelligent habit and intelligent habit" (55).

Academy personnel understand well the role of intelligent habits in ethical development, recognizing that their task is decidedly more challenging when students abandon constructive habits or acquire destructive ones, for a habit continues until school and external environments determinedly discard it (MW 14, 88). The "art" of selecting conditions and building environments (97), therefore, is systematically fostered by the Academy community and its social groups to ensure that educative conditions continue to be supplied for students who are making appropriate intellectual, emotional, and social growth; who are largely trapped in deep-rooted social and emotional grooves; and who are struggling to make regular progress toward a stable ethical life (46–52). Of course, the ethical needs of educators are rightly considered a part of the needs of schools. In view of the fact that educator preparation programs help shape aspiring educators' habits, one may ask what their roles are in the professional ethical development of aspiring teachers and leaders. Is an introduction to ethical codes, theories, and reasoning sufficient? Perhaps not. Would Olivia's situation be different if her studies and experiences at university included a carefully crafted emphasis on student communities of ethical reasoning, moral development, and problem-solving? An answer will no doubt be influenced by many considerations, e.g., Had Olivia's prior ethical development been left to her organismic propensities plus the random influences of culture, school, and university?

In the above discussion, Dewey's interest in virtues and vices is similar to that of many virtue ethicists (Pappas 2008, 129–30, 135–44). But, he thinks, when appraising who is a good person, "the influence of social custom as well as personal habit has to be taken into account" (MW 14, 26). That is to say, thinking that a person may be calloused or indifferent (LW 7, 194) or kind-hearted and empathetic (193–4) needs to be interpreted, in part, in the light of one's customs and habits as well as other considerations. More broadly, whether descriptions of traits and habits are

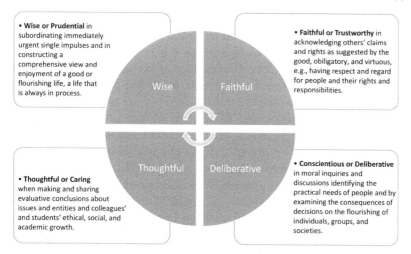

• **Wise or Prudential** in subordinating immediately urgent single impulses and in constructing a comprehensive view and enjoyment of a good or flourishing life, a life that is always in process.

Wise

Faithful

• **Faithful or Trustworthy** in acknowledging others' claims and rights as suggested by the good, obiligatory, and virtuous, e.g., having respect and regard for people and their rights and responsibilities.

Thoughtful

Deliberative

• **Thoughtful or Caring** when making and sharing evaluative conclusions about issues and entities and colleagues' and students' ethical, social, and academic growth.

• **Conscientious or Deliberative** in moral inquiries and discussions identifying the practical needs of people and by examining the consequences of decisions on the flourishing of individuals, groups, and societies.

Figure 6.1   Dewey's holistic interpretation of a good person

good or bad depends partially on the meanings of the concepts as employed, the contextual and temporal particulars of situations, the actual situational consequences, the type of interests involved, and "the *kind* of self" immersed in and emerging from a situation (295–7; emphasis original). While immensely important, Dewey is also interested in more than virtue development.

As noted above, Dewey's concept – the ethical educator – implies that becoming good or ethical is an unending process; for when a person believes his goodness has been attained, he begins drifting. When a person deems her ethical progress completed, former desirable attitudes and actions usually atrophy (MW 7, 272, 306). Understood through Dewey's lens, a dynamic self suggests that each autonomous person (302) is in the process of constructing and creating herself (306–7) and can be viewed as being a prior (304), an existing, and an emerging self (287). The good person, therefore, lives life in community with others where people plant and cultivate ethical potentialities and support each other as they collectively encourage a meaningful life (MW 14, 201). To repeat, virtue ultimately "resides in the quality of becoming" (MW 7, 306), not in what one was yesterday. Virtue, then, is found in one's becoming, being, and doing, involving one's thinking, feeling, choosing, and acting (Pappas 1997b, 447).

Figure 6.1 provides both an advanced organizer of forthcoming ideas and a set of lenses for the examination of ethical development and problematic situations. The figure foregrounds the four qualities that Dewey argues characterize a good or ethical person. Of course, combined with these four qualities are numerous others that help constitute the character of a person. In the four sections of the spherical portion of the matrix, the arrows represent interactions, interdependences, and interpenetrations (LW 7, 256–7). The sphere depicts the inseparable yet distinguishable and organic nature of wisdom or prudence, faithfulness or trustworthiness, thoughtfulness or considerateness, and conscientiousness or deliberativeness. The strength of any one quality or ability affects the capacity and development of the whole person. Collectively, these qualities and associated virtues constitute "the wholeness of virtue" (LW 7, 259). Associated virtues are invisible in Figure 6.1, obscured in a web of interwoven virtues. In the four outlying boxes, we use Dewey's original terms as the first in each of the boxes because of their interpretative importance when one reads his works. Of course, it is important to remember that these virtues are relevant to nearly anyone, not just to educators.

Wisdom in a Meaningful Life

Wisdom, if Dewey is accurate, stimulates a person to ask questions about contemporary life as a whole as well as specific situations that are approached by seeing one's self as more than a professional educator. Why is this the case? Briefly, he thinks that an educator's engagements, activities, and passions – while frequently broad and rich – may not be sufficiently "inclusive" to cultivate their growth as a more highly complex and expanding person, one who enjoys a comprehensive range of life-enhancing experiences. Similarly, he implies that a principal who sees their school family as merely or largely a means to becoming a better professional or their leadership position as a way to secure the resources to supplement their household income may be in danger of neglecting a more comprehensive satisfaction based on a broader, richer life (LW 7, 285). One's physical health, emotional well-being, spiritual fulfilment, aesthetic enjoyments, intellectual growth, and social relationships are, in a variety of configurations, facets of a more comprehensive good life. Fortunately, the educator who can give attention to an inclusive development of herself as a person likely enriches her professional and familial satisfactions and enjoyments too. She flourishes as a person. But, as Higgins (2011) observes, when educators are seen – and see themselves – as selfless helpers of students in inexcusable environments, they may neglect themselves as persons and lack needed self-regard. He (2011, 121–5), however, thinks Dewey's emphasis on the existential and aesthetic in his concepts of vocation and occupation, calling open the door for educators to recast their roles and, eventually, environments, leads to the enrichment of their work and lives with a deeper sense of purpose, a greater degree of beauty, and a more profound concept of meaning. Specifically, educators embracing this frame of reference are people who pursue cooperatively and continuously the ethical, aesthetic, emotional, and educational development of themselves and others in comprehensive ways that enhance personal, educational, and societal growth (Higgins 2011, 125–30).

What is wisdom and its link to a comprehensive understanding of life? Broadly, it is the utilization of knowledge or understanding that informs one's pursuit of "the better living of life" (MW 8, 163). Yet, it is more than intellectual conclusions; it is "a conviction about moral values, a sense for the better kind of life" (MW 11, 44). As an ethical term, "it refers to a choice about something to be done, a preference for living ... [one] sort of life rather than ... [another]. It refers not to accomplished reality but to a desired future [in] which our desires, when translated into [an] articulate conviction, may help bring into existence" (MW 11, 44). As Jeong-Hee Kim (2011, 225) concludes when visiting the Aristotelian roots of wisdom: "*Phronesis* is moral judgment to act wisely and prudently, which is more than the possession of *episteme* (general content knowledge) or *techne* (skills or techniques). It is the ability to put into action the general knowledge and skills with relevance, appropriateness, or sensitivity to a particular context."

In understanding Dewey's Aristotelian-enriched concept of wisdom, then, it is useful to revisit the phrase "the satisfaction of an immediately urgent single appetite" in the epigraph (LW 7, 285). An urgent single impulse, depending on the specifics of a situation, may have a mild to profound impact on broader personal and professional satisfaction (LW 7, 285). The immediate impact can be satisfaction, maybe even elation. But the wise superintendent and teacher, one may surmise, governs her appetites – whether emotional, material, aesthetic, sexual, or otherwise – so that her passions and emotions contribute to a fuller experience, an enduring, meaningful life. Thus, personal and professional gratifications deepen and expand when they are integrated with other elements of life, into a more comprehensive set of people-regarding values and relationships. An out-of-place appetite should be noted and governed, but not necessarily rejected, for, appropriately understood, guided, and transformed, it may become a vital part of a lovely life.

Nonetheless, when an urgent appetite arises, it is wise to "stop and think," for without pausing to think one may quickly undercut one's better or best interests and, by this means, one's ethical development (LW 13, 41). Reflective thinking stops one's impulse to act until one's reflections connect with other interests that are included in a broader plan of action (41). Reflection, then, postpones action until "it effects internal control of [an] impulse through a union" of an urgent longing with its consequences (41). Impulsively signing a contract, sending an email, flashing a sign, rolling the dice, dropping an untruth, releasing one's irritation, resigning a position, and posting on social media are possibilities that come to mind. Olivia telling Robert she would tutor him for a mathematics examination after he completed his nightly work also surfaces. Yet, the pleasure of an experience itself is not, Dewey argues, necessarily one's greatest challenge: the immediate rush of one's anticipated enjoyment or pleasure is (MW 5, 367); for, anticipated pleasures can overwhelm one's judicious inclinations. Robert's excitement in Olivia's class, for instance, may have impulsively caused him to miss his after-school job and go immediately to her apartment.

Consequently, it is important that educators' and students' wisdom and related habits (e.g., self-control, judgment, and foresight) be well developed. For reflectively developed desires and habits are needed to strengthen one against careless choices as well as guide one in making attractive decisions. Virtues can enable an educator to act responsibly rather than shriek at a colleague, censure an infuriating parent, or bully a testy student. Bringing to a conscious level one's long-term plans regarding one's family, friends, civic engagements, professional advancement, spiritual growth, and financial security helps preserve one's ethical integrity and secure one's future. Thus, one's ethical growth may, if one stops and chooses judiciously, be both secured and advanced concurrently. The kind of prudential thinking that facilitates "attitude and disposition" formation, Dewey continues, is "the *insight and wisdom* which is able to discriminate between ends that deceptively promise satisfaction and the ends which truly constitute it" (LW 7, 181–2; emphasis original). School moral development, as a result, involves helping an educational community distinguish between urgent, electrifying but later traumatizing possibilities and satisfying or flourishing options. Wisdom offers more, however, for it is "the nurse of all the virtues" (MW 5, 364).

Stop and Think

Identify what you consider an exciting impulse or appetite. How is this impulse addressed in different cultures, age groups, and religions? Are there school curricula where impulses can be best studied?

Dewey further clarifies his thinking about good and bad when he states that "there is nothing intrinsically bad about raw impulse and desire. They *become* evil in contrast with another desire whose object includes more inclusive and more enduring consequences" (LW 7, 187; emphasis original). Fortuitously, he pinpoints a twofold power of urgent impulses: "What is morally dangerous in the desire as it first shows itself is its tendency to confine attention to its own immediate object and to shut out the thought of a larger whole of conduct" (LW 7, 188). Restated, Dewey thinks that a person's heightened excitement forces out of one's attention the broader values of one's entire life (MW 5, 366). Conversely, wisdom gives a perspective on the relative value and worth of a desire "so that when we give up one good we do so . . . because we see another which is of greater worth and which evokes a more inclusive and a more enduring desire" (LW 7, 189–90). Introducing students to broader life possibilities and values, then, is important. To do this, in many cases, means seeking to alter or redirect some cultural and political forces.

Stop and Think

Assume that Robert thought wisely and inclusively before he and Olivia became involved. What factors and goods might he have considered? Which of his goods might have redirected his actions?

In keeping with his political views, Dewey does not impose his comprehensive set of values or ends on others. Instead, he argues that a range of options exist, e.g., the aesthetic, natural, religious, and ethical. These and other realms, separately or blended, illustrate his pluralistic orientation. In a comprehensive life that grows through streams of aesthetic experience, for example, one may recognize an "undefined pervasive quality" that connects experiential elements and makes them "a whole" (LW 10, 198). Whether enjoyed in arenas, laboratories, parks, classrooms, cathedrals, or galleries – the aesthetic can heighten a "quality of being whole and of belonging to the larger, all-inclusive, whole which is the universe" (199). Thereby, any person has the potential of seeing themselves as "a citizen of a vast world beyond" themselves and experiencing an "intense realization of its presence" as "a peculiarly satisfying sense of unity" (199). The quality of being whole and the feeling of "exquisite intelligibility" help explain "the religious feeling that accompanies intense esthetic intensity" (199).

When Dewey considers the religious or spiritual domain as a comprehensive end, he notes that some see it as "the most individualized" wide-ranging framework (MW 14, 226; Boisvert 1998, 139; Rockefeller 1991, 467), and it often includes "a conviction that some end should be supreme over conduct" (LW 9, 15). Moreover, a religious attitude may lead to a "deep-seated harmonizing of the self with the Universe" (LW 9, 14). Somewhat like Blake (see "Auguries of Innocence"), although holding very different metaphysical views, Dewey sees the aesthetic, religious, ethical, and natural potentially interwoven yet with each offering the opportunity "To see a World in a Grain of Sand / And a Heaven in a Wild Flower / Hold Infinity in the palm of [one's] hand / And Eternity in an hour" (LW 9, 14). In *Reconstruction in Philosophy*, Dewey concludes that religious affections are among "the unforced flowers of life" (MW 12, 201). Although rejecting the theism and atheism of his time for different reasons (Boisvert 1998; Rockefeller 1991), his naturalism retains the use of the term *god* – "Nature . . . is capable of being the source of constant good and rule of life" (LW 4, 45) – and said the term *god* refers to "the union of [the] actual with [the] ideal" (LW 9, 36). Still, he does not see the term *god* as necessary to his ethic or philosophy. Neither interested in restricting the expression of his own views nor forcing his students to adopt his beliefs, he promotes social intelligence and cooperative engagement among diverse peoples in order to secure the good or betterment of individuals, groups, and societies (Boisvert 1998 152–3). He (LW 4) does, however, critique dogmatic attitudes, beliefs, and practices.

Similarly, a life that grows richly in understanding ethical experience, he proposes, is both a means to and the embodiment of an inclusive, expanding good life. Among other suggestions, he indicates that an interest in virtue development (a concern for the kind of self a person is becoming) and an interest in social development (a concern for fruitful relationships with others) are connected to self-fulfillment and the common good. These interests are woven together in the fabric of one's self:

> The kind of self which is formed through action which is *faithful to relations with others* will be a fuller and broader self than one which is cultivated in isolation from or in opposition to the purposes and needs of others. In contrast, the kind of self which results from generous breadth of interest may be said alone to constitute a development and fulfillment of self, while [any] other way of life stunts and starves selfhood by cutting it off from the connections necessary to its growth. (LW 7, 302; emphasis added)

Obviously, Dewey thinks that multiple forms of experience can complement one another by clarifying aspects of growth, e.g., thinking, choosing, valuing, and living (MW 11, 44; LW 8, 163). His idea of wisdom, therefore, involves one giving a conscious priority to a complex of dispositions, habits, and experiences that are important features of a good life. But his view of a good life rejects class and intellectual elitism for, among other reasons, the riches of many cultures are needed in both schools and societies (MW 9, 22–7).

Trustworthiness in Human Relationships

Dewey's (LW 7, 302) reference to faithfulness or trustworthiness in human relationships is a second feature of an ethical person and extends his thinking about an ethical or good self. As implied above, Dewey (302) brings together, reconstructs, and demonstrates the potential compatibility of the ethical interests of personal growth, the common good, and virtue ethics. Now, his focus shifts to relational human ethics (regarding people, planning with them, and acting in their interest), although relational ethics is inclusive enough to include relationships with animals, the planet, and elsewhere. He maintains that being trustworthy, especially as it involves recognizing and attending to the needs, interests, and rights of others, is an essential social and democratic virtue. That he identifies its importance when discussing the claims inherent in social relations (LW 7, 285) is no surprise given his strong emphases on respect and regard for people (MW 7, 299). The authenticity and reliability required by a sincere regard for others is partially clarified in his phrase "regard for the welfare and integrity of the social groups of which we form a part" (LW 7, 299). Thus, he recasts aspects of a deontological emphasis on ethical duties and obligations to others, including social and professional groups (EW 4, 60–1; Strike and Soltis 2009).

In an early ethics essay, Dewey does not encourage a teaching of ethics per se in secondary schools but strongly supports studying "ethical relationships" (EW 4, 60). Using this approach, classroom activities should focus on clarifying "the interrelation of all individuals" (59), the "practical value" of analyzing "practical situations" (57), and explicating "*how to decide what to do*," not what to do (56; emphasis original). Using this approach, the teacher's aim is "*the formation of a sympathetic imagination for human relations in action*" and enabling each student to realize for themselves "the nature of the practical situations" in which they find themself (57; emphasis original). Ideally, an "actual scene" or situation needs to be consulted by students (57).

One may argue that the primary relationships educators have with one another and students entail a need for a robust and vibrant mutual respect and benevolent regard for the common good. Districts, schools, programs, and parent-guardian-teacher organizations depend upon a collective involvement and commitment to ensure open, cooperative, reflective, and productive decision-making and action. Keeping abreast of the interests and needs of one another through formal communities and associations and informal interactions is therefore crucial. But regularly thinking and working in isolation as individuals and as subunits can easily lead in time to an erosion of concern for district-, school- and class-wide well-being and integrity and to the thinning and virtual collapse of moral cultures or ecologies (Wagner and Simpson 2008). Even so, Dewey (LW 11, 347) expects schools to educate the public in matters essential to developing democratic societies.

Why are routine individual and small-group planning and decision-making activities possibly harmful? Dewey references reasons that are subsumed in the phrase "welfare and integrity of the social groups" (LW 7, 299–300). How are group welfare and integrity weakened, or even destroyed? The answer, in part, seems to be that the habits of working alone and in small groups, as is often required, can unconsciously lead to slighting certain obligations and relationships. Working alone can lead to overvaluing one's own and undervaluing others' interests. Meeting regularly with a small group can be very helpful, but it can also narrow interests primarily to that specific group. Hence, unplanned or accidental self-centeredness and small group-centeredness is easily facilitated by losing contact with the everyday interests and thoughts of colleagues, forgetting the consequences of partially informed decision-making, overlooking the professional well-being of others, and, thereby, undermining the integrity (e.g., wholeness, honesty) of membership groups. In the long run, a practice of working largely alone and in small groups can undercut both staff and student development of democratic personalities and cultural proficiencies (Edgar, Patton, and Day-Vines 2002). Likewise, they can make it more difficult to nurture caring communities and community-based school reform (Strike 2010, 50–65).

Educational statespersons (LW 11, 345–7), including many superintendents, principals, and teachers, should push for inclusive discussions that shape policy and practice. These leaders, if Dewey's advice is to be taken, need to affirm a vision of the school as "a cooperative community" rather than a collection of individual contractors (345–7). But a cooperating school community needs to be "a caring community" too (Noddings 1988, 223), one that is concerned about the opinions, needs, and rights of others. Leaders who are responsive to the needs, relationships, and activities of schools and one another enter into the heart of educational duties, goods, and virtues (LW 11, 346–7). But, as Rogers (2009, 243) notices, Dewey's ethic "struggles against the impulse of our age [and encourages people] to be unresponsive" to others. If so, educators definitely need to revisit their priorities in order to pursue rich, cooperative, and healthy school communities.

Second, when freed from, in part or whole, the indispensable contextual condition of interested others, their welfare and well-being is – comparably speaking – "pale, remote, negligible" (LW 7, 224). Unfortunately, routinely being outside of a person's or committee's interactive realities often results in being out of one's relevant population. The tendency to ignore the interests of invisible others (see Ellison's *The Invisible Man*) makes it difficult to "regard oneself as one among others and not as the 'only pebble on the beach'" (LW 7, 224). To think of oneself as one of a group, Dewey contends, "is perhaps the most difficult lesson we have to learn" (224). That is to say, a preoccupied, not just narcissistic, person may find it difficult to remain or develop into an empathetic and cooperative builder of school communities (346–7).

A third factor is that some struggles between two or more goods or desires may turn toxic, especially if some involved have turned into strangers. A common struggle is between the desire to act on the principle of regard for others, including groups, and the desire for one's own good (LW 5, 279; LW 7, 220). Embedded in double-or-triple-desire disputes for many is the flawed assumption that desires or goods are mutually exclusive, e.g., a superintendent's fervent desire for an exceptional middle school mathematics program and his passionate desire for an enhanced leadership-civics program. In such situations, a superintendent and a school staff may think they must support themselves or others. In reality, each group's good is involved in the well-being of others (LW 7, 220–2). Consequently, making clear mutual goods during decision-making processes is particularly advantageous; for, finding a way to clarify and meet mutual goods is a key part of pursuing social justice and educational progress. The superintendent who listens carefully to a principal and staff can act wisely in the interest of the school and district and, broadly speaking, the interests of parents, community, and society. Perhaps they can legitimately conclude that the scant district support for citizenship and leadership education is actually inexcusable and should be a vital part of the district's values or ethical emphasis. They may decide, then, that the award-winning mathematics program should be celebrated now and continue to make incremental progress rather than make another striking step at the present time. Perhaps, too, they and others answer openly the question: Who has the most to gain by an enhanced leadership and citizenship program, and who has the most to gain by moving the mathematics program from an excellent to a superb one?

Fourth, Dewey warns of those who, although intellectually aware of the rights and needs of others, think "quite literally *for* themselves, that is, *of* themselves" (MW 14, 50; emphasis original). When thinking for and of one's self, a person may act unethically in a particularly subtle way. That is, they may take advantage of the respect and regard colleagues have for them so that they can disregard their interests at opportune times. Specifically, their "wrong consists in *faithlessness* [or betrayal] to that upon which [he] counts when he is judging and seeking for what is good to him. He betrays the principles [and people] upon which he depends; he turns to his personal advantage the very values which he refuses" to embrace (LW 7, 230; emphasis added). The person who regularly thinks and acts primarily on their own behalf seems to form an ethical self that undermines student and faculty well-being. A lifetime of self-absorption can turn even a reasonably caring person into an educational highwayman.

Stop and Think

Should we interpret faithfulness as being responsible, dependable, and authentic? Should preference be given to other concepts? If yes, which ones?

Consider the Academy's assistant principal, Matthew Webb, who aspires to become a principal as quickly as possible and, thereafter, a superintendent. In the process, he goes out of his way to demonstrate faux respect and regard for select leaders even as he calculatingly drops hints of inadequacy about his perceived competitors. Envision too as Matthew attempts to draw from Yoon Yú, a counselor, the gossip she has heard about Maria. Matthew plans to use the gleaned rumors of speckled moments about Maria for his own professional advantage. His thinking is literally for and of himself. This kind of "so-called educator," Dewey tersely concludes, "is little more than a cheap politician" (LW 13, 346). Perhaps, Dewey could envision Matthew thinking that duties and obligations are really for others and that "his own immediate feelings" are his only authority (EW 3, 375).

On the other hand, Dewey maintains that having an authentic respect and regard for people indirectly constitutes support for their existing desirable qualities. Furthermore, there is a decided plus for each person who attends to school relationships. As Dewey claims,

The kind of self which is formed through action which is *faithful to relations* with others will be a fuller and broader self than one which is cultivated in isolation from or in opposition to the purposes and needs of others. In contrast, the kind of self which results from generous breadth of interest [in one's self as well as in others] may be said alone to constitute a development and fulfillment of self. (LW 7, 302; emphasis added)

Enduring personal happiness, Dewey claims, is not attained by its direct pursuit or in self-centeredness. Instead, happiness is largely a byproduct and an expression of a person who is steadily maturing intellectually, emotionally, socially, and ethically. One's regard for others and desire to see them flourish, therefore, are the "forces which lead us to *think* of objects and consequences" that promote or impede everyone's well-being and happiness (LW 7, 300; emphasis original). Thus, as Haidt (2006) concludes, happiness, to a significant degree, is found in healthy personal relationships (see also Noddings 2003, 240–61).

While Dewey recognizes the importance of principles, procedures, and conditions that cultivate the welfare of everyone, he also understands the importance of constitutional and charter rights, laws, and policies when initiating and sustaining a hospitable environment for the ethical development of school communities (MW 15, 169). In short, laws and policies are also needed to encourage personal and community welfare: "Every proposed measure of public policy should, therefore, be considered on the ground of its own effects on the welfare of the members of a community," not be enacted or retained because of loyalty to a private interest (LW 7, 337). Yet, a school environment that is based overwhelmingly on constitutional claims, legal rights, and codified prescriptions and prohibitions will be a hollow version of Dewey's democratically conceived ethical school community, a school that is differentiated by students and staff who aspire to be "*faithful* in [their] acknowledgement of the claims involved in . . . [their] relations with others" (LW 7, 285; emphasis original). Moreover, an arid abstract respect is insufficient to create a substantial view of persons (Strike and Soltis 2009); people also need to be warmly regarded (LW 7, 298) or cared for (Noddings 1988).[1]

---

[1] Dewey's view of the aridity of law echoes a well-known quote from Grant Gilmore in *The Ages of American Law* (Gilmore 1977, 111):

> Law reflects but in no sense determines the moral worth of a society. The values of a reasonably just society will reflect themselves in a reasonably just law. The better the society, the less law there will be. In heaven there will be no law and the lion shall lie down with the lamb. The values of an unjust society will reflect themselves in unjust law. The worse the

Above we intentionally employed the phrase "Dewey insists that being *trustworthy*," although Dewey's actual phrase – "faithful in acknowledgement of the claims involved in its relations with others" (LW 7, 285) – implies an unstated personal obligation to others' claims. Trustworthy indicates another's judgment of a person's faithfulness. Connecting faithfulness and trustworthiness is crucial, especially since some (Pappas 2008, 239) think trust is "a democratic virtue absent in Dewey." While the words *trust* and *trustworthy* are almost nonexistent in Dewey's vocabulary, his late nineteenth- and early-twentieth-century word options do not always serve him well today. But his use of words such as *faithful, integrity, reliable, confidence,* and other synonyms shed light on the import of trust for him. Thus, we use both the words *faithful* and *trustworthy* because the usage is consistent with Dewey's conceptual emphases and draws out in a richer way the connection between being faithful to values, relationships, and people and having the confidence or trust in one another to work together.

Stop and Think

Does faithfulness or trustworthiness differ from the concept of loyalty? If so, how? Could an educational leader be faithful to their colleagues but be deemed disloyal too?

Thoughtfulness in Evaluative Judgments

Dewey's term *thoughtful* (LW 7, 285) may be understood in at least two overlapping ways involving interpretations that are weighted toward either the affective (e.g., thoughtfulness) or the cognitive domain (e.g., reflective or thoughtful). He, however, does not empty either interpretation of affection or cognition. Likewise, both interpretations focus on the ethical responsibilities embedded in relationships with others. In the affective-leaning interpretation, the importance of the word *solicitous* as a synonym for caring, concerned, considerate, or sympathetic is instructive if not determinative. Here both virtue and caring ethics spring to mind. Hence, the implication is that one should be considerate or caring in evaluative

---

society, the more law there will be. In hell there will be nothing but law, and due process will be meticulously observed.

Here, Dillon's (1992) work on the concept of caring respect has much to commend itself.

situations. Dewey's second term, *thoughtful*, suggests a similar concept: a generous thoughtfulness. Together they call to mind Dewey's comment that an ethical interest in others is "intellectual and practical, as well as emotional" (MW 4, 274) and is based partly on the cultivation of "benevolent impulse and intelligent reflection" (LW 7, 298).

This idea is noticeably relevant to those who teach "sensitive and thoughtful" students who are not yet prepared for "the realities of the world" (LW 6, 125). Nevertheless, the idea is broadly applicable. Since Dewey connects solicitous and thoughtful to "praise and blame, [the] use of approbation and disapprobation" (LW 7, 285), his emphasis appears to be that thoughtfulness is particularly needed in situations where approval and disapproval are appropriate. In this case, the educator who is a caring navigator of evaluative situations springs to mind. Or, to restate the idea, a considerate professional contributes much in schools, especially in those situations that require a fair and kind appraisal of skills and competencies as well as virtues and vices. Almost everyone, Dewey argues, hopes for a considerate evaluation of his or her ethical and academic foibles (LW 7, 284–6). An empathetic person would seem well prepared to live up to these terms.

Thoughtfulness, the affective-leaning interpretation, also has various implications. For instance, an authoritarian and oppositional person may have qualities that are incompatible with many evaluative responsibilities (LW 7, 268). In particular, Dewey warns that "a person of strong will" may "attempt to impose his [or her] judgments and standards upon others in a ruthless way" (268). A dogmatic person, whether fostered by impulse, culture, tradition, or ideology, "is likely to become socially [and professionally] dangerous" (268). Similarly, Dewey speaks of the "vices of reflection" (MW 14, 137). Among the vices he lists the possibility of indecisiveness in the face of ethical problems and of preferring "remote and abstract matters" rather than attending to an "immediate situation" (137). More specifically, he alleges that people "who devote themselves to thinking are likely to be unusually unthinking in some respects, as for example in immediate personal relationships" (137). Instead of being modest in their claims, they may be petty and arrogant in "personal relationships" (137).

An inherently bright, meticulously observant person, if imbued with ideological hubris, is probably even more harmful. Dewey avers:

> Nothing can make up for the absence of immediate sensitiveness; the insensitive person is callous, indifferent. Unless there is a direct, mainly unreflective appreciation of persons and deeds, the data for subsequent

thought will be lacking or distorted. A person must feel the qualities of acts as one feels with the hands the qualities of roughness and smoothness in objects, before he [or she] has an inducement to deliberate or material with which to deliberate. (LW 7, 268–9)

Evaluative moments, certainly, are frequently emotional, for the person evaluated as well as for the evaluator (LW 7, 174, 269–72). Being irritated, fatigued, defensive, and judgmental are mostly harmful emotions, mainly during evaluative activities. Developing an evaluative thoughtfulness and language that is devoid of unnecessary negative connotations is indispensable. But overly exuberant language of approval is potentially dangerous too, especially after a private conversation winds its way through a faculty and staff of hundreds or into a district and neighborhood of thousands.

The main considerations of Dewey in this realm are that each person and ethical situation is unique and that approval or disapproval of one's conduct or action should facilitate reflective and respectful emotional, social, and ethical development. A fundamental evaluative aim in educational situations is growth, not punishment, much less humiliation. Of course, the variety of ways that educators manifest their reflective concern for others is nearly innumerable and may at times be easily misunderstood in culturally integrated situations. Thus, the educator's empathy during evaluative moments is invaluable. But what does thoughtfulness mean through the eyes of the evaluee or assessee, student or educator? Importantly, the evaluee who feels uncaringly or unfairly evaluated may draw incorrect conclusions and thereby weaken the evaluative relationship, resulting in strained relationships. Thus, responsibility for productive evaluative relationships and positive change seems to start with those who supervise and evaluate others. But those who have their performance evaluated are responsible too, especially for seeking clarity from supervisors and teachers and conveying to others accurately the comments that evaluators make.

The challenge of evaluative relationships is compounded because of the way some conceptualize schools: schools are often seen merely as places to instruct and train students, not as institutions that are designed to support people and build relationships, e.g., personal, social, emotional, and intellectual. Viewed largely as instructional and training centers, schools can become absorbed in correcting mistakes and misconduct of even very young students – and the newest of teachers. Moreover, when leadership adopts a business and assessment mindset, students are turned into little more than revenue units (LW 11, 346).

Yet, thoughtful policymakers and educators – with input from students, parents, and others – can transform schools into humane, educative, and relational centers. To do so, educators and policymakers need to be thoughtful in evaluative responsibilities, prudent in their decisions, and faithful in their relationships. Of course, being thoughtful in evaluative responsibilities does not mean that schools should merely be mutual affirmation centers. Educators are obligated to meet the educational duties "involved in ... [their] relations with" students (LW 7, 285). Hence, promoting student growth entails finding the most appropriate means to cultivate the acquisition of skills, understandings, and judgments. To do so, educators need "freedom of thought in inquiry and in dissemination of the conclusions of inquiry" (LW 11, 375) so that they and others can better learn to work together as learning communities.

A second but less plausible interpretation, in context, of a thoughtful person is slanted toward the cognitive domain but is still conspicuously imbued with affective qualities. In *How We Think*, Dewey claims:

> When we say a person is *thoughtful*, we mean something more than that he [or she] merely indulges in thoughts. To be really thoughtful is to be logical. Thoughtful persons are heedful, not rash; they look about, are circumspect instead of going ahead blindly. They weigh, ponder, deliberate – terms that imply a careful comparing and balancing of evidence and suggestions, a process of evaluating what occurs to them in order to decide upon its force and weight for their problem. Moreover, the thoughtful person looks into matters; he [or she] scrutinizes, inspects, examines. He [or she] does not ... take observations at their face value, but probes them to see whether they are what they seem to be. (LW 8, 175)

Continuing, he elaborates on the logical educator, student, and citizen: "The logical person inspects to make sure of his [or her] data" and "puts two and two together" and "casts up an account" (LW 8, 175). While the ethical person is thoughtful in this largely cognitive sense, the former sense – the affective leaning account – appears to be the emphasis of the present context.

Of course, being "solicitous and *thoughtful*" remain connected to "praise and blame" (LW 7, 285; emphasis original). Even though Dewey was cautious about forms of judgment, he affirms that it is a positive "thing for anyone to be made aware that thoughtless, self-centered action on his [or her] part exposes him [or her] to the indignation and dislike of others" (MW 14, 220). Thus, "others," especially students and staff, play a major role in the ethical and social development of classroom and school cultures (LW 13, 31–8). As a consequence, one of the most important aspects of ethical development in schools is creating a strong ethical community that is cooperatively planned and nurtured (Strike 2010). In the realm of associative ethical relationships, Dacher Keltner (2009, 6) draws on the Confucian idea of *Jen* to stress that bringing "the good in others to completion" is especially powerful: leaders and teachers take advantage of fostering the already existing and growing good in one another and students. The existing goods Keltner mentions include the emotions of love, tenderness, laughter, compassion, sympathy, and contemplation.

Decisions regarding praise and blame, understandably, should be made in the light of an ethical framework and culture. Goods, obligations, and virtues need to be examined along with unique participants and situations. The kinds of persons, schools, and communities that are desired and desirable need attention. Wisdom should intervene if hurried conclusions are being urged. In particular, Dewey notes that a solicitous thoughtfulness or caring involves a "love of truth [that] is manifest in [the] desire to understand rather than in a hurry to praise and blame" (MW 13, 308). Blending a love of truth with a love of others, he claims, is necessary, for the combination "discourages dogmatism and . . . intolerance; . . . arouses and heartens an experimental spirit which wants to know how systems and theories work before" giving them complete support, "militates against too sweeping and easy generalizations," "safeguards one from seclusion in universals," and "fosters a sense of the worth of communication of what is known" (MW 13, 308).

In the end, a person who is wise, considerate, inquiring, and thoughtful also needs to think with foresight or prospectively. For, "generosity in judgment of others as distinct from narrowness is largely a matter of estimating what they can grow into instead of judging them on the basis of what conditions have so far made of them" (LW 7, 348). Noddings (1988, 228) expresses a parallel conclusion: "just as we ask teachers to treat the success and failure of students with exquisite sensitivity, we should study teacher success and failure generously and report on it constructively."

Everything considered, is there room here for professional friends as well as family to support Olivia in her recovery process? Are there ways that her life chances can be well cared for? One's answer, in part, depends on whether she welcomes support. Another question is whether she wants to return to teaching. Also, one may need to know the final official adjudication of her situation with Robert. Was she formally charged for her activities with Robert? Was the rumor that Robert initially targeted Olivia because of a challenge by a senior clique confirmed by authorities? Did he, in fact, seek to seduce Olivia to prove himself? While many in Harbor School District discussed these issues, a tiny group of district students developed a plan of their own.

Stop and Think

If you were a school leader, how would you schedule staff evaluation feedback? If you could reconstruct your "dreaded moments" what would you recommend?

What does Dewey's view of the good educator suggest beyond his emphasis on being wise, developing a broad view of a worthwhile life, demonstrating faithfulness in human relationships and to one's related duties, and making clear, supportive, and thoughtful evaluative judgments? Where do his twin passions for truth and others lead? Conscientiousness in moral deliberations appears to be part of his answer.

Conscientiousness in Moral Deliberations

An emphasis drawn from this chapter's epigraph – "should be *conscientious* and have the active will to discover new values and to revise former notions" (LW 7, 285; emphasis original) – further clarifies Dewey's view. Of course, his words reinforce the idea that a good person is not stagnant ethically and, consequently, that educators should be interested in altering both school community and external community conditions and situations to create growth opportunities. Nor does the adjective *good* refer to people who are satisfied with who they have already become. Instead good people habitually seek relationships and interactions that facilitate their personal growth (LW 7, 272–3). Clearly, however, Dewey does not expect aspiring or beginning teachers or administrators to possess richly the qualities, dispositions, and abilities packed into the epigraph, much less those embedded elsewhere in his writings. His description of a good person is one that should become progressively manifest as one goes through life. He does, then, think virtuous people keep developing over their lifetimes as they mature and as they keep deliberating "the better" and "the worse" in professional and nonprofessional situations (LW 7, 274). Among other matters, this process involves ongoing deliberation about one's students, schools, and districts (LW 7, 274).

When did our topic change to the topic of deliberation? Actually, Dewey's discussion of conscientiousness feeds into his notion of deliberation. Hence, the direct answer to the question is that conscientiousness is "the name given moral deliberativeness when it is habitual" (LW 7, 272). Rephrased, conscientiousness is the habit of giving attention to "the potentialities of any act or proposed aim. Its possession is a characteristic of those who" profit from being wise and are not "unduly swayed by immediate appetite and passion," and who avoid behavioral "ruts" (272). Here Dewey connects the virtue of wisdom with that of deliberation so that the two virtues fuse and help a person avoid being overwhelmed by passions (285) or seduced into ethical inertia (272).

Stop and Think

What kind of learning situations lend themselves to using dramatic rehearsal? Is it suitable for every age group and all kinds of content? Are there cultural limitations?

Conscientiousness – or the habit of deliberation – is "the spring of the moral life," for it is "*a constant will to know* what should be, and to re-adjust [one's] conduct to ... new insight" (EW 3, 366; emphasis added). Here, Dewey, who seems to have obliquely addressed his personal tendency to be overly conscientious early in life (Martin 2002, 48–50), counsels against a "constant anxiety as to whether one is really good or not, a moral 'self-consciousness' which spells embarrassment ... morbid fear" (LW 7, 272). On the other hand, a healthy conscientiousness is "intelligent attention and care to the quality of an act in view of its consequences for general happiness" (LW 7, 272–3). Of course, "deliberation is a dramatic rehearsal (in imagination) of various competing lines of action" (MW 14, 133). Consequently, an ethically good person is conscientious or one who habitually engages in deliberating about the merits of different options to solving problems. This emphasis on deliberation clarifies that Dewey blends moral and intellectual virtues.

Happiness, therefore, is not independent of one's moral and intellectual well-being, e.g., experiencing community, fairness, freedom, friendship, and togetherness. Yet, efforts to identify the greatest happiness minus the collective misery of people may not serve well diverse populations because people have assorted and evolving interests and standards of happiness. Different kinds of questions may need attention – e.g., What conditions foster desirable forms of happiness for specific people, groups, or individuals? Which kinds of happiness lead to "alert, sincere, enduring interests in the objects in which all can share" (MW 7, 302)? Answers to these questions throw light on how individuals and groups can develop environments that facilitate personal and social growth and, thereby, satisfaction. But, Dewey claims, there is no current utilitarian calculus sufficiently sophisticated to warrant recommendation (MW 7, 198–9, 244–52; Westbrook 1991, 153–7).

Properly understood, Dewey argues, happiness is "a stable condition . . . the standing disposition of the self" (LW 7, 198). Educators, it seems, should work toward involving students in life-enhancing activities, not habitually promoting their direct pursuit of excitement. Happiness, of course, often emerges in the process of learning and school interactions as well as in a plethora of other relationships and engagements. Indeed, ethically maturing educators and students may "find happiness in the midst of annoyances; be content and cheerful in spite of a succession of disagreeable experiences" as long as they are also developing complementary virtues, e.g., courage and perseverance (198). Moreover, the "agreeableness [of school and other activities] depends upon the way a particular event touches" a person (198). Unsurprisingly, a variety of research studies (see Keltner 2009) helps to clarify the concept of happiness by analyzing how certain conditions and emotions contribute to the growth of other prosocial emotions. Pinker (2009, 393) claims that studies often identify happy people as those "who have spouses, friends, religion, and challenging, meaningful work."

When feasible, students should help educators build school environments that provide opportunities for them to accept and handle challenging situations and cultivate new interests and desires. Thus, Dewey concludes, "Happiness is a matter of the disposition we actively bring with us to meet situations, the qualities of mind and heart with which we greet and interpret situations" (LW 7, 198). To clarify, happiness is "an end-product, a necessary accompaniment, of the character which is interested in objects [e.g., nature, people, ideas] that are enduring and intrinsically related to an ongoing and expansive nature" (198).

To promote satisfaction, teachers and administrators should be keenly interested in students learning how to avoid, resolve, and solve ethical problems (EW 4, 54). Included in this learning, Dewey underlines deliberation or the process of "dramatic" or "imaginative" rehearsal (MW 14, 132; LW 7, 275), which is primarily "a method of *gaining information necessary for moral* judgment" (Welchman 1995, 171; emphasis original). Ideally, the dramatic gathering of and deliberation about data enables participants to make intelligent moral judgments that lead to actions that are fair, just, compassionate, and liberating. The term *dramatic* suggests that the students and teachers involved in ethical problem-solving are engaged as whole-persons, not as "cold blooded" analysts (LW 7, 269).

In brief, dramatic rehearsal is an enriched, complete-person deliberation that can be either factual or imaginary, although Dewey prefers "actual" situations (EW 4, 57). As participants acknowledge their impulses and intuitions and use their imagination to identify and test hypothetical ways of unraveling real problems and dilemmas, their confidence, satisfaction, and autonomy develop (MW 7, 272–5; MW 14, 132–8). As Dewey indicates in his synopsis below, dramatic rehearsal has the potential to enable students to utilize and extend abilities as they learn whether their plans are worthwhile (LW 7, 275). Thus, as dramatic rehearsal is entered into in an artistic fashion:

> we give way, *in our mind*, to some impulse; we try, *in our mind*, some plan. Following its [the impulse's] career through various steps, we find ourselves in imagination in the presence of the consequences that would follow: and as we then like and approve, or dislike and disapprove, these consequences, we find the original impulse or plan good or bad. (LW 7, 275; emphasis original)

Since deliberation is

> dramatic and active ... and ... intuitive, the direct factor [is] in it. The advantage of a mental trial ... is that it is retrievable, whereas overt consequences remain. They cannot be recalled. Moreover, many trials may mentally be made in a short time. The imagining of various plans carried out furnishes an opportunity for many impulses which at first are not in evidence at all, to get under way. Many and varied direct sensings, appreciations, take place. When many tendencies are brought into play, there is clearly much greater probability that the capacity of self which is really needed and appropriate will be brought into action, and thus *a truly reasonable happiness results.* (LW 7, 275; emphasis original)

Within this framework, one can readily see why Dewey, like Shelley (1792–1822), concludes that "imagination is the chief instrument of the good" (LW 10, 350), not simply because it offers the power of imaginative sympathy to access the inner emotions and thoughts of others but also because of its power to envision multiple ways to discuss and address knotty moral situations (350). But, as McVea (2007, 385) observes, Dewey thinks the conclusions reached during dramatic rehearsal have "provisional moral standing, subject to empirical results."

Here it is important to note that Dewey's view of deliberation was not the kind that results in deliberation by political elites and seldom by the public. Even his view of dramatic rehearsal is an egalitarian and unrestricted means of deliberation by anyone affected by an ethical issue in a participatory democracy, not just a means of answering some imaginary or theoretical problem. Dewey himself, although a deeply engaged professor, prolific author, and an involved community and family person, was involved in international affairs, presidential politics, antiwar activities, and equality and equity efforts. Likewise, he was a proponent of social justice, workers' rights, respect for immigrants, academic freedom, freedom of intelligence, and the rights of diverse peoples. In short, he engaged in and promoted a participatory democracy with its allied values (Martin 2002).

Stop and Think

What kind of learning situations lend themselves to using dramatic rehearsal? Is it suitable for mixed-age groups? Are there cultural and ethical limitations to its use?

Conclusion

The answer to the question, What are the qualities of an ethical educator? may be summarized, in part, as follows: they are a person who is wise in everyday life, including considering urgent impulses as less important than and, sometimes, detrimental to the development of a broader, enduring, and flourishing life; trustworthy in personal relationships, including relating to people in ways that demonstrate a warm regard for them and their interests; thoughtful when interacting with others, including having a sensitive approach to sharing judgments about and evaluative opinions with others; and deliberative, including seeking information that clarifies issues and identifies the consequences of proposed choices. In addition, these four qualities are woven into a web of interconnected virtues, where specific manifestations of them are alternatively foregrounded and backgrounded depending on circumstances. But there is more: the educator's understandings, affections, and choices are in the process of being transformed into "habits of refined moral sensitivity, discernment, and perception – habits analogous to those of an artist" (Fesmire 1995, 592). Then again, it is crucial that Dewey's idea of habit is understood as a powerful force: "It includes a sequence of acts following upon some cue internal or external [to the person]; it leads to the satisfaction of needs; and it is in itself energetic – quite literally harnessed for a particular purpose"

(Murphey 1988, x). Understood as strong tendencies, habits have a "hold upon" people (MW 14, 21).

Schools and districts should be evaluated by more than their academic and athletic achievements. Service projects, inclusion endeavors, community assignments, and international experiences need to be evaluated too. But to be reasonable, Dewey indicates that educators cannot be held responsible for consequences that stem from confused government policies, inadequate resources, and defective work environments, for these shortcomings partly, often significantly, abridge the agency and effectiveness of educators and students. Hence, societies, lawmakers, policymakers, and commerce are partially responsible for outcomes. This mutual responsibility should lead to cooperative communities (LW 11, 346–7) that lead to "*mutual responsiveness* – a kind of attentiveness to the claims of others that creates the framework necessary for thinking about moral situations from the outset," from policy contemplation and construction through resource allocation (Rogers 2009, 146; emphasis original). In Chapter 7, we explore the school as a democratic community.

Discussion Questions

1. Why do you think Dewey emphasized wisdom, faithfulness, thoughtfulness, and deliberateness in his view of a good person? Would you select a different set of virtues to describe a good person? If so, why?
2. Do you see how Dewey's emphases on thoughtfulness and thoughtful intertwine? If so, can they be fostered simultaneously?
3. Which virtues – e.g., justice, patience, harmony, gratitude, humility, honesty, freedom, courage, strength, appreciation – do you think are closely associated with Dewey's foregrounded virtues?
4. If you were asked to identify the primary areas of teachers' faithfulness or trustworthiness to students and colleagues, what realms would you identify? How would you answer the same questions about being faithful to or trustworthy with guardians and parents?
5. Which phrase – an enjoyable life, a good life, a flourishing life, or a meaningful life – best captures your idea of an ethical life? Why?

RELATED READINGS

Bergman, Roger. 2005. "John Dewey on Educating the Moral Self." *Studies in Philosophy and Education*, no. 24, 39–62.

Bergman deals extensively with Dewey's concept of the self and the insight it offers into his views of habits, character, social intelligence, and education.

Biesta, G. 2015. "How Does a Competent Teacher Become a Good Teacher?" *Philosophical Perspectives on Teacher Education*, 1–22.

Biesta identifies sound judgment as the quality that otherwise competent teachers must acquire before they become good teachers. His discussion of the interlocking nature of sound judgment and competence is noteworthy.

Campbell, Elizabeth. 2003. *The Ethical Teacher*. UK: McGraw-Hill Education.

Campbell's research examines the everyday ethical choices, behavior, responsibilities, and problems that educators encounter. Classroom decision-making is the focus of her book.

Dewey, John. 1922. "Character and Conduct." In *Human Nature and Conduct*. Vol. 14 of *John Dewey: The Middle Works, 1899–1924*, edited by Jo Ann Boydston, 1–189. Carbondale and Edwardsville: Southern Illinois University Press, 1988.

Dewey's theory of human nature and conduct is an essential element of understanding his approach to moral or ethical development.

Hare, W. 2007. "Credibility and Credulity: Monitoring Teachers for Trustworthiness." *Journal of Philosophy of Education* 41 (2): 207–19.

Hare turns trustworthiness upside down as he examines the feasibility of students considering the open-mindedness of their teachers. If credulity is to be avoided, Hare argues that students should learn to be questioning even with teachers.

Higgins, C. 2003. "Teaching and the Good Life: A Critique of the Ascetic Ideal in Education." *Educational Theory* 53 (2): 131–54.

Higgins argues that many traditional expectations for teachers – that they live and work as self-sacrificing professionals – undermine both their pursuit of a comprehensive flourishing personal life and a rich, fulfilling professional life.

Tan, Sor-hoon. 2019. "The Dao of Politics: Li (Rituals/Rites) and Laws as Pragmatic Tools of Government." *The Journal of School & Society* 6 (2): 81–103.

Tan's article on the Confucian idea of li harmony and western interpretations of democracy is a stimulus to evaluating Deweyan views, including the virtues he emphasizes.

Case Study: When All Seems Lost

"Are you okay?" Yoon Yú questioned as Maria sat at her desk. She knew Yoon wanted to talk about the eruption in the faculty meeting today between two teachers, but she simply was not up to processing what had happened or her jumbled feelings. She needed to think through things first before having any conversation about the meeting.

"I guess so. I need to ponder what happened and what to do next for a while. Thanks for checking on me; I hope you're okay too."

Today, of course, was not the first time there had been discord at an Academy meeting. The challenges teachers and staff faced daily often broke surface emotionally. But this was the first time two teachers had squared off so directly. Ultimately, the issue of the conflict is: What is the real duty of every Academy educator? That is such an intense and personal matter that most people keep their views to themselves or share them with a few others. There is generally a code among teachers that requires no one publicly challenge a peer on how they teach students: you take care of your business your own way.

These boundaries are difficult to maintain when districts impose modes of teaching so often, justifying them as "research-based" or associated with higher test scores. If classroom doors had always been the most precious tool to protect as much pedagogic autonomy as teachers could preserve, they were even more so now when districts impose "one best way" of teaching. And the more how teachers teach content became a matter of policy versus independent professional judgment, the more all matters of teacher behaviors with students became a question of freedom or judgment that teachers hated to discuss or judge. Maria was used to overlooking differences of her teachers if they were successful with students. She did not want them to believe she thought she knew their subjects, students, and duties better than they did.

Given these norms, it was especially unusual for teachers to argue with each other about the teacher's role. Correcting each other's work was just not a teacher's job. If a teacher was to be singled out for criticism, it was an administrator's job and perhaps the most delicate duty of administrators.

The meeting in question was largely focused on deadlines, events, and the daily tasks of running a school. Most of those issues were safe harbors. Academy meetings were viewed as necessary evils and not too technical since the whole group of kindergarten to twelfth-grade teachers did not share too many common issues.

So no one was expecting an eruption between two high school teachers. Mrs. Lewis, which is how she is addressed by everyone, was in her mid-fifties and had been teaching in the district her whole career. She taught science courses, and everyone at the school viewed her as formidable. She was somewhat close with a few teachers but reserved with all, including Maria. She was considered to be quite "old school" and stern with, but interested in, everyone. She also was usually quiet in school meetings. Today she had something to say. At one point a teacher made an impassioned plea that many of his students needed extra help in the form of helping them survive both school and their life away from school – what Maria called a typical "let's just do what's best for the students" statement. It was no surprise today's statement came from Tom Cisneros, a social studies teacher, who was in his late twenties and had been at the school about three years. His worldview was shaped by social justice activism and a deeply held desire to reform schools and society as a whole. He tended to blame the "system" for the achievement gap and greater disciplinary issues of poor and so-called minority students. Many of Tom's peers said he made them feel as though they were a key part of the corrupt system and charged with disinterest toward the most vulnerable students.

Generally, Tom's remarks were met with eye rolls or quiet groans, but not today. Mrs. Lewis responded acerbically by suggesting he get off his high horse. All the teachers and staff worked hard to help every student. She added that the causes of student difficulties were more individual than generic or group-based and mostly operated outside the control of the school, which could not provide competent parents or offset the effects of their overall lives on school performance. She asked Tom to stop in effect blaming everyone else at the school and taking the position of personal savior to the students.

Murmurs and expressions ranging from horror to real unease spread throughout the room. Tom said that he did not blame everyone, but that Mrs. Lewis and he shared enough students who trusted and shared with him that he felt safe saying she had little interest in the well-being of most students who couldn't do well easily in her classes and that she was totally inflexible to the many stressors and challenges in students' lives. Interrupting, Mrs. Lewis icily responded that she was organized and worked hard to ensure every student had a choice and a fair chance in her room, by offering tutoring after school and adapting materials, even testing, for students with academic challenges. And that her students did as well or better than any science teacher on state and district tests. She did what she could to help them learn science, but ultimately they had to choose to work.

Tom immediately responded to Mrs. Lewis, in a deeply emotional voice as tears formed in his eyes. "You're a part of the problem in this and every school. You want only the students who succeed and who can do so without bringing their home life into the classroom. You want them neat, orderly, and obedient. You do not go beyond the classroom walls to help them."

Mrs. Lewis replied: "That is utterly untrue and unprofessional of you to say."

Tom jumped up, with tears flowing, and said, passionately as ever, "Maybe you do more for some students, but not the brown students; I know that my students feel driven from your classroom and unimportant to you. If you care about students that struggle, it's just the black students. Everyone else is on their own." He bolted from the room. Silence prevailed.

Maria went immediately to the front of the room. She apologized for not intervening earlier, adding that she was responsible for allowing and monitoring open discussions. Neither Tom nor Mrs. Lewis was responsible for the outcomes, she implied. She was the responsible person. After saying some ameliorative words, she noted that she'd talk with Tom and Mrs. Lewis privately and plan with others some follow-up discussions. She also apologized to Mrs. Lewis. Thankfully, Maria thought, it is a Friday afternoon.

Later, Maria contemplated why she had allowed this short but caustic conversation to unfold. She could have stopped the conversation earlier before it became a disaster. She could have stopped Tom as soon he started, except he was not saying anything he had not said before, at first. Most teachers appreciated his commitment to students and his job. And while his pleas to change the outcomes at the school for the lowest achieving students seemed naïve to many, he lived to help students. He did make some people feel guilty that they did not accomplish enough, but no one seemed to believe schools alone could overcome what history and culture as a whole created.

In truth, Maria was not entirely unhappy Tom had stood up to Mrs. Lewis, even if his remarks were partly unprofessional. Maria also had to think more personally about her own reaction to what Tom had said to Mrs. Lewis. Some part of her agreed with him or felt Mrs. Lewis had some of what he said coming.

Maria's memory served up a teacher similar to Mrs. Lewis that she had in middle school. She was a stern, seemingly unfeeling and harsh teacher. It had been an awful year for her at home. At school hadn't been great either. She had struggled some, but most of her teachers gave her "the really good student's benefit of the doubt." Not this teacher though. She accused her of wanting more than other students got and riding on her reputation as a good student. Maria survived, but she remembered that teacher as the embodiment of a teacher who saw students only as a homework assignment and could not care less about their lives as a whole. She was the prototypical Mrs. Grinch, with a frown for every student. Did Mrs. Lewis remind her of that long-gone teacher? Was she unfair to Mrs. Lewis because of that long-ago experience? Was this part of what Dewey warned: seeing people – not to mention teachers – as good or bad?

As Maria left her office, Kenseisha, her administrative assistant, handed her a sheet of paper. Three sentences stood out: "The Steppingstones want misconduct addressed fairly, consistently and compassionately with the intent, when necessary, that students and staff are helped to enter legitimate realms of community and professional life. An example of a legitimate realm of employment is that our highly respected former mathematics teacher is scheduled to teach online mathematics courses next year in a nearby school district." On the backside of the page, another sentence drew her attention, "We think that ignoring the behavior of district and community leaders who violate community sexual standards and then harshly punishing students and staff for comparable offenses is a blatant form of hypocrisy."

QUESTIONS

1. What do you think Maria meant when she said she was responsible for the faculty meeting fiasco?
2. What steps does Maria need to take to address the anger and resentment between Tom Cisneros and Mrs. Lewis?

3. Given the broader racialized possibilities of the Academy, what kinds of emphases do Maria's future restorative plans need to provide?
4. How much weight should a teacher give to student criticisms of colleagues? When should they be reported to a principal?
5. Should Mrs. Lewis be asked to share her personal story? For example, Maria alone knows that Mrs. Lewis was traumatized by white youth during her school years. The most horrendous occasions included teens shooting over her head as she walked home in elementary school and when she was sexually assaulted after attending a secondary school football game.

CHAPTER 7

What Are the Characteristics of a Good School?

> ... the school becomes ... a form of social life, a miniature commu-
> nity and one in close interaction with modes of associated experience
> beyond school walls. All education which develops power to share
> effectively in social life is moral. It forms a character which not only
> does the particular deed socially necessary but one which is interested
> in that continuous readjustment which is essential to growth. Interest
> in learning from all contacts of life is the essential moral interest.
> —John Dewey, *Democracy and Education* (MW 9, 370)

Introduction

Dewey encourages schools to become more than places where students learn basic and advanced skills, develop a range of creative and scientific abilities, engage in inquiry and dialogue, nourish desirable dispositions and habits, and, on occasions, listen to lectures and presentations. In addition, he nudges schools away from the belief that ethical education is a discrete part of the curriculum. Instead, he explains that ethical growth occurs daily at school. In ordinary activities, all students are encouraged to develop the "power to share effectively in social life" (MW 9, 370). Moreover, instead of urging schools to focus largely on students and educators as individuals, he encourages them to help everyone recognize that they are considerably more than an individual; they are a social being who should enjoy human interactions and responsibilities including: coteaching, cooperative learning, and, in the process, becoming a more conscious and contributing member of school and external groups.

Specifically, Dewey champions social groups within the school community and advances the need for internal school communities to interact regularly with external ones (Simpson and Jackson 1995; 1997, 119–26). He employs the term *social group* to describe what classes, friendship groups, sports teams, academic clubs, student government, and, perhaps,

166

video games are capable of becoming academic and social entities (Waddington 2015, 2020). Schools and classes ought not be just a collection of individuals meeting in a room with an educator (MW 9, 368). As small communities, schools have the capacity to nourish a warmer, more robust sense of togetherness and belongingness as well as a fuller sense of responsibility than do larger communities. But small groups and schools have to be developed reflectively and experimentally; they do not flourish simply because of their size. Nor are they automatically democratic (Strike 2010). In fact, they may be inclined to be autocratic. Importantly, Dewey thinks these positive activities and more develop as students acquire the "power to share effectively" in school life (MW 9, 370). Ethical understanding and behavior, therefore, is not an add-on curriculum but part of living and learning together in well-designed communities. Of course, school communities, especially when Deweyan-informed, will vary noticeably. They are creative and should regularly look to more than one complementary theory for insight into schools and ethical development.

For example, a heartbreaking experience compelled the Academy to consider what it means to be a welcoming community. Nocona Parker, a thirteen-year-old Comanche student, took his life. While students and teachers knew he was often alone and missed his extended family and tribal friends, few recognized his depression. No one knew that he was decidedly estranged from the Academy, episodically missing classes. The Academy's new student alert system failed miserably. Predictably, guilt, grief, anger, and responsibility prompted the Academy to rethink its alert system. After considerable inquiry, the Academy decided to reconstruct the system and add an applied version of Ruitenberg's (2011) Derridean-informed approach to guiding the introduction of newcomers to schools. A core thesis of the approach is that those who inhabit a place, e.g., school or community, do not own it. Thus, newcomers are invited to share in a school's development and cultures as they change daily. Among others, inhabitants have a responsibility to help newcomers understand their new worlds. But the introduction should take place in an ethos of hospitality. Volunteer guides think of themselves as hospitality personnel, but not just any kind of hospitality workers. Derridean hospitality workers should encourage newcomers to deconstruct and reconstruct their school environments as well as add new environmental features.[1]

---

[1] For a discussion of Dewey and Derrida's ideas of construction, deconstruction, and reconstruction, see Garrison, Neubert, and Reich's *John Dewey's Philosophy of Education* (2012, 70–5).

The death of Nocona led to two new district committees. The first was designed to help the Academy keep abreast of the causes, signs, and consequences of social isolation and, overlapping with its emerging hospitality guidelines, effective ways for the district to foster belongingness without compulsion. Students and teachers successfully argued that a site-based administrator should also be on the committee. Moreover, a second committee, composed of a school psychologist, students, teachers, and parents, was charged with studying and nurturing a better understanding of the mental health needs of students. In this context, a student maxim arose spontaneously as discussions captured the new emphases on the values of togetherness and belongingness: "We belong together."

Unfortunately, few in the Academy initially understood the significant cultural, structural, and ideological barriers to developing a hospitable belongingness, especially with newcomers (Ruitenberg 2016, 83, 132). The barrier of hidden expectations can be especially important when it comes to understanding conceptions of hospitality. In many situations, a person is both obligated to accept an invitation and also indebted thereafter to reciprocate. Derrida's (Ruitenberg 2016, 7, 83, 200) conception, however, is much different: "The other may come or he may not [when invited]. I don't want to programme him, but rather leave a place for him to come if he comes." Thus, "we belong together" cannot ethically mean the newcomer belongs together spatially or philosophically with classmates or teachers. Yet a teacher or student is regularly available to help guide newcomers.

The Academy also initiated curricular changes, including integrative historical, cultural, and aesthetic studies of and by relevant people groups, including Indigenous peoples, new immigrants, and underserved populations. The Academy also employed a new counselor to help address the challenges of students. The Academy's entire curricular offerings were examined to learn where diversity and inclusion studies should become a portion of the common curriculum. But the year Nocona died, nothing eased the pain of his death or expanded the understanding of his peers more than when his parents served as mentors to sixth- and seventh-graders. As a consequence, students recommended that at least one component of the external collaborative community should be composed of newcomers.

As we examine Dewey's claims about the characteristics of an ethical school, five interwoven conceptions act as the focal points: a democratic (and, as a consequence), a conflictual, a caring, a learning, and a cooperative community. Contrarians may think schools can be communities but object to the idea that they should be conflictual ones. Indeed, being ethical regularly entails seeking to reduce conflict as much as is reasonable, does it not?

Dewey's answer is a qualified yes and no, for he understands communities both scientifically and aesthetically, i.e., as entities with rhythmic movements from peaceful to conflictual or from states of equilibrium to disequilibrium. His view coheres with Keltner's (2009, 65) claim that "conflict is synonymous with human social life" but that people can also solve problems and reconcile their differences. Hence, Dewey encourages a balance of harmony and conflict that involves a "continuous readjustment" of internal communities to one another and of internal communities to external ones (MW 9, 370). He understands the critical need for both external and internal communities to work together to identify and resolve challenges and not spend their energies on blaming one another for social and educational problems.

In studying Dewey's claims, we examine his answers to five overlapping questions: What is a democratic community? A conflictual community? A caring community? A learning community? A cooperative community? While these questions could be addressed in an integrated way, only the third and fourth questions about caring and cooperation are folded into the other topics. We address another question too: What are the desirable characteristics of leaders in democratic school communities?

Educational leaders, obviously, should be well-educated, richly experienced, and ethically prepared persons. But what additionally have they learned that enables them to lead well in democratic schools? For certain, leaders are not identical because imaginative, creative, and reflective people are diverse. But being ethically prepared includes understanding that people habitually collaborate as they make group-related ethical decisions. Leaders cannot be ethical recluses; for, ethics is concerned with others as well as with one's self. Of course, everyone needs to think for themselves but also understand that they work in "administrative contexts," settings where people should attempt to create solutions that integrate *multiple competing goods*" (Mehta 2016, 19; emphasis original), and not allow themselves to think largely in terms of one's goods versus others' evils. They also resist the lure to enter and win each argument and the enticement to take credit for group accomplishments.

Stop and Think

Assume you are a staff support person and prepare comments for Superintendent Amematine to consider as he reviews staff. This year it is clear that a board member thinks that good schools should have better personnel than the Academy does. Which staff members would you suggest Amematine should be prepared to discuss with the board member? Why?

A Democratic Community

What is a democratic community? This question invites a plethora of diverse answers regarding the nature of democracy and community (Cunningham 2002; LW 16, 399–406; Stout 2004; Terchek and Conte 2001). Dewey's contributions to the discussion about democracy are scattered in his writings, as are his explanations of what constitutes a community. In *Liberalism and Social Action*, Dewey maintains that democracy is a "form of social organization" (LW 11, 25) that extends to "all the areas and ways of living, in which the powers of individuals" are freed, developed, and guided (25). To be an effective and ethical democratic school community, therefore, requires ongoing learning about school and district organizational operations in order to evaluate and guide staff and student development. It also "demands that the method of inquiry, of discrimination, of test by verifiable consequences, be naturalized in all the matters" (25). It requires that people become empowered by community learning, thinking, and decision-making.

The shared leadership and governance that requires cooperation helps transform schools from places to work and study into democratic learning communities. Each person's growth, in turn, is rooted too in "the principle of moral, self-directing individuality" (MW 3, 235). Beyond seeking to develop a community of self-directing individuals, a critical question is: "What are the ways by which can be secured more organic participation of teachers in the formation of the educational policies" and practices of schools (LW 11, 223)? School leaders should also ask, What are effective ways for students to learn about, participate in, and contribute to the development of schools and societies?

Since school experience is one of the earliest potentially sustainable democratic experiences of many children, its social organization, activities, and values – its culture – should be a primary concern of district and school personnel. Just how important is the democratization of districts, schools, and classrooms? If Dewey's musings are accurate, the democratic relationships that develop in schools are "second only in importance . . . to those which exist in industry and business," but, he adds, perhaps "not even to them" (LW 11, 225). Often, schools and businesses are not known for encouraging a spirit of democracy: "the efficacy and responsibility of freed intelligence" (MW 3, 239). Why, then, does Dewey draw the conclusion that schools, as educational communities, are among the most important entities in society for the promotion, practice, and progress of democracy?

The Academy spends considerable time learning and relearning how a democratic community involves the development, appreciation, and practice of social values (e.g., respect, regard, justice, freedom, compassion, honesty, authenticity) that, in turn, may constitute normative criteria for personnel and students. But to develop these concepts and qualities requires that the Academy members "communicate with one another . . . [and, in time and for cogent reasons, come to] agree with one another in action because they share in a common understanding" (LW 3, 342). This extended scenario – communicate, understand, share, agree, act – is, Dewey asserts, "perhaps the most difficult and the most important" (342) of human challenges: cultivating people who cooperatively move toward and achieve in substantial ways a mutual understanding and practice of democracy and community. Predictably, a few educators annually leave the Academy because of its emphasis on democracy and community. The two reasons they most often give for leaving is that democratic community building takes too much personal time and is too stressful.

Maria and most faculty, however, now find it easier to enjoy, even as they continue to struggle with specifics of creating a democratic culture and community. They also quickly realized that they have seldom experienced authentic democratic cultures outside of schools. But where else would educators and others learn how to discuss their differences, deliberate about solutions, disagree agreeably, and work to advance common public interests? In family rooms, bars, backyards, clubs, worship centers, warehouses, stadiums, boardrooms, social media venues, colleges, and chat rooms? To a degree, yes. Many kinds of discussions advance democratic values. But the quality and depth of discussion is immensely important. How, then, can the quality of typical social discussions be augmented?

Which of the aforementioned locations, if any, have the necessary ingredients – e.g., educational missions, discussion leaders, information portals, intellectual obligations, and learning accommodations – to provide democratic learning contexts for discussing complex issues in a productive manner? Which of them regularly devotes sufficient time to developing the necessary respect and regard to produce important moments of agreement rather than repeatedly fostering resentments? The aforementioned spaces have educative roles, but they are likely more effective when they contribute collaboratively with schools by both communicating and engaging common concerns (Waks and English 2017, 15).

Difficult or not, the route to meeting diverse personal, social, and institutional challenges, Dewey asserts, entails a constant, multilayered

cooperative journey that employs democratic means and promotes democratic outcomes. He argues, too, that when a school wishes to foster ethical
beliefs and behaviors, it needs to select democratic or ethical means to
cultivate democratic goals. Why? If either official or informal school leaders
act undemocratically in the pursuit of what they deem democratic educational goals, they engage in contradictory and self-defeating practices:
they engage in the process of developing, using, and justifying undemocratic behavior that conflicts with and undercuts their professed
democratic goals.

Questions arise, therefore, when an educator's practice is inconsistent
with their avowed democratic theory: Are they really committed to democratic values and the common good? Are they willing to engage collaboratively with others who have different views? Or will they act arbitrarily
when they think that their family, career, friends, class, ideology, or culture
seem better served by disregarding others' contributions? The invitation to
ignore democratic practices in order to sustain so-called democratic communities and organizations is worth spurning. Plus, the overserving of
one's self raises serious questions about one's faithfulness to and trustworthiness with others. This is not, however, to say that strikes, boycotts,
demonstrations, walkouts, lawsuits, and many other political and legal
actions are undemocratic. Democratic peoples and constitutions rightly
authorize these and other actions. They should be built into the social and
legal fabric of societies. Citizens and aspiring citizens, therefore, have the
right and responsibility to use their political powers and freedoms to insist
on a reconsideration of issues and decisions (LW 11, 1–65).

Democracy and Communication

To increase the probability of a school learning democratic values and
means requires that a school community consciously chooses both democratic means (e.g., communication and deliberations) and goals (e.g.,
common understandings, ends, and practices). Coherence between the
desired goals, goods, and virtues and the desired means, environments,
and conditions is a needed alignment; for community requires open,
sustained, and cooperative problem-solving. In time, many claims can be
confirmed and others disconfirmed by educators and collaborators. Still
other claims will remain uncertain. Each warranted claim, Dewey argues,
should be envisioned as a hypothesis, not a final report, to be employed
and tested, and, when appropriate, revised or rejected. The educational
challenges (e.g., curricular, structural, personnel, financial, organizational)

examined need to be cooperatively addressed by the school's community, e.g., staff, students, administrators, and others. But collaborating communities should not expect every inquiry and deliberation to result invariably in unanimous agreement or, as Dewey prefers, a consensus. Working and inquiring together in the presence of strong disagreements is unavoidable when one discusses important concerns. The purposes of reflection include, among other ideas, finding ways to work better together. Coercing others to agree usually indicates leadership and community failure.

Respect, regard, and tolerance, therefore, are necessary virtues if school communities are allowed to think and speak. In view of the critical need of respect and tolerance, Freire (1973, 10) observes that a genuinely radical community member "is convinced he [or she] is right, but respects another's prerogative to judge himself [or herself] correct. He [or she] tries to convince and convert [a disagreeing community member], not to crush his [or her] opponent." Crushing colleagues makes a farce out of both democracy and community. Facilitating student, educator, and parent rethinking of controversies, therefore, is part of the art of fostering a community of Freirean radicals. Likewise, searching for legitimate action involves fostering wise and deliberative leaders and committees. Equally needed, Dewey suggests, is a collective perseverance, for "it takes time to arouse minds from apathy and lethargy, to get [people] thinking for themselves, to share in making plans, to take part in their execution" (LW 7, 347). Failure to persevere in these activities is at times interpreted as a failure of democracy. Perhaps it is better viewed, at least occasionally, as a failure of schools and societies to promote leadership habits or people who persevere as they reconstruct environments and institutions. The impulse to decide immediately strangles reflection.

Why is extensive time for communication and understanding important? In a sense, communication and understanding constitute a, if not *the*, lynchpin for living, learning, and working together; they are intrinsic to building and enjoying a good, free, and meaningful life. For Dewey, however, communication must meet a high standard: it only occurs when there is a "common understanding" that is evidenced by reasonable and open discussion and is measured by whether people actually "*agree with one another in action*" (LW 3, 342; emphasis added). Open discussion and unforced action, of course, result in planned and unplanned consequences, some desirable, others questionable, still others objectionable. Likewise, when people communicate, they often disagree; but they also, if they persevere, can deliberate until they agree on more issues and learn to act together for additional common goods. On occasions, communication means people determinedly ask, Is that really required (MW 9, 370)? Why should we consider this particular outcome acceptable? Importantly, Dewey advises that "the best thinking occurs" when perplexing issues are balanced with less stressful topics, not when there is an uninterrupted flow of agreeable or discordant discussions (MW 8, 350).

Elaborating, Dewey asserts that as people "arrive at an understanding they come to agreement, and agreement is committal to a common cause: it is reciprocal engagement and mutual confidence" or trust (LW 3, 342). Note Dewey's outcomes of common-cause work: "reciprocal engagement and mutual confidence" (342). The former (give-and-take engagement) is partially responsible for the development of the latter (mutual confidence or trust). Trust, admiration, and other desirable emotions are nourished as people demonstrate their authenticity and dependability even in contentious situations. Thus, more than a narrow understanding emerges from communication, for it helps ensure an equitable involvement in processes and outcomes (MW 9, 7). Communication includes listening to what others say and responding reflectively to their suggestions. Moreover, cooperative activities foster the growth of "emotional and intellectual dispositions" (7). Hence, actually hearing the ideas and reasons of others can lead to more personal and social growth and to a richer democracy. Pappas (2008, 233) argues that "Genuine listening, especially to those who speak against our beliefs, does more on behalf of participatory democracy than voting." Conversely, the tendency to prepare our rebuttals while others are speaking constructs an invisible wall that stymies learning and problem-solving. The Academy staff learned a sad lesson after Matthew Webb became the new assistant principal; that is, a seemingly ideal colleague can lack "sympathetic intercommunication" and, thereby, reveal "disrespect for [colleagues' and students'] experience" (LW 6, 21).

Democracy and Expectations

Community expectations include a swath of sympathies and may include cross-cultural "manners" (MW 9, 22), a concept that metaphorically refers to "the oil which prevents or reduces friction" (MW 13, 37). Cross-cultural manners, therefore, are deemed important to pursuing goals together. In many, perhaps most, cases, it is possible for people to reach their goals by crafting a "common understanding" and "a common intent" (MW 9, 35–6). Freedom to participate or act is not an innate ability or right of a few but emerges as freedom of intelligence is developed via cooperative inquiry and problem-solving (MW 11, 217–25). Hence, Dewey claims that "the basic freedom" for everyone "is that of freedom of mind and whatever degree of freedom of action and experience is necessary to produce freedom of intelligence" (MW 11, 220). The pursuit of freedom of intelligence entails also "education of the public" (LW 11, 347). This kind of education, although a facet of "interaction ... beyond school walls" (MW 9, 370), can be an invaluable campus-wide endeavor, too (Abowitz and Stitzlein 2018). Schools, therefore, are not merely isles of deliberation but outreaching deliberative communities. Superintendents wisely become diplomats or ambassadors, even educational statespersons (LW 11, 345–7), when working with internal and external communities.

When professional desires are not approved, how should such situations be handled? By declaring verbal war on the contrarian ideas of colleagues? Or, perhaps, on the contrarians themselves? Before deciding, answer these questions: e.g., Is the desired nonfunded item a necessary item? Can a purchase be reasonably delayed? Did the budget committee deliberate about all options? Did its members show wisdom and provide justification in the selection of requests? Were decision-makers sufficiently faithful or attentive to different groups' interests? These questions may uncover patterns that indicate that decision-makers have a healthy regard for every group and person – or not. When the items selected for funding seem to advantage the already materially and educationally advantaged, it seems appropriate to ask Rawls' (1991) question: Will an injustice be committed against the economically challenged and educationally underserved? (See also Apple 2009; hooks 2014; West 1994.)

Dewey's (MW 9, 370) ideas in Chapter 6 about thoughtfulness in making evaluative remarks emerge as practical necessities while pursuing controversial expectations (MW 7, 297–311; LW 6, 123–30). Since working with others on weighty matters is usually a cross-cultural and a multi-paradigmatic endeavor, thoughtfulness in making evaluative or audit-like comments assumes a particularly important role (Foreman-Peck 2015, 159–60). While having respect for a person who makes candid statements is essential, it may also be well-advised to clarify that aggressively stated ideas are sometimes intimidating and considered attacks by certain people. Plus, antagonistic comments sometimes silence would-be participants and, thereby, undermine an essential democratic dialogical quality: equitable participation (Strike and Soltis 2009, 123–7). Thus, educators often need to negotiate dialogical styles to ensure that it is clear to everyone that exchanging ideas sometimes requires modifying social and personal speech patterns. People, occasionally, may prefer to "inflame ...

opinion for the sake of ... party advantage" (LW 11, 517) when they could instead think more about the common good.

Stop and Think

When, if ever, is it ethical to inflame students' or educators' feelings toward a person, a practice, or a theory? Illustrate your ideas.

On the other hand, educators need to remember that people are not always predisposed to value so-called wisdom, caring dispositions, persuasive arguments, and reflective engagements (MW 7, 298). They may have experienced these activities as tactics to delay action, especially to escape dealing with equity concerns. Or, alternatively, some may rely on raw power and intimidation to force their views on others, including schools that are attempting to be dialogical and cooperative communities. What, then, should district and school leadership do if they want to be democratic with educators and parents who seek to force colleagues to agree with their priorities?

Consider an occasion that confronted Superintendent Amematine, the Harbor School Board, and Maria. Years prior to this incident, the district had implemented its now largely obsolete plan to prepare staff and students to engage in constructive interactions and reduce conflicts and hostilities. The popularly called peacekeeping plan required teachers to limit or avoid discussions of political, religious, economic, and ethical topics in classes because they were labeled potentially disruptive. Since approval of the plan, a small Ethiopian population had settled in the city. Like other district parents, Ethiopian parents were prepared to submit their children's applications for possible attendance at specialty schools. During the spring, three new board members were elected, one of whom, Catherine Bump, stated immediately that the existing board should guarantee that diversity overload is not allowed in any school and ensure that the peacekeeping and educational capacities of all schools are not overwhelmed. In addition, she proposed a reconfiguration of the English as a second language (ESL) program at the Academy to include the accepted Ethiopian students and the existing Academy ESL students. Furthermore, she proposed that student conflicts be addressed by a zero-tolerance policy regarding disruptive behavior: any student who disrupts classroom learning or threatens the safety of others will automatically be given an off-campus suspension. She announced too that she intends to ask the board president to set up a meeting with the superintendent and principals of affected schools to determine if there are other matters that need immediate attention.

Incongruously, Harbor School District's less-than-sterling peacekeeping plan and the Academy's community engagement plan contain ideas that are advantageous during the new board quandary. Both stress the importance of strengthening the school community and its social groups by having much higher participation rates in both social groups (beyond school classes) and more school community activities. Likewise, the plans note the importance of understanding students and creating, when desirable, additional social groups and identifying external communities to attract their participation. Additionally, the community engagement plan stresses the ideal of selecting external communities that align with the interests of students who are outliers in the school community.

The Academy's community engagement plan also attends to the importance of constructing "a common store of experiences" (LW 3, 342) that will strengthen inter-social group engagements and affinities. A desired byproduct of these engagements is fostering voluntary, reflective commonalities. In pursuing reflective common experiences, the Academy's internal and external learning communities utilized the "process of living together" in and outside of school to educate (MW 9, 9). Thereby, the Academy "enlightens experience; it stimulates and enriches imagination; it creates responsibility for accuracy and vividness of statement" (9); and it shapes dispositions that "arouse and strengthen" desirable habits and behavior (20).

The construction of cooperative communities also creates allies for Academy educators as they cultivate democratic processes and values in students' cultures (MW 9, 171–87). But notice, in particular, an important outcome of effective interaction: "responsibility for accuracy" (9). Living in virtually any community can sharpen and dull one's tendency to be accurate and, thereby, influence data collection, presentation, interpretation, and truth telling. Accuracy, especially when describing others' lives, views, and values, is a crucial virtue and communicative necessity, one that is invaluable when talking about others' identities, faiths, and cultures. Consequently, everyone needs an environment that nurtures epistemic accuracy and thoughtful analyses; for, democracy is based to a large degree on a fair and accurate description of facts and data. Similarly, schools that depend heavily on narrative ethics, like the Academy, depend heavily on being communities of accuracy. For example, Kunzman (2016) argues that it "makes no sense to speak of generic" religious or nonreligious and, by extension, conservative or liberal people. The details and the nuances of each person's beliefs are relevant if typecasting people is to be avoided.

Democracy and Evaluation

In *Democracy and Education* (MW 9), Dewey highlights aspects of everyone's learning: "in close interaction with modes of associated experience beyond school walls," and "from all contacts of life" (MW 9, 370). Given these emphases, it is apparent why he argues that "the moral and the social quality of conduct are . . . identical" (368). His criteria for school evaluation, therefore, extend beyond scientific, artistic, historical, and sport indicators to include "a spirit of companionship" (368). He claims that "the measure of the worth of the administration, curriculum, and methods of instruction of the school is the extent to which they are animated by a social spirit" (368). In addition, he asserts that "the great danger which threatens school work is the absence of conditions which make possible a permeating social spirit" (368) and that "the great enemy of effective moral training" (368) is a lack of esprit de corps.

School leaders, if Dewey's ideas are plausible, should be "animated by a social spirit" and involved in identifying social activities and conditions that foster esprit de corps (MW 9, 370). He underscores too that largely focusing on tangible quantifiable school outcomes and slighting qualitative outcomes (e.g., attitudinal and affectional) greatly impede a student's growth as a whole person. Plus, he implies that when the common good of a region or nation is not a high priority of leaders, the possibility of many people learning about and leading good, meaningful lives is undercut.

Why is the qualitative so important? To begin, we should clarify that Dewey does not make a dichotomy between qualitative and quantitative interests. Each suggests the other. More specifically, qualitative indicators are present wherever appraisals or judgments of value exist (e.g., about teaching mathematics, chemistry experiments, sport competitions, artistic performances) and are a part of judgments regarding actions and behaviors that enhance or diminish human existence (e.g., protecting animals and the natural environment). In short, wherever decisions intersect with the well-being of people, the planet, and beyond, ethical questions are nearby. As Hansen (2001, 90) implies, the qualitative deals largely with answers to the question of what difference a decision makes to the way a person thinks, feels, aspires, appreciates, and shares.

The wealth-and-poverty-gap problem for Dewey is significant, in part, because it is not a quantitative-qualitative stand-alone question; it compounds the challenges of creating laws, policies, and systems that promote the common good or nurture opportunities for free, equitable, and caring communities. Educational disparities proliferate. Moreover, enormous wealth and power by a small minority frequently accentuate objectionable unemployment and retirement outcomes. In short, a superabundance of wealth by a small portion of people provides them with immense possessions, privileges, and powers and, simultaneously, deprives the many of the needs connected to their pursuit of meaningful lives. Plus, even the minuscule power of the poor is abridged by politicians who act primarily in the interest of wealthy banks, corporations, groups, and individuals (LW 11, 130–45). As Jonathan Kozol (1991) records, a nearly unbridled access to almost unlimited capital and privileges results in *Savage Inequalities*. Once many may have been tempted to think it is reasonable to conclude that the privileged, politicians, the middle classes, and the poor in sufficient numbers would work together to enact laws, policies, and programs to humanize the economic, health, and social systems that often incapacitate people. Yet this kind of thinking now appears largely wishful and should disappear as realities keep revealing that the interest and the will to cooperate in the pursuit of humane and just outcomes is regularly resisted.

How is the national good to be measured? Dewey suggests, in *The Public and Its Problems*, that it is measured in part by the extent to which it relieves the individual from "the waste of negative struggle and needless conflict and confers upon him [or her] positive assurance and reinforcement in what he [or she] undertakes" (LW 2, 280). One may ask: Which nations significantly relieve their peoples' undesirable struggles for food, health care, meaningful employment, and housing? Unfortunately, this list has been and remains short. So short, in fact, that Dewey made more equitable dissemination of resources and the democratization of power a lifelong concern (Chomsky 2000, 37–56). Fortunately, this important effort for an equitable dispersal of political power and economic justice continues as proactive people face barriers of indifference, greed, and antidemocratic ideologies (Delgado and Stefancic 2017; Ladson-Billings 2003).

> **Stop and Think**
> Which nations have made significant progress at enhancing the overall well-being of low- and middle-income families in recent decades? How did they achieve their goals?

As world democratic practices budded, bloomed, shriveled, died, and then budded again, Dewey's faith in the potential of well-informed people who are characterized by democratic attitudes and habits seems to have remained largely unshaken. In view of what he saw, however, he warned of the violence that often results when governments, corporations, and banks continue to exploit the majority of people. Thus, when speaking at a South African Education Conference, he expressed deep frustration about the future of world democracy:

> In a mad, often brutal, race for material gain by means of ruthless competition the school must make ceaseless and intelligently organized effort to develop, above all else, the will for cooperation and the spirit which sees in every other individual an equal right to share in the cultural and material fruit of collective human invention, industry, skill, and knowledge. The supremacy of this aim in mind and character is necessary, not merely as an offset to the spirit of inhumanity bred by economic competition and exploitation but to prepare the coming generation for an inevitable new and more just and humane society which, unless hearts and minds are prepared by education, is likely to come attended with all the evils of social change by violence. (LW 9, 203)

The economically and politically powerful, with few public exceptions, do not appear open to the idea that their values and practices often deprive the disadvantaged of necessities. Nor do many seem open to arguments that coercive power constitutes and promotes acts of violence. Dewey (LW 15, 173), therefore, counsels that we "need to make sure of the grounds of our faith in the ideals and methods of a free society, and we need to make sure these grounds are moral and religious in quality, not matters of external prudence, policy, material gain, ease and comfort." Here he argues for shaping democratic dialogue; the issues are moral and religious issues, not merely about policy matters, wealth acquisition, and comfortable lifestyles. The deeper issues involve the common good and the ethical well-being of all people, not merely about whether social elites should be allowed to determine what is best for everyone with de-ethicized arguments and practices.

Dewey's idea of a good school is obviously a complex construction with a democratic community orientation. Figure 7.1 identifies a selection of his emphases.

Stop and Think

Imagine you are Superintendent Amematine when Catherine Bump is elected. What would you do, given the future board member's public proposals as well as community and district reactions? How does Figure 7.1 help you understand the challenges triggered by Bump?

Indicators of a Democratic School Community
Each person is the moral equal of any other individual.
Each student is entitled to share in the resources that will enable them to engage successfully in educational, economic, and political activities.
Each educator and student should have normalized opportunities to participate in a school's reconstruction of policies and practices.
Educators and students are responsible for fostering civic and leadership abilities that enrich democratic life.
Educators are responsible for engaging students in developmentally appropriate deliberative and problem-solving activities.
School communities should nourish freedom of inquiry and creativity in order to enhance their students' and others' understanding and enjoyment of a free, good, and meaningful life.
Schools should ensure that every student is engaged in groups and activities that provide opportunities for social and emotional development.
School communities should evaluate episodically the outcomes of their policies, programs, and practices.
Schools should foster common purposes and academic interests through cooperative inquiry, discovery, and projects.
Educators and students should ensure that school communities and social groups regularly interact with parents and external communities.
Students should learn to face, manage, and overcome the fears that obstruct their personal development.

Figure 7.1   Indicators of a democratic school community: a Deweyan framework

Democracy and Agency

Before examining Dewey's view of an inherently conflictual community, it is useful to note his emphasis on human agency. Recognizing that an opportunity for freedom may exist in a person's next choice, he observes that Aristotle rightly stresses that each agent or actor should possess a particular "'state of mind'" when making a moral choice:

> First, he must *know* what he is doing; secondly, he must *choose* it, and choose it for itself, and thirdly, the act must be the expression of a formed and stable *character*. In other words, the act must be *voluntary*; that is, it must manifest a choice, and for full morality at least, the choice must be an expression of the general tenor and set of personality. It must involve awareness of what one is about; a fact which in the concrete signifies that there must be a purpose, an aim, an end in view, something for the sake of which the particular act is done. (LW 7, 166–7; emphasis original)

Unpacking Dewey's thought is ideal but immediately deferrable. Suffice it to say that he seems to describe activists as people who are emotionally, intellectually, and purposively prepared. They understand that they will face formidable, well-financed opponents and that such work demands wide-awakeness.

Greene (1978), in "Wide-Awakeness and the Moral Life," clarifies what is involved in agency even when feeling somewhat incapacitated. She argues that feelings of powerlessness

> can to a large degree be overcome through conscious endeavor on the part of individuals to keep themselves awake, to think about their condition in the world, to inquire into the forces that appear to dominate them, to interpret the experiences they are having day by day. Only as they learn to make sense of what is happening, can they feel themselves to be autonomous. Only then can they develop the sense of agency required for living a moral life. (43–4)

Greene's personal journey was exceptionally challenging, every so often lacerating, but characterized by consciousness, inquiry, and sense making. She recognized that if agency is left undeveloped, autocrats and tyrants will flourish.

A Conflictual Community

Given Dewey's description of democratic communities, one can appreciate why he analyzes their conflictual natures and sees disagreements as ongoing opportunities to address problems. Conflicts, at least those that are reflectively addressed, need not be dreaded; for, they exist, to a substantial degree, because of individual organic needs, human interactions, and social demands. Conflicts, therefore, are potentially instructive and productive.

Certain conflicts, of course, can be unproductive if the causes and measures to address them are not well understood, the involved parties are not respected and respecting, and entities, including schools, are not well-prepared to guide open inquiries. At the Academy, analysis of disagreements is a vital part of school and social responsibility preparation: students are taught to argue productively and work collaboratively to shape political ideals, policies, laws, and practices.

The Roots of Conflict

Dewey identifies what he deems the roots of conflict: they are embedded in existence and manifested in impulses, desires, purposes, and diverse views of goods, rights, and virtues (LW 5, 279–88). Not only are there personal conflicts related to these factors, but personal conflicts also bleed into social ones. Conflicts can also be heightened by miseducative experiences (LW 5, 396–7). Thus, educators should plan for likely conflicts, including those that may multiply when educators, students, and families interact. Nonetheless, school-related conflict, when guided by experienced educators, can stimulate judicious discussions, decisions, and actions. All too often, when specific topics are declared conflict-free subjects for a dozen or more years, schools and societies forfeit incredibly valuable opportunities to examine problems, find solutions, and promote meaningful lives. The unofficial silent years, roughly ages five to eighteen, however, perpetuate boredom, miseducation, and social evils.

The growth of political hostilities and legislative stalemates is, in part, a sign that silencing schools is counterproductive. In effect, children and youth are forbidden to become their better selves and more effective adults. People, including politicians, fail to understand that students mature as humans and members of society through "give-and-take communication" (LW 2, 332). Using his early Congregational church vocabulary, Dewey concludes that depriving children of citizenship education means the "old Adam, the unregenerate element in human nature, persists. It shows itself wherever . . . [there is] attaining results by use of force instead of by . . . communication and enlightenment" (LW 2, 332).

Speaking from personal experience, Dewey says "Conflict is the gadfly of thought. It stirs us to observation and memory. It instigates to invention. It shocks us out of sheep-like passivity, and sets us at noting and contriving" (MW 14, 207). When schools and districts think, observe, recall, invent, awaken, note, and plan together, imaginative solutions can be tested, processes democratized, and thinking enlarged (207). Yet, without an appropriate education and social development, friction and conflict easily become unproductive. Dewey, therefore, urges that educators and students work toward the creation and enhancement of conditions that clarify each person should be equally respected and regarded even as all ideas are evaluated by their educational, social, economic, and political consequences and their impact on the common good. This implies that all ideas are not equally meritorious and that not everything is tolerable. Ethical questions often have clear-cut right answers (Harris 2010, 28), and some answers are toxic and antihuman (27–53).

Rights and Duties

Among qualities to develop in schools, if Dewey is consulted, is the democratic ideal "that every individual is to share in the duties and rights belonging to control of social affairs, and . . . that [new or proposed] social arrangements are to eliminate those external arrangements of status, birth, wealth, sex, etc., which restrict the opportunity of each individual for full development" (LW 7, 348–9). This ideal requires that school personnel, parents, and students share responsibilities for decision-making and that irrelevant human traits should not foreclose one's input. Shared responsibility and procedural fairness, then, broaden democratic involvement in "social [and school] affairs" (349).

Neither element – sharing in rights and duties or disregarding irrelevant differences – suggests that an influential individual or group should be allowed to dominate discussions and conclusions nor that educators should be stripped of their voices much less their legal and professional responsibilities. In addition, shared decision-making does not connote that equal credence can be given to every idea (LW 11, 219–20, 296–9). If equal credibility is expected for every idea, evaluative thinking and solving problems are truncated. Hence, each opinion about a curricular, organizational, or fiscal matter is not necessarily of equal epistemic and professional value with others (MW 11, 219–20; LW 7, 340–50). Still, everyone's right to speak and potential "to judge wisely" need constant affirmation in silencing cultures (LW 7, 346).

Stop and Think

Assume Superintendent Amemantine creates a committee to study the teaching of controversial issues because the current peacekeeping plan is overly restrictive. What clarifying questions would you ask Amemantine? Do you know of any relevant guidelines that should be examined by the yet-to-be formed district committee?

Discouraging news about conflict includes the fact that it may add stress, at least immediately, to an already fatigued profession (Nias 2005). More stress is especially likely if educators are neither disposed to nor prepared for discussing controversial subjects. Where staff readiness is concerned, districts are obligated to strengthen both staff problem-solving skills and their ability to lead developmentally appropriate inquiries. Time for examining effective ways of interacting and discussing issues is clearly necessary (Hess 2009, 158–68). Early in the preparation, clarifying when and how to handle questions about local history, politics, religion, wealth, and poverty may be needed (LW 9, 158–68). Imaginative educators, of course, can enhance their abilities to engage in controversial topics, particularly if they collaborate with parents and community agencies that have common interests (LW 9, 109). At the Academy, emphasis on fostering student leadership and social responsibility provides a ready-made context for learning to examine and discuss complex topics. The Academy is also advantaged because teachers have periodic staff development designed to cultivate the integration of societal issues (LW 13, 79) and "already stirring" student interests (LW 8, 324). They also know that discussing controversial issues does not necessarily absorb enormous amounts of time and, eventually, can become a commonplace habit.

Dewey encourages educators to examine prickly issues with colleagues and students for democratic reasons. In essence, he sees schools having democratic duties to prepare youth for democratic participation. To facilitate understanding and addressing ethical issues, Figure 7.2 depicts his analyses of different kinds of conflict. But, first, we note that Dewey (LW 7, 322–8) rejects the notion that controversial matters are reducible to the individual versus the social, claiming "*no* question can be reduced to the individual on one side and the social on the other" (323; emphasis original). Instead, he avows that "society consists of individuals, and the term 'social' designates only the fact that individuals are related to one another in intimate ways" (323). He acknowledges also that there are "conflicts between *some* individuals and *some* arrangements in social life" (324; emphasis original). To this individual lens, he adds three others that can assist in analyzing socio-political-organizational disagreements that frequently involve power and control interests among educators, parents, and students, and ultimately include issues regarding greater degrees of respect, freedom, equity, inclusion, and justice (LW 9, 107–11). His trilogy is amplified as follows:

Types of Conflictual Situations	
Individual Conflicts	*Examples*
1. Particular Individuals – Specific Social Arrangements	Individual Conflicts: Two administrators disagree over how to discipline two students who were involved in a cafeteria brawl.
Social Unit Conflicts	*Examples*
2. Dominant People – Existing and Rising Classes or Groups	Power Groups: Established Political-Civic-Business-School Board-Leaders disagree with Young Professionals and Parents. Religious Group vs. Nonreligious Group. Central Office Staff Development Agendas vs. Site-Based Agendas. Majority Ethnic Group vs. Minority Ethnic Groups.
3. Old – New Forms of Association and Organization	Generational, Paradigmatic, and Content Groups: Existing non-union leaders & staff disagree with union-orientated personnel. School-based Consensus Building vs. Content-based Negotiations.
4. Private – Public Action Orientation	Advocacy Orientations: Educators United for Funding of Public Schools vs. Parents for Educational Vouchers for Schools. Parental Support for Music-Art-Theater Programs vs. District Funding for STEM Programs.
Methodological Conflicts	*Examples*
5. Rational, Traditional, Religious – vs. Experimental Methodologies	Epistemic Orientations: (e.g., Traditional) Reason, Precedent, Intuition, Culture, Hybrid Methodologies, Revered Literature vs. (e.g., Experimental) Scientific Inquiry, Hybrid Methodologies.

Figure 7.2 Analyzing conflictual situations: a Deweyan framework

First, the struggle between a dominant class and a rising class or group; secondly, between old and new forms and modes of association and organization; thirdly, between accomplishing results by voluntary private effort, and by organized action involving the use of public agencies. In historic terms, there is the struggle between class and mass; between conservative and liberal (or radical); and between the use of private and public agencies, extension or limitation of public action. (LW 7, 328)

Dewey (LW 2, 284) rightly notes too that a gerontocracy may exist in a group, not because older people ipso facto are wiser and better experienced, but because "A principle of inertia, of least resistance and least action, operated. Those who were already conspicuous in some respect, were it only for long gray beards, had political powers conferred upon them" (284).

Subsequently, Dewey identifies a fifth conflict, a methodological one, which may intersect with any other kind of conflict: "a genuine difference of conviction as to the way in which ... conflicts should be met and managed" (LW 7, 324), e.g., major differences between using traditional, rational, religious, humanistic, or scientific methods of addressing conflicts. In a traditional vein, one may find people thinking that since they are community leaders, they and their families should remain such in perpetuity. A proliferation of sub-conflicts within and among these types of conflict, of course, is also possible, e.g., traditional versus rational. Likewise, some people are largely scientific in their educational interests as, say, engineers and physicians but traditional in their personal interests as parents. Thus, Figure 7.2 does not explicitly capture these nuances and complexities. Likewise, certain religious groups often want their values represented in curricular activities. Hence, Figure 7.2 should be a stimulus for imaginative applications, not a definitive window on conflict.

In Figure 7.2, we group the five types of conflict into three general categories: Individual Conflicts (1), Social Unit Conflicts (2, 3, 4), and Methodological Conflicts (5). While there are distinctions among and within these conflictual types, there is also overlap, e.g., a particular individual conflict, when examined in depth, may be situated in or change into a social unit or a methodological conflict. In addition, Dewey (MW 7, 299–301) describes interests – which may be manifested in one's point of departure or in the weight given to one side or the other of social unit conflicts – that arise in philosophical discussions and lead to conflicts between conservative-progressive, institutional-individual, secular-religious, and scientific-ethical explanations.

Analyzing conflict types is instructive but does not routinely identify specific solutions to ethical problems. Nor is an analysis likely to reveal immediately whether a problem is an at-large one or systemic one. Educators and students need relevant arguments, data, principles, and other particulars before they can work toward conclusions about what should or should not be addressed. But learning to identify how different individuals and groups may be inclined to think methodologically; how class and cultural differences may influence but not determine beliefs; how generational, gender, and paradigmatic backgrounds oftentimes contribute to preferences; how economic, political, and religious differences partially shape actions; how sexual identities, political propensities, and regional allegiances may predispose some sympathies; and how ethnic and racial experiences and professional commitments may influence perceptions of conflicts and their resolution is important. Pursuing a knowledge of relevant details is necessary for resolving educational conflicts.

To an experienced teacher who regularly engages in ethical inquiry, the fog around individual-social unit-methodological elements of conflicts may suddenly clear. This clarity may occur, at first, by (a) direct apprehension of the meaning of pertinent information and, then later, by (b) "indirect, mediated" comprehension of more evidence, including learning more via deliberation about a situation and proposed solutions (LW 8, 228). Of course, this kind of person is distinguishable from the individual who habitually stereotypes specific populations, fails to inquire into conflicts, and offers stale answers and clichés for new problems (MW 7, 331–8). Likewise, they are markedly different from "the intellectual bungler" (LW 8, 214) who slipped past the district human resources department. The seasoned ethical inquirer is also alert for situational novelties as well as different strands of conflict. Obviously, ensuring that there is no stereotyping of people because of the individual-social unit-methodological framework is essential for fair-minded analyses and attempted resolutions too, for commonalities and differences cut across all dynamic categories and diversities in every grouping (Kunzman 2006, 35–58).

The methodological differences Dewey mentions flow into numerous social and theoretical conflicts. Tradition, with considerable variety, may assume "the existence of final and unquestionable knowledge" to resolve particular kinds of issues (LW 7, 329). Today traditions are more complex as societies have become more diverse. Thus an environment of "free inquiry and ... discussion" remains necessary (329). Consequently, Dewey reasons that the experimental method is "the method of democracy, of a positive toleration which amounts to sympathetic regard for the intelligence and personality of others, even if they hold views opposed to ours, and of scientific inquiry into facts and testing of ideas" (329). Dewey's description of the experimental approach allows for the possibility of using precedents and authorities to inform situations much as do "personal memories" (330). He considers the experimental method "the method of democracy" (329), because everyone can use scientific methods to inquire into issues, but not everyone can readily use dissimilar ideological beliefs, religion-specific sacred literatures, scores of cultural traditions, multitudes of individual experiences, and conflicting paradigms as methods of problem-solving. Even so everyday life helps clarify how many people understand their experiences and responsibilities in social and political democracies.

Democracy and Power

The contradictory forces of personal and social desires, goods and demands, and of social, political, economic, and government entities form the cultural backdrop for school conflicts. Likewise, families, neighborhoods, and schools play roles in conflicts (Stein et al. 2003). One need not wonder, consequently, why Dewey explains that conflicts and power are extremely important to understand. Covert and overt power – e.g., personal, economic, religious, ideological, and governmental – are ordinary forces in society and, indirectly, in schools. Thus, he judges these forces and powers as necessary studies for a well-informed community and teaching profession. Knowledge of civics, law, economics, politics, and government can empower educators and students throughout their lives. Without a knowledge of these areas, democracy probably has little chance of being of, by, and for the people. Instead, democracy is corrupted and is of, by, and for financial, political, and government planners who aid and abet wealth and power collectors.

Power or, as Dewey often says, forces are important because "the simple fact is that power rules and the real government is carried on not necessarily in Washington [Ottawa, Beijing, New Delhi, or Cairo] ... but wherever power resides" (LW 9, 163). Many wealth designers and creators, individually and collectively, act "in ways that are not open and clear" and are "entangled at every point with politics" (163). The capital footprints of these affinity groups cannot always be traced easily, but the affiliations and clients of lobbyists, the trails of multinational corporations, and the proposed laws of legislators reveal important information (Fraser and Gerstle 2005). In view of the past and present actions of many wealth accumulators, Dewey's warning of returning to a past that allowed "an orgy of so-called economic liberty" and a "reckless and extravagant exploitation of natural resources" and workers is still headline news (LW 11, 250–1; McDonald 2003). Yet, developing antipathy for the privileged ignores Dewey's emphases on mutual respect, regard for everyone, and working toward the common good. On the other hand, he recognizes that an oppressive pursuit of wealth must be aggressively and consistently resisted, for group, class, religious, ideological, and race exploitation is inimical to democracy. Philanthropy, although based at times on compassion, is not the answer to societal economic and material needs, for it is only a patchwork effort, not a public policy answer to systemic problems.

One of the more contentious situations – with several forces at work – that the Academy has encountered regards methodological conflicts that evolved into a tangle of interwoven questions. The initial inquiry from a curriculum committee was twofold: How can we help students learn to discuss ethical, religious, ideological, and political issues with one another and help ourselves as educators address related curricular, pedagogical, and legal concerns? Fortuitously, the district decided that the question should be examined by an ad hoc district committee. In the initial stage of the process, the Harbor School District called upon a set of informed and interested people for their input. While district and community leaders were cautious, they were also convinced that the school district could not consider itself effective or successful if educators and students could not at least openly inquire into controversial values.

Following extensive discussion with Harbor personnel, parents, consultants, and curriculum specialists, the committee eventually recommended that Kunzman's (2006, 2012, 2016) approach to teaching values be examined and, if appropriate, adapted. To facilitate the process, Kunzman's ideas were further studied. District personnel and interested parties discussed his research and identified issues related to the implementation of his ideas. In the process, they learned he (2006, 111) focuses on "what civic virtue requires in an ethically diverse, liberal-democratic society." Among other ideas, he (2006, 79–97) stresses that rigid restrictions on students' comments in schools are unproductive. He, therefore, created a framework for understanding the overlap and differences between private and civic (including political) speech spheres. He (2011, 234) concluded too that people, including students, "must be willing and able to explain to others why ... [they] advocate certain laws or policies, and [be] open to hearing reasons that others have for believing otherwise." His approach rests on developing "mutual understanding, respect, and goodwill" (234). He (2012, 45–8) found it necessary for students and staff to learn a "civic multilingualism," including operating on seven useful claims:

> (1) "Focus on respect instead of tolerance." (2) "Respect doesn't mean endorsement." (3) "Reasonable doesn't mean right." (4) "Religions are internally diverse." (5) "Focus on civic implications, not the beliefs themselves." (6) "Public and private [concerns] mix but shouldn't match." (7) "Students should know their teacher's convictions – about respectful conversation."

The Academy's adaptation of Kunzman's pedagogical approach helped it make small, then substantial, differences in its approach to discussing controversial topics. In addition, open discussions led to a special cadre of teachers volunteering to study economic, political, and religious views that they did not necessarily share but that were shared by some students and parents. These teachers became co-explainers, when well-advised, of their students' and their parents' ideas. At first, Genie Tan, an agnostic elementary teacher, volunteered to study the beliefs of different forms of Islam because she off-and-on saw negative body language and heard censorious remarks by a few of her students about classmates' beliefs. Other teachers later volunteered to study nonreligious, religious, and political beliefs that were held by various Academy students and families. The major purposes of teacher volunteers were to help classroom discussions flow smoothly and to help adherents of diverse beliefs become more comfortable in explaining their ideas. But teachers realized early that most students – and many parents – often do not understand the details of their or their parents' faith. Thus, learning about religions was a means of teachers ensuring that classroom comments were educative and fostered parent-student-teacher interactions.

Later, students with friends who were atheists, Jews, and Buddhists followed the example of Tan and decided to study and then contribute to discussions about their friends' nascent beliefs. From Tan's insightful step, the Academy eventually became known as the school where students could disclose their economic, gender, political, and religious identities without being ridiculed and ostracized. Among the challenges the Academy faces when discussing the political and religious beliefs of students is distinguishing between students explaining their opinions and promoting them. The Academy's first emphasis on understanding beliefs was followed later by students learning the grounds for their opinions. Issues regarding separation of state and religious institutions have arisen intermittently. The community and the district seemingly accepted the idea that the Academy is a school of choice, an experiment in democratically educating diverse peoples in respectful, caring, and reflective ways. Controversial claims are regularly discussed as challenges to be addressed by reasonable and reasoning students, parents, and educators. Yet one afternoon in a recent faculty meeting Maria was told that a group of parents became irritated when their children told them an Academy teacher is seeking to persuade students to become secularists.

A Learning Community

A well-prepared conflictual community is characterized by ongoing educative learning opportunities (Chomsky 2000, 4–10). For Dewey, learning experiences are planned and guided yet often spontaneous and serendipitous. They arise in multiple ways: from student desires to teacher constructions to political and fiscal forces. Fortunately, when conflicts – or, disagreements – are imaginatively addressed, they can yield meaningful and effective learning; they can stimulate problem-solving situations. As a democratic learning community, the Academy is becoming a place of cooperative learning groups; it is an interactive community that explores the questions and problems that students encounter in school and in their broadening worlds. As a result, Academy students frequently experience the joys of playing, creating, and communicating; the pleasures of inquiring, discovering, and constructing; the benefits of understanding, questioning, and respecting; the discomforts of disagreeing, reconsidering, and reconstructing; and the relief of achieving, reconciling, and problem-solving.

Democracy and Learning

In time, Academy classroom and out-of-school challenges led to the activities of, among others, electricians, peace officers, artists, technology specialists, historians, plumbers, religious leaders, grocers, political scientists, physicists, and military personnel. Engaging in the kinds of thought and activities these experts pursue enables students to more broadly understand their worlds and to address problems (Bell and Stevenson 2015; DeFalco 2010). Students form competencies and develop behaviors that lead to personal satisfaction and social growth.

But we have jumped ahead of Dewey's question: "What is learning?" (LW 11, 238–42) and, thereafter, the questions: What is a learning community? What kinds of activities are effective and ethical ways of learning? Should people learn naturally throughout life (LW 17, 213–25; Simpson and Liu 2007)? As expected, Dewey's theory of learning interfaces with other elements of his educational theory, e.g., his understanding of students, teaching, and curriculum. His broad educational theory emerges from his philosophic bent to examine everything in its context (MW 9, 335–6).

Beginning by considering his views of the child's instinctive tendencies or "'active needs'" is useful (LW 11, 239). These needs, while not at first "conscious purposes," are immediately "dynamic moving forces" (239). They urge the infant, child, and youth to search their environments for "materials which will bring satisfaction" (239). The organismic abilities of infants and children include seeing, smelling, tasting, touching, crawling, hearing, reaching, and so forth. Feelings, emotions, and thinking enter the picture too. Later, more reflection and deliberation are perceptible. Immediately, however, an unmet need becomes "a demand" that is met by students interacting with "objects and forces" (239). The child, therefore, begins as an active, not passive, person; they "decide" which environmental objects will bring satisfaction and, later, the objects become forces for "further activity" (239).

The active demands of the student, therefore, help clarify four factors about learning and, thereby, the construction of learning conditions. First, every child has organismic needs: "inner pressure[s]" that are so powerful the objects in the immediate environment "naturally and almost inevitably provide means of satisfaction [for the child] and hence of . . . growth which is learning" (LW 11, 239). Urges and interests propel the child toward understanding "the properties of things and the nature and meaning of his [or her] own powers and acts" (239). Students, thus, are not just active; they are active learners. Second, certain environmental conditions contain powerful attractions for students: classroom materials and physical objects are the means of satisfying a child's active needs and learning interests (239). But it is obvious that an environment requires enrichment if a child is going to keep learning and growing. Caregivers and educators, therefore, must add conditions that meet the emerging needs of each child. In each learning situation, caregivers and educators, who provide material conditions, constitute the essential human conditions. From early in children's lives, guardians and teachers constitute a critical environment, including the conditions of a child's growth, and, at times, the curriculum that is learned. In irreplaceable ways, Academy educators realize that they themselves should be the superb conditions and curricula of a student's world.

The third point is that each child has their own internal learning indicators: the "criterion of success is internal rather than external. Satisfaction is personal; an unaided success in an attempt to stand or walk gives the sense of elation . . ., and this same sense of progressive achievement is the motive power which, joined to need, will carry the child on to greater external perfection" (LW 11, 240). Shifting largely from internal satisfactions to external rewards, however, can create a disequilibrium that wreaks havoc on learning, making it more difficult and less satisfying, inhibiting natural learning inclinations. Sustaining a balance of internal and external satisfactions, then, is achieved as a teacher becomes a student of their students as well as the curricula.

In Dewey's *Educational Lectures before Brigham Young Academy* (LW 17, 213–25), a fourth feature of natural learning is underscored that links two phases of learning that inform the educator of a student's success: the "sensation, or impressions [phase] ... [and the] expression or movement" phase (LW 17, 218). That is, the fruitful flow of a child's needs lead to impressions and then expressions that constitute a complete learning cycle. Without a clear manifestation of the second phase (expression), there is little assurance of the success of the first phase. Dewey also claims that natural learning is a suitable theory for K-16 schools, including university students.

As Dewey further explains his natural learning theory, he raises key questions: Is the learning that occurs in my school community largely educative, miseducative, or noneducative (MW 13, 1–62)? Does the learning produce the power for immediate and ongoing growth of ideas, abilities, and habits? Do students learn that their and others' affections are worth understanding and appraising; their sympathies are worth exploring and evaluating; their inclinations are worth developing and focusing?

Democracy and Curricula

A somewhat common process for curricula selection – minus the linear implications – often includes the ongoing input of business and corporate leaders who usually make valuing leading-edge research more challenging. Moreover, legislators, policymakers, and bureaucrats inject their beliefs about curricula throughout the selection process. Guardians, parents, and educators are invited to make known their experiential and professional opinions too (Pinar et al. 1995). Understanding the pressures of economic-political-class-professional sifting of curricula, Dewey still contends that the ability of educators to make professional judgments about each subject and child is essential if schools are to meet the needs and interests of each student (MW 2, 271–91).

In preparing for their roles in curriculum development, a cadre of Academy faculty examined Dewey's three recommendations about general curriculum selection to evaluate their usefulness. His proposals involve decisions for constructing (a) a "simplified [classroom and school] environment" so that students are not overwhelmed by massive amounts of information, (b) a "purified medium of action" so that the selected curricula do not introduce toxic ideas and gratuitous external demands, and (c) "a broader [classroom and school] environment" to offer more diverse learning conditions than a family or community may want or can provide (MW 9, 24–5). In each of these realms of curricular selection, Dewey claims that "the prudent thinker selects warily," because she is aware of the complex set of political, economic, and educational variables that influence decision making (LW 8, 215). Restated, Dewey's threefold conclusion is that each school has an ethical responsibility to ensure that select learning conditions, pedagogical means, and learning experiences should be personally flexible, developmentally suitable, educationally worthwhile, and experientially broadening. He observes further that each teacher should understand that "respect for [each student's] individuality" is fundamentally manifested in their understanding of a child's emerging, growing, and declining interests and needs (LW 9, 198) and should be "a student of the pupil's mind" as it matures and expands (LW 8, 339) and recognize that to study a student's thinking is fundamentally an "*intellectual* study of the individual" so that the teacher's "sympathetic understanding" of the person informs her or his choices (LW 9, 198; emphasis original).

Dewey predictably argues for collaborative educative experiences that flow from a common mission and set of aims that promote the general end of growth, the "all-around development of the [students'] capacities," especially their attitudinal development, including "a sense of positive power" that is manifested in the "elimination of fear, of embarrassment, of constraint, of self-consciousness" and "of failure and incapacity" (LW 9, 140). He claims too that the fostering "of a confidence, of readiness to tackle difficulties, of actual eagerness to seek problems" to solve is incredibly empowering (140). Moreover, educators, he stresses, should nurture (a) "an ardent faith in human capacity" and (b) "a faith in the capacity of the environment to support worthwhile activities" (140). The crowning attitude to be developed by students is the "willingness to reexamine and if necessary to revise current convictions," because this approach to thinking promotes a lifetime of growth (LW 7, 330).

Closed-mindedness, then, is not admirable; it is an enemy of personal and community inquiry and renewal. Dewey's emphases mean, therefore, that in developmentally and epistemically appropriate ways students need to move beyond just understanding one another and each other's values: they should grow in their understanding the grounds of one another's political, economic, historical, aesthetic, and religious beliefs. The Academy's approach to some epistemic questions includes inviting vetted local representatives of diverse theories to talk through issues and differences with faculty before students and teachers discuss related topics. Vetted representatives are aware of the Academy's orientation to epistemic questions from elementary into middle school through high school and are required to attend a two-hour orientation session before they participate in the school discussions. In part, they are selected for their depth of understanding of particular topics and peoples, their respect in their own communities, and their respect in other local communities.

Dewey concludes, too, that if schools are effectively democratic, they should make "adequate [experiential] provision for all the elements of personality, for the manual [and technological] and overtly constructive powers, for the imaginative and emotional tendencies that later take form in artistic expression, and for the factors that respond to symbolic statement and that prepare the way for distinctively abstract pursuits" and second, schools should constitute "a community in which special aptitudes are gradually disclosed and the transition is made to later careers, in which individuals find happiness and society is richly ... served" (LW 11, 242). Aims that align with these curricular foci include "the progressive development of what is already experienced into fuller and richer and also more organized form, a form that gradually approximates that in which subject-matter is presented to the skilled, mature person" (LW 13, 48). But Dewey observes that school experience "that does not tend to knowledge of more facts and entertaining of more ideas and to a better, a more orderly, arrangement of them" is miseducative (LW 13, 55). Failure to develop these qualities in a student's emerging "adult mind" (MW 2, 279) and mature personality (LW 13, 48) reveals unmet obligations.

Democracy and Education

Of course, Dewey reasons that schools constitute just a small, important aspect of the multiple forces of a democratic education (LW 17, 476), for education itself, broadly speaking, involves:

> everything that shapes what men [and women] really believe, what they most desire, what they are loyal to – the purposes for which they strive and for which they are willing to sacrifice. Schooling is important but its work hardly goes beyond furnishing the tools, the instruments, with which to strive for realization of the deep affections of the heart and the steadfast and informed aims of the head. [Thus education] ... is nothing less than making of character and of mind and the prime question is whether the young are going to have their characters and minds made for them by outside pressures or they are going to have an active share themselves in the making of the world in which they will live. (LW 17, 476)

Three conclusions, at least, are embedded in Dewey's comment: first, societal entities – from school rooms to courtrooms and boardrooms to barrooms – are forces for ethical and unethical formation and, second, every student should have the freedom and a share of the responsibility of shaping their ideas, dispositions, and worlds. Third, to expect schools alone to meet the educational and ethical needs of society is akin to expecting them to ensure world peace and prosperity. Thus, to believe schools constitute a panacea for all or most societal ills is manifestly wrongheaded. Only after rejecting this enticement can societies and schools devote resolute attention to constructing a clear and effective role of ethical development in schools – and elsewhere in society. Only after rejecting false representations of what schools can accomplish will society and its diverse entities be able to think and act more intelligently about plans of ethical development.

When considering a potential overlapping matter, Dewey rejects the idea that an educator has a right to indoctrinate or propagandize students (LW 9, 158–68), even if one claims to be fostering democratic values (LW 11, 414–16). Likewise, he opposes the imposition of ideas designed for adult consummation on children (LW 13, 1–62). Instead, teachers should nourish reflective (LW 8, 111–39) and deliberative thinking (MW 14, 132–45) by means of sound ethical and pedagogical theory and practice. Through these means, educators and students can pursue "active, intelligent participation in the ... eternal rebuilding ... of a genuinely democratic society" (MW 13, 295–303). Educators, then, should not undercut "the moral cause of the dignity and the worth of the individual" (303) by means of demagogue-like pedagogy. Instead, they should reflectively promote "give and take, the pooling of experience" (303). By supporting both respect and open-mindedness, educators support a growing experimental foundation for their democratic faith. Thus, everyone

> should work toward success in carrying on this experiment [of democratic living] in which we are engaged ... the greatest experiment of humanity – that of living together in ways in which the life of each of us is at once profitable in the deepest sense of the word, profitable to [her- or] himself and helpful in the building up of the individuality of others. (303)

For a moment, reflect on Dewey's depiction of an ethically good student or educator: a person who is wise, caring, trustworthy, and deliberative (LW 7, 285). Much more also helps build good school communities, including ensuring that the community is rooted in a democratic philosophy that fosters sympathy, justice, compassion, and freedom on its campus and, with well-planned community involvements, transplants these qualities elsewhere. Doing democracy or living and educating democratically involves "intelligence, energy and courage" (LW 11, 180). As courage, especially, is nurtured in and through democratic schools, this quality provides a stronger platform for spreading democracy into other societal entities. But each societal entity needs to accept its responsibility for cultivating courage and, thereby, a satisfying, meaningful society.

Some falsely consider conscious teaching a prerequisite to learning. Of course, an explicit examination of ethical problems and ethical relationships needs special attention. But the largely implicit elements of communicating values (MW 14, 47) – i.e., habitually living with colleagues and students and supporting defensible features of a collateral curriculum (LW 13, 29) – are necessary too for character and cultural formation (MW 14, 33–42). Nonetheless, ethical concerns should be raised to a conscious level. This is the case because the "conscious life" offers "a continual beginning afresh" each day (MW 9, 370). A largely unconscious life, as Freire (1973) demonstrates, is prey to the random and planned oppressive forces of society.

Here Dewey draws again on his aesthetic understanding to argue that there needs to be a "rhythm of the unconscious and the conscious, of going ahead and of analysis ...in all fruitful thinking" (LW 8, 342). Since everyone "takes some system of ideas for granted," the unconscious system – the taken-for-granted beliefs – should be evaluated intermittently, especially when the system's proposed solutions to problems are ineffective, or even counterproductive (343). One's disposition to question existing assumptions and practices, therefore, is crucial; for, "there is no test of the success of an education more important than whether it nurtures a type of mind that maintains a balance of the unconscious and the conscious" (343).

Studying Dewey's emphasis on teaching practices and their aesthetic and artistic dimensions offers a way to balance the unconscious and conscious elements of his recommended pattern of teaching and learning (EW 5, 94; MW 10). Dewey's memorable aesthetic/ethical figure of speech is worth mentioning: what "the wisest parent wants ..." (EW 1, 5). This wish does not allow a parent to impose their desires on a student but, instead, the parent provides the conditions and context for the maturing child so that they learn to think, feel, act, and live fruitfully as a member of multiple groups. Societies, communities, and schools that work together to provide the necessary material, educational, and human resources for each child, consequently, help create ethically attractive schools and communities. To do less for the child of an*other*, reveals a deep, if sometimes largely hidden personal and societal ugliness, and, over time, a hideousness that is revealed in numerous disparities (Levitsky and

Ziblatt 2018). If Dewey's analyses are defensible, any reasonably prosperous society that has large numbers of children and adults who are materially, emotionally, and intellectually ignored seems to have insignificant interest in democracy or people.

Another aesthetic tool for Dewey, one introduced earlier, is dramatic rehearsal, an ethical-empathetic essential, not just an insightful and enjoyable technique to utilize (LW 8, 200, 320). The artistic process is an imaginative instrument for obtaining a view of and feeling for an ethical situation and its participants. Moreover, it is a tool for evaluating the likely consequences of different hypotheses about handling or solving a problem. Plus, it is an invaluable mechanism for drawing together the thinking of students, parents, and educators. As participants think and learn together with foresight, "deliberation pictures shoals or rocks or troublesome gales as marking the route of a contemplated voyage" until "the various factors in action fit harmoniously together" and "there is a picture of open seas, filled sails and favoring winds" (MW 14, 134). Dewey alludes here both to solving problems and to consummatory aesthetic experiences (LW 10). Dramatic rehearsal, at its best, is an imaginative, experimental, and affective experience that tests solutions to real ethical problems. The process engages not only the whole person but also entire groups.

To further underline the importance of dramatic rehearsal, it seems reasonable to say that an educator, whether addressing their own challenges or working with students on their problems, cannot model doing ethics democratically and effectively without contributions by others. To move in and among crucial ideas, delicate issues, growing students, and, intermittently, disenfranchised adults, educators also need to access current research findings about learning, curricula, students, and artistic practices since education demands "the most perfect and intimate union of science and art" (EW 5, 94). When using Dewey's moral science method – examining an issue, addressing a problem, or evaluating an intervention – educators also need to exercise the "ability to seize what is significant and to let the rest go"; to think like "the expert, the connoisseur, the *judge*" (MW 8, 213; emphasis original). But "the greatest and commonest mistake" that is made is that of forgetting that learning itself is "a necessary incident of dealing with real situations" (MW 8, 212).

Out of appreciation for law, science, and the humanities and arts, the educator gains insight into teaching as well as into learning, leading, and community building. When an educator, official leader or not, has this expanding intellectual background and mentored practical experience, Dewey argues they are able to practice successfully "the supreme art" of "giving shape to human powers" (EW 5, 94). The imaginative, creative, passionate, and forward-looking person society considers a teacher is described by Dewey in myriads of ways (Simpson, Jackson, and Aycock 2005), but the description of the teacher as "a great orchestral conductor" (LW 11, 544) is, perhaps, his most beautiful. The balancing of multiple duties with different individuals and groups by a principal or superintendent is likewise a great artistic undertaking; for, they need to be mindful of the minds, bodies, and personalities of students, colleagues, and parents while foregrounding, at least for themself, moment-by-moment disclosures, that point to compelling data and potential fulfillments. Indeed, sometimes, "the controlling features" of a problematic situation are perceived and comprehended during the educator's most engaged moments (LW 13, 32).

Dewey scatters other pedagogical tidbits throughout his writings. In *How We Think* (LW 8), for instance, he writes that the educator needs to uproot ambiguities and fuzzy thinking (244), foster a delight in thinking (298), avoid dominating class interactions (313), develop a "rhythm between the extensive and the intensive" study of issues (322), possess intellectual depth in order to focus one's thoughts on students (338), exhibit tactfulness when guiding discussions (326), diagnose student needs quickly and accurately (326), identify triggering or central problems (329), question artfully in order to probe deeply (331), require reasonableness as well as participation in activities (324, 334), allow time for "leisurely mental digestion" (336), appreciate the volatility of "*emotionally* colored" issues (340; emphasis original), and serve as the "director of [the] processes of [intellectual] exchange[s]" among students (LW 13, 37).

Conclusion

What are the characteristics of a good school? That is a question that can be answered partially and episodically but not categorically. Also, adopting Figure 7.1 as a checklist is counterproductive since checklists are often converted into mechanical processes; they stop being stimuli for reflection and deliberation. Of course, there are many ethical continuities and empirical generalizations that enlighten diverse contexts and situations that require flexibility as well as form (Pappas 2008, 51–5, 255–9). For example, a comprehensive answer for one population group is seldom, if ever, the precise answer for all students and schools. Besides, each school that wants to be democratic should grapple with the construction of its ethic, mission, and curricula. Similarly, no one ethical framework is likely to provide sufficient insight into what constitutes good peoples, schools, and societies. Indeed, any answer to this question needs room for the judgments of well-informed and richly experienced local educators, updating by growing bodies of experiential and scientific knowledge, and refining by researchers, parents, citizens, and, always, contrarians. The absence of definitive answers should not be considered a problem; for education and educators can and should continue to work toward the improvement of classrooms and schools as knowledge advances and societal needs change.

The foreseeable future seems to offer many families, students, and educators the opportunity to live and learn in democratic communities. Communities should grapple not only with the question of what is a good person, school, society, and world but with questions about what characterizes good or ethical means of reaching these ends. Similarly, searching for answers to the question of who a good leader is will continue to need attention. Accessing ethical, empirical, and interdisciplinary studies (Bitterman, Goldring, and Gray 2013; Eisenbeiss 2012; House et al. 2004; Starratt 2003) is likely to require more attention than has been given by many schools in the past. Likewise, a good school community understands and develops its powers, especially its student powers. In doing so, it clarifies how personal and community power can be organized for the good of students and society. Ultimately, good schools foster their and others' powers in order to promote the individual and common good.

Dewey argues that a good school is a deeply democratic community that is characterized by respect and regard for everyone, including students and their intellectual, social, emotional, and physical development. The school is also an engaged learning community that is characterized by cooperative inquiry, open discussion, and reflective dialogue. Moreover, it facilitates students' demonstration of wisdom, their construction and pursuit of meaningful lives, their trustworthiness in human relationships, their thoughtfulness in interpersonal evaluative situations, and their deliberativeness when attending to personal and social problems. The "moral measure" for graduates is how activities, environments, and proposals influence individual and group "impulse[s] and habits" (MW 14, 202). They ask many questions: Does a recommendation "liberate or suppress, ossify or render flexible, divide or unify interest? Is perception quickened or dulled? Is memory made apt and extensive or narrow and diffusely irrelevant? Is imagination diverted to fantasy and compensatory dreams, or does it add fertility to life? Is thought creative or pushed one side into pedantic specialisms?" (202–3) Ultimately, does education, formal and informal, "foster conditions that widen the horizon of others and give them command of their own powers, so that they can find their own happiness in their own fashion?" (203).

Discussion Questions

1. Does Dewey dwell too much on economic and political forces and power? How do you support your answer?
2. Which three features of a Democratic School Community (Figure 7.1) do you think are most important? Why did you select these three items?
3. As you think through Dewey's ideas about democracy, which points do you find most insightful? Most troublesome?
4. Identify an ethical problem embedded in the Academy that seems insufficiently addressed. What are the competing goods in the situation?
5. What would you revise, subtract, or add to Dewey's qualities of a good school?

RELATED READINGS

Callan, Eamonn. 2016. "Education in Safe and Unsafe Spaces." *Philosophical Inquiry in Education* 24 (1): 64–78.

Callan offers a careful analysis of "dignity safety" and "intellectual safety" in schools. Parsing various issues, he affirms the necessity of the former as a classroom ally of "students' equal dignity" and classroom civility but rejects the notion that student ideas should be safe or protected from reflective analysis.

Dewey, John. 1903. "Democracy in Education." In *Essays on the New Empiricism*, 229–39. Vol. 3 of *John Dewey: The Middle Works, 1899–1924*, edited by Jo Ann Boydston. Carbondale and Edwardsville: Southern Illinois University Press, 1977.

Dewey discusses what he labels the ethical principle on which public education rests (the responsibility of society to free people's minds) and the democratic ideal of individuality (the responsibility of each person to use their abilities to make decisions).

Forrest, Michelle. 2008. "Sensitive Controversy in Teaching to Be Critical." *Paideusis* 18 (1): 80–93.

Forrest's approach to classroom issues is rooted in her high school and university teaching. Through the lenses of a caring, empathic feminist, she discusses what, if anything, a teacher is obligated to say when residents attribute racist attitudes and behavior to local peace officers.

Greene, Maxine. 1978. "Wide-Awakeness and the Moral Life." In *Landscapes of Learning*, 42–52. New York: Teachers College Press.

Greene notes the powerful obstacles that seek to limit and destroy identity and agency and stresses the need to become liberated. Becoming wide awake is an essential part of developing a sense of self, agency, and freedom.

Hytten, Kathy. 2015. "Ethics in Teaching for Democracy and Social Justice." *Democracy and Education* 23 (2): 1–10.

Hytten clarifies why she supports teacher preparation in both social justice issues and the ethical dimensions of classroom teaching. She encourages the development of reflective humility, open-mindedness, and sympathetic attentiveness.

Kunzman, Robert. 2015. "Talking with Students Who Already Know the Answers: Navigating Ethical Certainty in Democratic Dialogue." In *Religion in the Classroom: Dilemmas for Democratic Education*, edited by Jennifer Hauver James with Simone Schweber, Robert Kunzman, Keith C. Barton, and Kimberly Logan, 79–89. New York: Routledge.

Kunzman discusses how ethical certainty often obstructs dialogue in schools and how educators can help students better circumnavigate potential dialogic blockers. He emphasizes distinguishing four sets of concepts: understanding-endorsement, public-private realms, humility-relativism, and deliberation-consensus.

Saltmarsh, J. 1996. "Education for Critical Citizenship: John Dewey's Contribution to the Pedagogy of Community Service Learning." *Michigan Journal of Community Service Learning* 3 (1): 13–21.

Saltmarsh provides insight into both Dewey's thoughts and how they may be employed to engage students and staff in service learning for critical citizenship. His identification of the five ways Dewey informs critical citizenship experience is discerning.

Case Study: The Either/Or Situation

"This is getting complicated," Maria said to Yoon Yú, her most trusted colleague. In two weeks, a majority of students were planning to walk out of school to lead a protest march they had largely created. They saw it as the ultimate responsibility of a socially responsible person, an engaged citizen, to help correct the marginalization, if not demonization, of immigrants in the country if not world.

The issues that had galvanized her students were recent changes in immigration policy, the incarceration or deportation of families and, in general, the description of newcomers as criminals and destructive forces. It was a set of issues that had affected Maria and her extended family her whole life.

She was proud that the Academy students were in the vanguard, organizing the march that now would include community members, politicians, celebrities, and people of all backgrounds. The local figures who resisted the project had described her students as puppets of all sorts of agendas, but the media coverage made clear that some of her secondary students had sparked the idea and provided the energy and planning for the march. Consequently, they were blamed or credited with turning the march into an international event. For Maria, the event would epitomize the identity and overarching goals of the Academy: to develop students into informed, engaged, and committed citizens.

Most of the faculty supported the students and planned to participate. Many were giving academic credit, especially for active roles in organizing the march. The schools' parents were largely thrilled and proud of their students and supported them in various ways. It had brought together a substantial portion of the school community in a collaboration for children and families locally and spurred similar activities nationally and internationally. In fact, students of all cultural backgrounds from many schools had enthusiastically joined in the process, just as their parents had.

There were students, faculty, and parents, however, who were reluctant to be associated with the march or have the school identified as in some sense sponsoring it. Some simply disagreed politically, but others were nervous about the children being involved. The march had clearly become larger than just a local project, as supporters and antagonists had voiced opinions through media and via the Internet, from all over the world. There were opponents that were planning countermeasures the same day and a lot of anger expressed on various sides and perspectives, as was not surprising since the event gathered the attention of all sorts of people and groups.

Some student leaders had rapidly become public figures – Maria was pleased some were captivating in front of audiences and cameras. But a public person gets trolled and threatened on social media, and several students had received critical remarks and even threats to their lives. Such degradations arose both locally and across social media. It was often ugly and frightening for the students and their parents. In the school, the issues of security for the march got more complicated and serious as publicity got broader and some reactions more vitriolic.

Within the school, there was much unity balanced by opposition of some faculty and students. Some saw the whole event as a distraction from academic work. They said the students were distracted and that some discounted the importance of "just doing school" versus changing the society and making a powerful statement for justice. There were arguments, to be sure, among students and faculty. Maria told everyone – faculty, students, and parents – that no one *had* to participate and that academic duties needed to be attended to as well. Plus, students not participating could earn extra credit.

Some faculty, students, and parents disagreed with the whole idea as well as the values that underlay the march. It was not easy to oppose an idea when so many people inside the school and beyond were passionately opposed to the anti-immigrant movement in the country. One argument offered from many sources was that school was for education, not indoctrination, and this whole event was too political and was being forced on lots of students and others. Locally some pressure was brought against the school board to stop it and the city council to deny the parade license, but the mayor, some city council members, and some of the school board had announced they would walk with the students, especially after a few celebrities promised to come and march.

The key planning issues dealt with how to handle school personnel and students who did not want to go. The elementary grades were more complicated because some parents were uncomfortable with the idea of preteens marching with all the uncertainty of what might happen. Of course, some parents were more than ready to take the whole family, including young kids. It was a celebration in some sense as much as a statement of discontent and anger. Logistically, it was not that difficult, apart from the fact that the teachers' students who stayed behind would have to be supervised. In other Harbor schools, plenty of students and faculty wanted to participate, but in differing proportions to the Academy; in some, the majority of parents clearly were opposed to releasing students for the march. The board felt divided on how to handle the situation. A minority of the board said they could not condone losing half a day of instruction for the march, but in all schools there were currents for and against letting any student who wanted to march have the opportunity. The board in general believed they were all caught between a rock and a hard place, even if they were, in theory, a supporter of the march and its goals and principles. They did not see a win-win situation for them, nor for central administration. Both groups were cautiously trying to please as many people as possible and intoning platitudes about protecting the right not to participate as being as important as providing the opportunity so long as it was safe and "developmentally appropriate." They offered support about the importance in allowing free speech and an opportunity for responsible actions and criticism about governmental policies and actions.

The march was a few weeks hence and Maria needed to keep the school climate peaceful and ensure classrooms were kept focused on school and curriculum during that time. As blowback started to crystalize, some supporters were getting angrier at the students and teachers who either opposed the march or just opted out. Those who were not enthusiasts felt more under pressure – like they were being driven to leave the school community as skeptics. She felt that she needed the help of the student leaders and the teachers to help keep the school calm and ensure space for those who opposed the march or opted out. She wanted to avoid having a disciplinary event just as she wanted the staff and faculty to remain colleagues and a team after this event was over. She knew how volatile a school could be when filled with true believers and a loss of empathy or tolerance. She needed to protect all students and support all faculty, irrespective of her own views and passion. She needed a clear statement of her role in this whole megillah. She needed to make all the school community understand that she would be fair and loyal to them as well as those they disagreed with.

Then another shoe dropped. The student leaders for the march came to see her and asked her to march with them, at the front of the march as a clear statement of her commitment to the fight for justice. They said that everyone agreed she was a symbol for everything the school stood for. She was the face of the school. If she did not march, supporters would feel abandoned. One student said, "This is a situation where we must stand together. We are only asking you to speak and act as a leader in this school and its community for justice and fairness. We need you, but you need us and this march to show that what you say is what you do and who you are."

Maria's thought as the young woman spoke these words was how magnificent the student was and that she and her peers represented a culmination of where she might have to choose between what she had worked to be and become her whole life and her role or career in this district. She remembered her grandmother's words: "It is one or the other, no alternate route."

Within minutes of deciding what she would do, Yoon, the school counselor, brought her new information. Matthew, the assistant principal, was colluding with an ambitious board member who hoped to come out of this situation with support to jump into a higher political position – mayor. The board member believed that with this event he could leverage a campaign based on his opposition to the march. And if there was conflict, he might ride the revulsion to the mayor's office. He offered Matthew a place on his coattails if he would stir things up. Matthew would promote the rumor that the march was a step towards getting the city to become a sanctuary city and to stack the city council and school board with liberal people. If Maria is publicly connected to the march, the narrative would be this scenario had been her's and others' plan from the beginning.

So far, she had not been a huge figure in all this furor, focusing on keeping things relatively calm in the building and assuaging intra-district and central administration fears as best she could. But walking at the front of the parade would make her a target to her enemies, as well as generating more enemies. It would be seen as putting ideology before her professional duties.

Was her grandmother right and was this the moment when it was finally just one or the other? If she had to lose the trust of some groups of people, who would she choose? There was a moment when she wondered if she could find a narrow option that allowed her to survive without sacrificing her sense of integrity, as she had been forced to do so many times before, each one seeming a slice had been taken from her. This time the choice was inextricable. At least she was aware of her situation.

She had to choose, she believed, and she also believed that her action would go a long way toward defining her career and her selfhood. She hoped that her students would learn, without any guilt, of the consequences – whatever they would be – of her choice to join the march. Should she, she wondered, make her answer contingent upon the student leaders' acceptance of three conditions?

QUESTIONS

1. How easy would your decision be in the above situation if you were Maria? How difficult would it be if you were yourself in a similar situation? Why?
2. Is Maria ultimately the person responsible for the students' plans? What responsibilities do the superintendent, board, faculty, and supporters have?
3. If you were new Superintendent Amemantine, what type of conversation would you have with Maria?
4. If you were Maria, what kind of final details would you mention to faculty, staff, and students? What priorities would you mention?
5. If you agreed to march with the students, would you make your participation contingent upon any student agreements? If so, what agreements would you underline with the student leaders and participants?

Epilogue

The very idea of democracy ... must be continually explored afresh; it has to be constantly discovered, and rediscovered, remade and reorganized; while the political and economic and social institutions in which it is embodied have to be remade and reorganized to meet the changes that are going on in the development of new needs on the part of human beings and new resources for satisfying these needs.
—John Dewey "The Challenge of Democracy to Education" (LW 11, 182)

Dewey's ethical thought is more complex and nuanced than we have had time to disclose, and, as this epigraph indicates, democracy is dynamic and open to ongoing research, reflection, and reconstruction. Political, economic, social, and educational institutions too need reconstruction, as societal change, research, and dialogue inform people that certain social challenges are not being addressed as equitably or successfully as others. The need for a school's or district's transformation is merited when, for example, it is not based on the best available research, theorizing, experience, and reflection. This means that intelligent transformation cannot be rooted in fads, whether prompted by misinformed legislation, pedagogical fashion, quasi-psychology, or pseudo-philosophy. Among the great opportunities and tasks of educators, including professors, is that of collaboratively sifting through and contributing to educationally informed bodies of knowledge so that students, societies, and aspiring and practicing educators are better educated and increasing proportions of children have a reasonable opportunity to pursue a meaningful life.

To continue fostering educational practice that enables people to pursue a meaningful life, we revisit aspects of Dewey's approach to ethics to highlight and enlarge upon them. In Chapter 1, we note Dewey's answer to the question of what educators can expect from ethics. Among other matters, he claims that ethical study is a worthwhile, significant, and transdisciplinary inquiry (MW 14, 204–5). This means, first, that doing ethics is a meaningful pursuit because it asks questions about one's life and profession, including personal fairness and social justice, and, second, it suggests answers that are characterized by warrant or confirmed knowledge claims. Answers to ethical questions should lead to inquiry, data collection, analysis, cogent arguments, and warrant. Third, it means doing ethics clarifies concepts, arguments, problematic situations, and choices. Ethics too offers clarity about living well, working productively, and disagreeing fruitfully but does not on every occasion indicate precisely how to resolve or solve a problem. But the inquiry is still valuable. That is, inquiry into a controversy can inform a group of educators that they should continue to care for one another and work together without a consensus on an important pedagogical or curricular question. For instance, coming to understand that an inclination to coerce staff agreement is professionally and democratically problematic and can indicate that freedom, not force, is merited because more data and deliberation may reveal a clearer choice. Fourth, it is clear that ethics frequently offers enlightenment into how ethics itself should be undertaken: when viewed comprehensively as an ethical science it is not a stand-alone method of inquiry but inquiry that draws on and contributes to a variety of fields, including psychology, law, education, aesthetics, neuroscience, and anthropology.

Dewey himself relies heavily on philosophy, psychology, anthropology, biology, history, and the arts. He notes that doing ethics is not a dogmatic process but a democratically reflective one that is based on listening to alternative opinions and revising one's own view as merited. Thus, the ethically minded educator understands – given the complexities of the fields that clarify contemporary ethics – why schools "have to be remade and reorganized to meet the changes that are going on" (LW 11, 182). When there is an ethical stalemate, it may reveal the need to ask: Do we need to (re)explore other disciplines that may better inform this issue?

The remaining threads of Dewey's thought issue from his first question: What Can Educators Expect from Ethics? The second thread we consider is in Chapter 2, What Does Sympathy and Empathy Have to Do with Ethics? When discussing this chapter, we observe that his use of the word *sympathy* appears to include the contemporary ideas of both the affective and cognitive aspects of empathy (Maxwell 2008, 25–35). "Sympathy is the animating mold of moral judgment ... because it furnishes the most efficacious *intellectual* standpoint. It is the tool, *par excellence*, for resolving complex situations" (LW 7, 270; emphasis original). Embedded in Dewey's comment are the ideas of an "animating mold," "*intellectual* standpoint," and "tool, *par excellence*" (270). In his understanding of sympathy, there is organismic animation, insight, and inquiry. The sympathetic educator, therefore, evaluates their affections and cultivates their and others' sympathetic insight into students and colleagues.

A person, conversely, could immediately indulge "a dominant emotion," and move instantaneously to overt behavior, giving way to what Rogers (2009, 180) terms "emotional intensity." Dewey (LW 7, 191; emphasis original) concludes, "many ends *seem* good while we are under the influence of strong passion" but turn out to be, upon contemplation, "bad." He asserts too that "a desire may be inflamed to a practically uncontrollable degree by dwelling upon [envisioned] . . . pleasures" (LW 7, 194). Being intoxicated with the envisioned pleasures of pseudo-justice, anger, or revenge, in online, face-to-face groups, or semi-private settings is an emotional indulgence that is likely to produce harmful consequences.

But emotional intensity itself, even if bypassing reflection on occasion, can be entirely appropriate. Most people do not need to process an in-depth meaning of the term *excellent* on a paper, an A on a chemistry examination, or a "yes" to the question, Are you free Saturday night? One can smile, do the pre-medical school jig, or erupt with joy without delay. Similarly, in ordinary circumstances, one can break into a series of high fives after reading the words: "Neat writing, Dilber." "Terrific feedback, Heejin." These kinds of intense emotions are constituent elements of healthy living. Conversely, the well-planned conversations and demonstrations that lead to more funds for students, staff, educators, and school facilities are also part of healthy living.

The shadowy emotional side, nevertheless, can show itself, too, e.g., as when immediate anger leads a person or group to disseminate hate messages. An entire class, group of followers, listserv, or scattered strangers can skip from intense feelings of identification with the reported pain or mistreatment of another to anger and outrage in a millisecond, without any provocation, except an electronic message containing unverified information. Revulsion and disgust can transform someone into what appears to be an entirely different person, someone determined to punish immediately a whispered offender who is actually blameless. Establishing one's self as a personal dispenser of justice is filled with ethical concerns, especially since many people can be emotionally manipulated easily.

Later, Dewey (see Chapter 6) writes of the role of wisdom in leading one to consider and govern strong, sudden impulses that may seriously impair one's present and desired future. But in this context, he also describes the beauty of sympathy or feeling with those who are experiencing pain and pleasure. Likewise, he mentions the temporary assumption or understanding of others' perspectives so that they are better understood, related to, taught, and welcomed into communities, schools, and beyond. He (LW 13, 1–62) says, in principle, that the impulses that have been developed into desires, plans, and ideals can protect a person from intense, underdeveloped impulses by integrating them with other well-considered and developed interests and purposes. Thus, impulses are not necessarily destructive. But they need to be asserted "deliberately" (MW 14, 62). To develop into a sympathetic educator ideally indicates that one is a growing ethical person and professional.

Our next questions – How Are Ethical Principles Useful? and What Does Regard for People Imply? – appear in Chapters 3 and 4. In terms of focus, Chapter 3 provides a general overview of how Dewey understood ethical principles and Chapter 4 provides his interpretation of, possibly, his umbrella ethical principle, the comprehensive principle of respect or care for people that offers insight into how other principles may show a specific regard for one's self, others, groups, and, ultimately, for the common good. Certainly, the principle of regard or caring for others may mean that staff and students conclude that they should demonstrate concern by including new people in their broad friendship circles, inviting the isolated to events with them, and evaluating them generously, not judgmentally. Dewey further argues that principles, when warranted, should basically displace ethical rules; for, principles are intellectual instruments used to examine problematic ethical situations. Specifically, he identifies the relationship between personal experience, developed principles, direct consequences, immediate values, and personal judgment in resolving a practical dilemma:

> a principle evolves in connection with the course of experience, being a generalized statement of what sort of consequences and values tend to be realized in certain kinds of situations; ... [it] is primarily intellectual, a method and scheme for judging, and is practical secondarily because of what it discloses ... (LW 7, 276)

Dewey (LW 7, 280) clarifies later that "A moral principle gives" an educator or student "a basis for looking at and examining [or a "method or scheme for judging" (276)] a particular question ... It holds before him [or her] certain possible aspects of an act; it warns him against taking a short ... view ... It economizes his thinking supplying ... the bearings of his desires ...; it guides his thinking ..." Thus, teaching students to show respect or deference for people requires reflection that goes far beyond encouraging them to give their subway seats to the elderly or injured. A principle's serviceability evolves as other situations arise and require reflection. A principle provides perspective, emphasis, warnings, bearings, and guidance.

Rogers (2009, 177–9) adds an interesting slant on Dewey's approach to principles. He claims they ultimately constitute a "cumulative wisdom" that enables school and district leaders to make appropriate decisions. Given the discussion of the ethical or good person in Chapter 6, it seems appropriate to add too that ethical principles, duties, and virtues constitute important aspects of the intellectual and experiential knowledge dimensions of wisdom.

The central question in Chapter 5, What Is a Problematic Ethical Situation? may seem to have a simple answer: it is a situation that is characterized by doubt, conflict, disequilibrium, and complexity among people and their desires, obligations, and virtues and, for many, right and wrong ends (LW 5, 279). But the nature of a situation, its characters and participants' dispositions and habits are unique dimensions in each situation. Therefore, educators need to work collaboratively to understand "the arbiter" (LW 6, 5) of the meaning of each person's comments, the "range and vitality" of one's experiences, interests, and passions (LW 6, 20), the power and uniqueness of both an external culture and an internal "culture of mind and spirit" (LW 7, 320), and the environment and conditions that frame a problematic situation (LW 13, 25). But educators know they cannot possibly understand all of these things about hundreds of students, colleagues, parents, and guardians without drawing on the knowledge of others. They collaborate as they investigate.

Wisdom, based in part of one's growing knowledge and understanding, facilitates the recognition, and resolution of problematic moral situations. When complex ethical situations arise, therefore, it seems well-advised in principle that a school's best prepared and growing problem-solvers be involved in appropriate ways. Ideally, pools of sophisticated school problem-solvers exist and are expanding. Given that ethical situations are constantly arising and virtually every school-based educator encounters them daily, ongoing preparation of staff is necessary.

The Academy's typical emphases in ethical development sessions includes preparing a new cadre of educators and students each year in the following areas: understanding the knowledge bases of school or community-based ethical decision-making; developing the ability to make immediate, delayed, and gradual ethical judgments and interventions; and recognizing the limits of one's expertise and the need for collegial and professional support. Among the most popular staff- and student-recommended topics at the Academy are "Confessions of a . . .; How

I Learned Classroom, School and/or District Ethics," and "What Do I Need to Understand in Order to Enter the Ethical Worlds of My Students/Teachers?" Popular student topics include: "Is This Really an Ethical Question? Why?" "How Can We Make the Consequences of Behavior More Educative?" And "Is It Appropriate to Give Students a Greater Voice in School Ethical Decision-Making?"

Another popular educator topic came from *Ethics*: "There is no better evidence of a well formed moral character than knowledge of when to raise the moral issue and when not. It implies a sensitiveness to values which is the token of a balanced personality" (LW 7, 170). The Academy leadership and faculty agree that since they have decided from the beginning it was important for educators to take measured risks, staff development would include other topics too. The most controversial discussions center around the phrases: "a well formed moral character," "when to raise the moral issue and when not," "sensitiveness to values," and "balanced personality." Dewey's final two sentences of the above partially quoted paragraph close with a threefold concern: "so callous or so careless . . . so unbalanced" (LW 7, 170). When addressed, outside professionals often address this trilogy.

Our penultimate question in Chapter 6 could easily be phrased differently, e.g., What are the qualities of an ethical person? What types of behaviors might one expect of a good person? What skills, abilities, attitudes, dispositions, and habits characterize a well-developed ethical educator? Even though we like the details identified in the immediate prior question, we selected the title What Are the Qualities of an Ethical Educator? because, in part, it facilitates both affirming and denying particular answers. Affirming Dewey's earlier thoughts is often easy: the good self should be

> *wise* . . ., looking to an inclusive satisfaction and . . . subordinating the satisfaction of an immediately urgent single appetite; . . . should be *faithful* in acknowledgement of the claims involved in its relations with others; . . . should be solicitous, *thoughtful*, in the award of praise and blame, . . . and, finally, should be *conscientious* and have the active will to discover new values and to revise former notions. (LW 7, 285; emphasis original)

One can, of course, attribute to Dewey via contemporary assessment lens an almost purely quantifiable set of interests: skills that are delineated in measurable details, abilities assessed on a scale of zero to ten, and attitudes, dispositions, and habits listed and specified in observable ways. These kinds of assessments alone, while often informative, will miss or distort the heart of Dewey's ethic. Definitely, it is crucial that an educator have the skills that will help them to address ethically problematic situations. But following an essentially quantifiable paradigm they will fail to attend seriously to the qualities that are needed in personal ethical development: "character consists of an abiding identification of impulse with thought in which impulse provides the drive while thought supplies consecutiveness, patience, and persistence, leading to *a unified course of conduct*" (LW 7, 190; emphasis added). To further clarify, Dewey adds, "*Mere* thinking" (190; emphasis original) will "not lead to action; thinking must be taken up into vital impulse and desire in order to have body and weight in action" (190). Hence, a person must have a "spontaneous sense of the claims of others" in order to address their rights and needs (270). Which personal and professional behavioral patterns should a candidate consistently exhibit? "In truth," Dewey asserts "only that self is good which wants and strives energetically for good consequences; that is, those consequences which promote the well-being of those affected by the act" (288). In schools, educators, students, and parents should be involved in identifying and clarifying these consequences.

How can ethical educators be recognized? Candidly, they may not be recognizable initially and at times thereafter, for being ethical is not easily observed when only isolated bits of public information are known. Dewey's answer, therefore, encourages looking for "a unified course of conduct" (LW 7, 190). What do personal engagements of two-three-four months and years say about her interests, desires, and activities? What is she like on stressful occasions, with students and parents, and in leadership roles? What does he post on social media? What do his offhand comments convey about fairness, freedom, and professional responsibility? How diverse or uniform are others' impressions of him? Also, one might conclude that Dewey would advise against giving too much weight to the "*mere* thinking" (190) of people – and probably mere talking and credentialing.

Answers to the following questions may also be useful: How has wisdom shown itself in prior and present positions? What ethical principles guide her decisions? Which virtues and qualities characterize his everyday life? How approachable and reasonable is the person when working with colleagues, staff, parents, and students, especially when there are serious disagreements? Does the person foresee problems and help others avoid them (LW 7, 191–9)? Does the individual reveal a personal understanding of the need for balance in the areas of regard for personal desires and regard for others' desires (220)? Does the person exhibit behaviors and attitudes of being the "'only pebble on the beach'" (224)? Does he welcome inquiry into rules, policies, and practices (230–1)? Is sympathy noticeable? Do those who know him well provide examples of his "kindliness, . . . sincerity and fairness" (242)?

But there are a multitude of other valuable questions. For instance, Dewey says there are legitimate and worthwhile insights offered by intuition theories, aesthetic capacities, and ethical sensitives:

> A keen eye and a quick ear are not of themselves guarantees of correct knowledge of physical objects. But they are conditions without which such knowledge cannot arise. Nothing can make up for the absence of immediate sensitiveness . . . A person must *feel* the qualities of acts as one feels with the hands the qualities of roughness and smoothness in objects, before he has an inducement to deliberate or material with which to deliberate. (LW 7, 268–9; emphasis original)

Moreover, he (271) claims, like Aristotle, that a good person has "a fine and well-grounded character" that enables them to respond immediately to simple problems but is likely to admit to being "perplexed as to what to do in novel, complicated situations." But, finally, fault-seeking inquiries are, candidly, unfair and unethical and should not be a means of evaluating current or prospective colleagues.

Our final chapter, What Are the Characteristics of a Good School?, focuses on creating a school community that fosters the desirable qualities of learning, cooperating, deliberating, respecting, engaging, disagreeing, planning, sharing, leading, understanding, agreeing, and behaving. As "a miniature community and one in close interaction with modes of associated experience beyond [a] school," it is designed to help create the "power [of students] to share effectively in [school and external] social life" (MW 9, 370). In the process, "it forms" student character that is "socially necessary" and that is "interested in that continuous [learning and] readjustment which is essential to growth" (370).

But there may be much more to a Deweyan-informed school. Ideally, it is a small school that is characterized by democratic organizational values, policies, and practices, a casual but planned culture, one that is staffed by professional educators, frequented by other adults who share their expertise, and are noted for intergenerational learning groups (LW 9, 136–40). In addition, it is concerned for every student and each aspect of their development. As such, it attends to social, emotional, intellectual, physical, and ethical growth. Critically, it ensures that each student and staff member has ample opportunities to develop a rich sense of belongingness, a togetherness that helps build confidence, courage, and interest in the common good. In this mission, a student is educated in such ways that they can become "a voter," a parent, "a worker" (EW 5, 58). The formal curriculum includes at least inquiry in "science, in art, in history; command of the fundamental methods of inquiry and the ... tools of ... communication; it means a trained and sound body, a skillful eye and hand; habits of industry, perseverance, and, above all, *habits of serviceableness*" (58; emphasis added). Habits of serviceableness, in formal and informal ways, are interwoven into good schools as they promote skills, attitudes, and habits of leadership and social and personal responsibility. In this way, habits learned at school become "animated by the breath of moral life" (63).

In good schools, educators are aware of the kinds of people they and their students are becoming; they understand their weaknesses and virtues, they recognize the emergence and blossoming of more comprehensive views of a good life. Similarly, they recognize the growth of students' diverse insights into and portrayals of "decencies" (EW 5, 58), "loveliness and grace" (MW 5, 373), "nobility and dignity" (373), and "enduring grace and charm" (LW 10, 57). Plus, they appreciate the complementary roles of justice and mercy in judging matters (MW 5, 372–3). Educators also learn with students about "the beauty, grace and loveliness of the universe" and their responsibility to help care for it (EW 2, 280). But they also understand that people are not born with robust views of democracy, that the concept is not static, and that no one understands how it should be operationalized in every cultural, economic, educational, and political detail (LW 11, 181–90). Educators, therefore, have the tremendous opportunity to support the creation and reconstruction of democratic learning communities and, thereby, become an integral part of the social and intellectual forces that impact directly and indirectly democratic schools, districts, and societies.

What are educators' most admirable motives and rewards for engaging in this democratic project? In "Democracy in Education," Dewey (MW 3, 239) provides a partial answer:

> In education meet the three most powerful motives of human activity. Here are found sympathy and affection, the going out of the emotions to the most appealing and the most rewarding object of love – a little child. Here is found also the flowering of the social and institutional motive, interest in the welfare of society and in its progress and reform by the surest and shortest means. Here, too, is found the intellectual and scientific motive, the interest in knowledge, in scholarship, in truth for its own sake, unhampered and unmixed with any alien ideal. Copartnership of these three

motives – of affection, of social growth, and of scientific inquiry – must prove as nearly irresistible as anything human when they are once united. And, above all else, recognition of the spiritual basis of democracy, the efficacy and responsibility of freed intelligence, is necessary to secure this union.

Of course, many other Deweyan ideas seem relevant to educators. Charles Wood (MW 13, 426) mentions one set of ideas in his interview of Dewey, shortly after his return to the USA from a twenty-six-month visit to China (Martin 2002, 314–27). Wood notes that Dewey did not

> care whether a student of his is radical or conservative, Orthodox or heretic, Christian, Jewish, Confucian or infidel: what he is concerned with is whether any particular student's mind is alive and doing well. Is it advancing? Is it coming out? Is it feeding well on the truths it is discovering? Or is there some bias, some prejudice or, more important, some fearsome dread which is keeping it from developing into a serviceable mentality? (MW 13, 426)

This orientation is consistent with Dewey's great concern for social, political, and school communication. In *The Public and Its Problems*, Dewey claims that "the essential need [of the public] . . . is the improvement of the methods of debate, discussion and persuasion. That is *the* problem of the public" (LW 2, 365; emphasis original). This problem seems to remain for many, if not most, publics a cardinal conundrum. If one focuses on the school context as a part of the public, Dewey's statement may require tweaking and must be understood in the light of the somewhat hidden but essential virtues of listening and sympathy, for "communication . . . is the process of creating participation, of making common . . . meaning and definiteness to the experience of the one who utters as well as . . . those who listen" (LW 10, 249). In democratic contexts, everyone plays a vital role in addressing these speaking and listening challenges.

Equipped with the aforementioned streams of reflection, Dewey argues that each generation of existing and former students (LW 14, 271–2) needs to struggle together for the rebirth of democracy (266), otherwise it will wither and die. For a people to succeed democratically, each generation must renew its commitment to communication, cooperation, fraternity, and freedom (266, 277–9). Among other valued outcomes, intelligence – energized by passion – enables fraternity, justice, equity, and peace. Fraternity, Dewey claims, is the "essence of cooperation" (277); it fosters understanding and acceptance as well as avoidance of conflict, animosity, and war (278).

An Interview with Maria

We arrived at Maria's home shortly after lunch. She greeted us at the door and welcomed us in. We were soon settled in a sun room. We had arranged the interview through Zoe Jackson, Maria's professional friend. When Doug asked Zoe if she would like to recommend any former students for us to interview for our research project, "A Glance Back: The Administrative Life," she immediately said yes. In fact, Zoe added, you know the person; you worked with Maria a decade or so back. Maria retired about two years earlier from a position as clinical professor at the university. She would be happy to talk about her twelve years as the Academy's principal. Not many principals get to open a school of choice, especially one centrally focused on the development of civic responsibility. Maria opened the conversation to whatever issues and experiences would help us in our research. But she had one condition: "I don't have to remember any sources!" We agreed.

We talked about our choice of John Dewey's ethical ideas as the conceptual lens for our and her work. She had read some of Dewey's work in graduate school but not much. She admired his pedagogical and curricular ideas, as best she understood them, but had not read any of his ethics writing until we worked with the Academy's teachers. We noted that we were not there to evaluate her; we wanted to hear her experiences and ideas about ethics drawn from her roles as an educator. We noted that everything she told us, if we incorporated it into a book, would be treated in a manner that ensured confidentiality for her, her students, teachers, and other actors in her narrative. The paperwork we signed, along with university policy, ensured confidentiality. She laughed and said that one essential virtue of retirement was that she had few fears about what was thought and said about her life, although she was relieved to hear our commitment to protecting the privacy of others associated with the Academy. Details aside, we began our conversation.

The Beginning

We first asked Maria about putting the new school together and the challenges she dealt with in forming a school of choice with some specific promises made to faculty, staff, families, and the community (most of what follows is our understanding of her comments with questions from us interjected).

One of the most interesting aspects of starting this new school was that unlike taking over an established school when an entering principal must learn the givens – the history, people, stories, culture – of the school she inherits, Maria had to help create a "there" as well as to choose who would best fit into what they could only partially anticipate. For the Academy, theoretically, no faculty or students would be automatically assigned to the school. Although the state and district would import many parameters (as yet not entirely known), the Academy ostensibly had considerable freedom to do things differently. It was conceived by some as almost a district-owned charter school, and by others as just another district school. In truth, no one really knew just what autonomy and differences would be tolerated in the Academy and its sister newcomer school of choice, The Fine Arts Academy, by central administration and the board, or even the Department of Education.

The emergent nature of the school meant that Maria and others already committed to the school did a lot of work in the summer before it opened. Members of central administration also were part of the planning that summer. Unfortunately, not everyone who would work at the school was identified as early as the work needed to begin to get it open for fall. Moreover, since students were not captured by geography but through application, they knew there would be a mixture of students living both proximate to the building and from all around the city. Students were added until the first week of classes, especially in secondary grades because those filled slower. The school opened as a kindergarten to tenth grade, with eleventh and twelfth grade added over the next two years. That was because Maria, who had asked for kindergarten to eighth or ninth to start, felt the initial graduates needed time to be immersed in the school's distinctive aspects and curriculum. When the Academy opened, most of its students had been socialized in traditional schools, and their parents brought with them expectations for how schools ought to work, as did the teachers and all other personnel. The unknown was how much the Academy's processes would diverge from prior experiences and expectations and whether that would be a problem for student and adult adjustment.

Historically, public schools were expected to produce effective, ethical citizens to function in a democratic, capitalist society. Also ethics, especially if conflated with morals, often created an uncertain role for schools as a significant portion of people and policymakers were not at all comfortable with government schools instilling morals in the nation's children. Other people sought access to public students to provide religious training of one sort or another. That meant boundary lines for the Academy had to be cautiously set and monitored. Thus, using terms like social responsibility, citizenship, and ethical codes or standards would help keep discussions and activities away from more divisive concepts. How ideas were framed, embedded in curricula, and presented as curricular goals would require educators to be on the same page. Also, it would be important to anticipate how to manage situations where parents, the general public, and especially students did not understand or respect particular boundaries. The history of church-state interaction as envisioned in the Establishment Clause of the First Amendment and related to public education was quite complex and could be fairly called muddled. The Academy would inherit that chaos and, given its specialization, might encounter greater problems than many schools. It could not be assumed parents and educators would embrace a distinction between secular ethics and sacred principles.

To the extent that becoming a responsible adult in our society and accepting and living by ethical principles would be an outcome intentionally taught represented a significant challenge for the educators. And to the extent that introducing the principles and behaviors of an ethical person was a duty for all educators, a lot of planning, professional development – not just for teachers but for the Academy's whole staff – and ongoing dialogue would be necessary. Teacher applicants and other potential personnel were required to explain their interest in and value to the Academy. Few teachers have much experience with teaching or learning the ethical development that would be part of the Academy's curriculum.

As for curriculum, formal and informal, in the school building and beyond, integrated and more freestanding, there were schools that professed a similar set of goals, both historically and presently, that could be models to help guide the Academy's development. That was normal when setting up a specialized school: look for parallel institutions to draw ideas and experiences from. However, the Academy would rise in a specific place and time, which would mean context would have to be respected and adapted to face its immediate challenges. Leadership, Maria to start with, could never assume successes elsewhere or in other times could be transported intact and imposed on the Academy because it is an institution nested in a community and district. Nor could the school always expect policy formation to function via a consensus adoption process. In addition to a constant interaction with external politics, the same forces would operate within the walls and require processes that were flexible and reliable enough that challenges to practice could be met with reasoned consideration and changes as growth and experience revealed. In fact, an awesome task faced the Academy: its culture would be selected, constructed, and reconstructed ad infinitum.

The Processes

Maria believed that the procedures through which the Academy and its members made decisions, resolved conflicts, and adapted to experiences were essential to achieving its goals. While many aspects of the school's operation could be codified into policy, no one could anticipate the issues and challenges that would arise over time. Therefore, how the school responded to events and actions in terms of applying policy and deciding when policy did not clearly cover a situation was critical. So often in schools an event occurs and policy does not entirely direct how educators should react because this event was not anticipated. Maria brought up situations where there was a clash between positive values, for instance. Speech issues were often at the heart of such situations, as when competing beliefs led to speech that was unexpectedly disruptive to a classroom or another school context. If the clash or disruption was sharp, a natural tendency was to suppress or moderate the scope of permissible speech or to punish one or more of the speakers. This reaction was often explained by a desire to protect some students or even adults from hurt or alienation, and the rationale was often to protect immature children from hearing divisive or harsh speech. Meshing free speech values with protective instincts regarding disruption or discomfort was a matter that arose many times.

Maria always tried to find time to investigate a situation fully, rather than quickly reacting. She would gather information from multiple parties affected, which could include all members or categories of members in the school. There is a deeply embedded norm in public education that many forms of speech are too dangerous for schools to tolerate. In a K–12 school, the developmental levels of students range widely as do their ages. A complicating factor, social media exposes children to too much information and vicarious experiences. Students bring more information and perhaps more actual experiences to school at earlier ages now. Trying to block children's access to knowledge is often a losing battle. Thus, speech issues are pricklier at every age as children try to make sense of endless information, no small amount of which is inaccurate.

When a student, faculty, or staff member's words or actions apparently transgress school or district policy, there is often a panicked effort to resolve the issue by enforcing a policy and imposing punishment. Often complexities in a situation are overlooked or minimized in the moment. The immediate desire is for a neat and final resolution and a confirmation of the rules and the authority of the school to impose them. Of course, since the 1960s, the legal requirement that students, faculty, and staff receive protections created by the Bill of Rights, many statutes and policies, and even as local as classroom rules, ensure as much if not more accountability and scrutiny as they do freedom. Moreover, the Academy sought more than students' compliance with rules; it fostered independent ethical conduct and participation in adapting rules and principles as circumstances changed.

Maria said the greatest issue was finding the time to implement processes that reinforced ethical thinking and action. Students needed experiences that allowed them to make decisions and understand effects and consequences. They needed adult models from whom they learned and received guidance. They needed direct involvement in policy creation and amendment. The Academy had to provide this curriculum to every student and ensure through scope and sequence and assessment everyone had an opportunity to develop. For the faculty and administrative staff, creating this educative environment and extending it to all students was incredibly complicated. In most schools some students had the opportunity to learn these elements of personal and social virtues – Maria used that last term because she remembered reading a 1983 book titled *Managers of Virtue* by David Tyack and Elisabeth Hansot that affected her understanding of her profession and public education. All students learned the necessity of being responsible, but only those who attracted mentors or who were widely involved in Academy activities had experiences that shaped their ethical thinking. One thing the Academy provided for any student was after-school programming that was intentionally educative. Many community organizations were involved with the school providing experiences that meshed well with the overall Academy goals. These programs were well received. Most students were at school until 4–4:30 p.m. or later every day. External funding was required to meet the children's needs, but setting that up became part of the school-community relationships.

We asked Maria more about slowing down consideration of dilemmas. If the situation received publicity, like a conflict among different groups of students, it was often difficult to get the time necessary to gather information and consider all the intersecting forces at play. If the situation created fears or anger among parents or others, there was pressure to bring things to a swift conclusion. When someone was clearly harmed, there was a push for a clear resolution and imposition of consequences. However, the decisions involved might be less than clear or certain as information was acquired and Maria had to find ways procedurally to let the information be gathered and the decisions be reached based on full reflection. That meant deciding who was a party directly and whose voices must be heard, and what information could be shared with whom. Finally, after an event with big ripples, time had to be made to consider whether the policies in place and processes followed led to a fair decision for those involved.

Maria did not feel as though these principles were unique to the Academy or her administrative duties. In many respects, the dilemmas that arose and the competing values and forces in play were those that every public school must confront. She did feel as though the Academy's name and express goals made it a lighthouse school where all issues involved in educating the young toward effective participation in society had to be addressed in a curricular fashion. The function of discipline could not be primarily order and efficiency but the development of the students as members of society.

Every event in the school was a form of curriculum, its ecological curriculum, and every dilemma an opportunity to demonstrate how adults and institutions could act in a manner befitting a democratic society (Simpson 2006, 59–69, 100–9). These expectations added layers of complexity to the processing of experience and creation of meaning with students. Why did this conduct matter? What duties were owed to all persons in the school? How were the principles taught and praised mirrored in the large and small interactions and events of the Academy? The constant flow of events and interactions among the Academy's community fueled these and many more questions. And often the answers were less than certain and constantly new events challenged the current de facto rules. One of Maria's favorite axioms as new issues or questions burst forth was from Judge Learned Hand: "The mark of a free man is the ever-gnawing uncertainty as to whether or not he is right" (something she had read online somewhere). Maria's overriding hope was to leave a legacy of accepting questions and embracing processes that led to more confidence in the fairness of policy and processes when dealing with subtle or outrageous situations – a habit of care and patience when decisions must be reached.

What Matters and for How Long?

When Maria mentioned what her hopes were in terms of the Academy, we asked if we could shift somewhat and ask her about her experiences and achievements as head. Had she left in place what she had hoped, and had that lasted? She said, first of all, that she believed that her position in opening and establishing the Academy helped her grow the most in her career. The twelve years there were the culmination of her work in public schools and were exactly where she wanted to end her years working pre-collegiately. When she left, she had no qualms or doubts. It was time to go. She believed that she had established a norm for decision-making and participation that fit the values and goals for the Academy, but she also knew that the life of the Academy as a specialized school existed at the pleasure of the board and would not necessarily be compatible with a new superintendent's plans or fit the new reform programs or state policies or even the demographics and needs of the community. The overall design of schools stayed stable over time, but intentional changes and reforms seemed to flow and ebb. The growth of privatized and other forms of traditional school replacements, especially in urban districts, as well as online education, had impacted some districts significantly. The Academy at present seemed stable and unlikely to be replaced, but she was a believer that in teaching and schooling there was no never or always.

She had worked hard from the beginning to bring in students and families from other parts of town. Some administrators had told her that her most important job for the Academy, apart from keeping decent test scores, was to attract and keep some students from the more affluent parts of town and to keep her school at least as white as the district and preferably more so. That would keep people with access to power more interested in the existence of the school. Of course, the politics of the district meant the Academy had to be successful with all types of students and families. It didn't necessarily have a board member to protect it, as many families lived outside the section of the district where it was built and could not vote for the member representing that section. Moreover, the area where the Academy was located was home mostly to minorities and some resented that whites were bussed into their neighborhoods, while some other low socioeconomic status communities and schools believed the Academy cherry-picked some of their best students away. She had never been in a school that was not serving a contiguous area geographically and had to learn to operate with constant district-wide political awareness, a new and sometimes frustrating experience. Maria struggled to buffer the school's community from these city-wide political issues while making the many decisions that arose within the school. It could not always be done, and sometimes a decision involving a particular child or family or teacher was taken from her hands by central office. She found, as so many building administrators do, that the rules mattered until something mattered more.

Most days, the school operated through the interaction of people, resources, and needs based on who belonged, following the processes and policies in place. That was not always simple or pleasant, but at least there were boundaries and expectations most members of the school community accepted. People generally recognized Maria was not a knee-jerk decision-maker. When a decision heavily impacted an individual, a group, or the school as a whole, she wanted to hear their views, review all the information she could collect, and, when possible, operate on some process of consensus or voting. If changes were brought forward, either as new requirements or policies or from members of the school as new ideas or improvements, she again wanted deliberations to be as wide as the likely scope of impact. She tried to involve students in real decision-making and got the elementary teachers involved in preparing younger students for broader participation through various forms of decision-making at the classroom and grade levels. As widely as possible, participation by groups most affected and opportunity to vote and use their voices was the preferred process in the Academy. She used the term *subsidiarity* to explain this principle – that those most affected by a policy or decision should have a role in making and implementing it as much as possible.

One set of policies and practices the Academy had to spend time on as well as adapt through experience involved sending students into the community for service and opportunities like internships. The Academy was committed to all students having learning experiences beyond the four walls of the school early and often. Being situated near the center of the city meant there were many opportunities in the public and private sectors. Also, some of the areas around the school were low to moderate income, and there were needs and opportunities to be of service to families. One tradition Maria helped set up was working with Habitat for Humanity to build an Academy house each year for a chosen family. Students were given the opportunity to work on the house, and many did, along with their family, and each year as part of graduation, student representatives presented the keys to the Academy house to the new owners. There were many opportunities for leaders in school-wide projects like this one. With experience, wonderful relationships arose with institutions, businesses, civic community groups, and local foundations that ensured support, opportunities for student experiences, and collaborative projects of all sorts. The Academy's aim of creating experienced and effective community members was a strong attractor, and preparing students to perform in myriad settings and being welcomed as a source of pride made the community relations aspect of administering a school a big success and a source of influence for the school with a varied set of community actors.

Sometimes that influence protected the school from people who were less enthusiastic about it inside the district and in the broader community. Cultivating that support took time and vigilance far beyond Maria. The school sent children across the school years into many settings. The Academy's houses meant sometimes a multiage group would go, while some activities were age specific. In any event, supervision and preparation were essential. Because the activities were part of every year at the Academy, students developed skills and awareness of expectations that were reinforced each year. However, sending children into less confined and controlled environments meant mistakes and embarrassments would happen. The important thing was to build from those experiences to hone the pedagogic and operational aspects of the different learning experiences. When new partners were joined bringing new experiences, the Academy knew it had to vet the people, activities, and setting, both for safety and value purposes. Each year the personnel at the Academy got better at preparation and implementation of experiences. The presence of Academy students working and serving in the community became a defining hallmark of the school. Maria believed this aspect was safe as long as the school existed because so many community sources participated and contributed. For a decade the Academy had employed a director of community learning who was paid for by private funds and did enormous coordination work. The Parent-Teacher Organization also assisted the director as parents opted to serve by supervising and otherwise supporting these distinctive learning experiences for all students.

We asked if anything made this whole process fragile or at risk before it became institutionalized and widely praised. Maria said there were mistakes and a few minor injuries that had to be cleared before limits were imposed that would have prevented the growth of partners and experiences. A relatively big seed grant from a trio of local foundations created positive vibes early on (such as opportunities for the superintendent and the board to have pictures taken with the foundation heads and express gratitude for their support of the district). The hire of the director of community services after the Academy's third year meant someone had eyes on the programs and time to establish and support the key relationships. The Academy was able to hire as initial director a retired colonel who had grown up in the community and was a great manager of details and people. Maria was relieved because her military service, she believed, gave them a special understanding and trust.

Maria also learned boundary management. Every person who became connected to the school had some role to play in some decisions. Few persons outside the Academy had a role in all the educational decisions, especially within the school. As Maria said, the Academy had a lot of moving pieces, and the issue was which pieces belonged as a part of which decisions and which parties belonged at the table when the actual decision was made. She had a preference for inclusion but learned that operationally, decisions had to be made often in tight timelines and not all decisions affected every party directly. However, one guiding principle was there were many more decisions students could participate in than most schools permitted. She also realized that people accustomed to power found mere influence unsatisfactory sometimes, and even people who wanted to help might have their own agenda and desire to be included in decisions where they really should have some voice at best. Her relationship with Reverend Smith was a great example. He would inevitably push past boundaries because he believed sincerely his involvement would lead to better decisions. Occasionally they would have a spirited discussion about his role in the school. He was at least overt about his actions. The local political types, starting inside the district and scattered across the community, were less straightforward and might have dubious motives. One thing the district did that caused her difficulties more than once was choose her assistant principals for her. She never persuaded the central office that her administrative team needed to be her people foremost because she had to trust them. Central administration was not interested in school heads having their own people dependent entirely on them. Thus, some assistant principals caused her real troubles from divided loyalties.

One particular issue had to be confronted during initial planning: What would the Academy do about extracurricular activities, especially sports? A secondary school without organized sports could easily have trouble attracting or keeping students. The other specialty school, for the arts, just replaced sports with arts of all sorts. There are plenty of opportunities to compete and perform for their students and the breadth and depth of arts-related opportunities made the school a haven for certain students (and parents) who wanted those experiences foremost in their children's development. The experiences of service and community-based experiences with a focus on developing productive and effective adults in the community was a less natural passion for most students. The initial plan was to have intramurals in sports and other forms of competition among the school's houses. That would allow vertical integration of students in various activities and competition, creating leadership and mentoring roles for the older students. It was not that hard to find this option as it drew neatly on *Harry Potter*'s Hogwarts and the houses there. Unlike the Hogwarts approach, students would be assigned not based on shared personal characteristics but more on a model of diversity and balance. Also, house competitions need not be limited to sports but could be patterned on an annual schedule and be a mix of challenges that would draw on different skills and interests. This model actually worked out well, and the houses had community sponsors that helped provide resources (banks seemed especially drawn to that role). Over the years, some students were elite athletes and met those needs through premier league sports outside of school. The ongoing process of interhouse competition could be tied to most extracurricular activities and could incorporate easily academically related clubs and performances. Every student had opportunities and obligations to participate in various ways and thus engagement was pervasive and not dominated by the students with more immediate talents.

We finally came to the point where we asked Maria why she left. She headed the school for twelve years through a decade of graduating classes. She said she believed the Academy was stabilized and had many people engaged and advocating for it including businesses, public interest groups, foundations, and families. The test scores were as high as any school in the district at the secondary level, and a significant percentage of graduates went on to post-secondary education. In fact, the percentage of students graduating was higher than any high school, and the students in the lower quartiles still graduated and most proceeded to college, vocational programs, or the military irrespective of the overall circumstances of students' lives. That culture of success had been developed early when the school received a grant to increase graduation and improve transition to work or college and hired A. Jay Johnson to set up and run its Destination Diploma program. His leadership produced results for at-risk students unlike any in the district or any other district in the area. He was sort of like the colonel – he managed the program with little need for monitoring or requests for help. After the grant finally ran dry, the superintendent hired Johnson and his team and was trying to replicate the program in every high school in the district.

So, again we asked her why she left. Maria sighed and paused. "It was not my choice," she said.

> Near the end of my last year at the Academy, a group of my students decided to stage a march to support immigrants in the country, including their children who were often separated from their families. The policy issues were very intense and divisive across the country. The district wanted to stay on the outside of the issues because even the board was divided on many of the issues, and the new superintendent was clear that the district would stay away from debates or any other connection to these matters. When word of my students' plan to march, joined by many people and groups in our city, got to central office, the superintendent and others initially ordered me to shut down the march or ignore it officially (e.g., if students were absent or left school to take part, it was an unexcused absence). Also, faculty and staff were unofficially cautioned to play no role in the march. My student organizers came to me and asked if I would march with them. It was my fight too, they said, and my presence would give all the people heart and show that at the Academy, they were taught that being an effective and engaged member of society included fighting for social justice and against bias and hatred. They said I was their heroine and without me, the march would not seem a full success.

And you did what? we asked. Maria said she talked it over with a few friends, mostly not from the district. They all said this action would certainly put her job at risk and to consider carefully the likely consequences. She decided to march. She arranged things so any student whose parents marched or agreed to have their child be part of it could go with no consequences except a writing assignment in social studies or English class. Faculty and staff could go as long as the remaining students were supervised and the office covered. What did Superintendent Amemantine say? There was an eerie silence, Maria said. No threats or bombast. By that time, many local politicians and national public figures were marching. The idea gathered force before it occurred with national media coverage and lots of conversations for and against. Going after Maria publicly at that point would have been risky. Instead, he waited until the summer and then announced he was promoting Maria to assistant director of professional development for building administrators. She felt that she was being buried alive.

[Below we write in Maria's words as faithfully as possible, because what she said was so personal, we do not want to risk misrepresentation. As we have indicated, she read this part too and agreed this was what she meant to say and presumably did.]

I knew – and Amemantine understood clearly too – I could not work under professional quarantine. A job was open at Zoe's university where I could supervise administrative internships and perhaps teach some courses on bilingual education and policy. I applied and got the position. I was an instructor, not a tenure track faculty, so I was off the radar screen and could attend to students that came under my care.

I enjoyed the position immensely. I learned things about myself and, more generally, about administrative work in education. I am a hands-on person, and in all my jobs, I had people I supported and advocated for. As a school principal, my direct reports and responsibilities were primarily staff and teachers. That worked alright for me, because by helping them, I helped enhance the quality of experience for the students. I did work as directly with students as I could, but it was not the same as being a teacher. My primary duties were to protect and improve the school as a whole. I did not have "my students" like a teacher does, and I needed to stay as neutral as possible in conflicts among the school community members and put the whole school before the individual. I also had to make decisions that fit that ethic. I had to do things I found distasteful, perhaps even wrong because the consequences of not doing so might hurt more people or the Academy. There was no way to maintain fully clean hands per my own personal values. There were a few times, in retrospect, I turned my back and walked away, abandoning someone to unnecessary consequences. There were times when there was no win-win solution or even a clearly right solution. More often, there would be a necessary solution for the common good. It was one thing when that happened to an adult, but when it happened to a student, it could overwhelm me. I could be imposing or acquiescing to a consequence that seemed to constitute giving up on the student. Rationally, I know we cannot protect or rescue everyone, nor ensure a consequence is just or proportionate. We cannot totally prevent careers and lives from being squandered. There are losses in a school every year and over time they pile up and reappear in memories or similar, new situations.

I know these facts and accept them, but I cannot help feeling these facts too. Inside me I have many scars. I try to be okay with the notion that we did the best we could, but I know that is not really true. Or if it is true, that is not enough. I think of myself as an ethical person. As I've said before, I'm a good problem-solver and policy creator. I was an effective principal by all the standards around me. What I did not fully realize is that I am human, an emotional person, and have strong and enduring feelings. As a principal, it was best that I manage my feelings carefully and strategically. I always said that spontaneity is an indulgence unless carefully planned. I smiled, laughed, occasionally hugged. But I suppressed showing anger unless there was a good purpose in showing it. I shaped my feelings to fit whatever purpose seemed most useful to me or the school. I left a lot of me at home, and that was a good thing professionally. Being a leader does not require someone to become a dishonest person, but dishonesty seems intrinsic to the role. It does not require you become uncaring, but caring is not as central as it should be. You do not have to live as an unethical person, but you do approach the margins frequently.

When I decided to march, I understood destructive consequences were almost inevitable. I wanted to be with my students and faculty as an advocate, for them, for my people. I did not want to be analytical, balanced, and safe. I wanted to live in the passion of that moment and know for whom I was fighting and why. Because it felt right, altogether right. It was part of finding my purpose as a person. I was never more aware of the love I felt for those around me. Of our strong, shared connection. I lived in that identity as a teacher at the university with more confidence and happiness than I ever felt before. I just stayed out of the annoying politics and worked with my students and helped a few school people along the way. I did not abandon my cognitive processes and analytical skills; I just lived as a whole person – one with a mind, feelings, and spirit, as Parker Palmer taught me, all in operation and all functioning. I revived parts of myself and being more of a person made me more effective in relationships and decision-making because I recognized the whole person that others were as well. By seeing more in situations and others, I brought more to the responsibility of serving and guiding others. I could accept the losses where situations were beyond me because I more clearly understood what it meant to do the best I could for others and in discharging my responsibilities as a person. But nothing I did ever surpassed the satisfaction I experienced working with K-12 students and colleagues. Along the way, I understood better what Dewey meant by developing a broad, enriching, and satisfying life.

That seemed to us a proper moment to conclude a long conversation. Maria said she enjoyed the reflection and that she needed to get ready for her goddaughter and her family. We thanked Maria and drove quietly home, immersed in our thoughts. As we approached my home to be dropped off, I said to Doug, "My grandfather used to say that we grow too soon old and too late smart. I think we can grow wise only as we grow older, but it does not seem too late to me." Doug said, "That sounds about right."

References

Citations of the works of John Dewey are to the critical edition published by Southern Illinois University Press. Volume and page numbers follow the initials of the series.

Dewey, John. 1882–98. *The Early Works* (EW 1–5). Edited by Jo Ann Boydston. 5 vols. Carbondale and Edwardsville: Southern Illinois University Press, 1967–72.
 1899–1924. *The Middle Works* (MW 1–15). Edited by Jo Ann Boydston. 15 vols. Carbondale and Edwardsville: Southern Illinois University Press, 1976–88.
 1925–53. *The Later Works* (LW 1–17). Edited by Jo Ann Boydston. 17 vols. Carbondale and Edwardsville: Southern Illinois University Press, 1988–91.
Abowitz, Kathleen Knight. 2007. "Moral Perception through Aesthetics: Engaging Imaginations in Educational Ethics." *Journal of Teacher Education* 58, no. 4 (September/October): 287–98. https://doi.org/10.1177/0022487107305605.
Abowitz, Kathleen Knight, and Sarah Stitzlein. 2018. "Public Schools, Public Goods, and Public Work." *Phi Delta Kappan* 100 (3): 33–7.
Anderson, Elizabeth. 2010. "Dewey's Moral Philosophy." *Stanford Encyclopedia of Philosophy.* Last revised January 12, 2013. http://plato.standford.du/entries/dewey-moral/.
Apple, Michael W. 1982. *Education and Power.* London: Routledge and Kegan Paul.
 2002. "Does Education Have Independent Power? Bernstein and the Question of Relative Autonomy." *British Journal of Sociology of Education* 23, no. 4 (December): 607–16.
 2009. "Is Racism in Education an Accident?" *Educational Policy* 23, no. 4 (July): 651–9. https://doi.org/10.1177/0895904809334371.
Bell, Les, and Howard Stevenson. 2015. "Towards an Analysis of the Policies That Shape Public Education: Setting the Context for School Leadership." *Management in Education* 29 (4): 146–50. https://doi.org/10.1177/0892020614555593.
Biesta, G. 2015. "How Does a Competent Teacher Become a Good Teacher? On Judgement, Wisdom and Virtuosity in Teaching and Teacher Education." In *Perspectives on the Future of Teacher Education*, edited by Ruth Heilbronn and Lorraine Foreman-Peck, 3–22. Oxford: Wiley Blackwell.

Bitterman, Amy, Rebecca Goldring, and Lucinda Gray. 2013. *Characteristics of Public and Private Elementary and Secondary School Principals in the United States: Results from the 2011–12 Schools and Staffing Survey.* National Center for Education Statistics. Washington, DC: US Department of Education.

Boisvert, Raymond D. 1998. *John Dewey: Rethinking Our Time.* Albany, NY: State University of New York Press.

Brinkman, Richard L., and June E. Brinkman. 2005. "Cultural Lag: A Relevant Framework for Social Justice." *International Journal of Social Economics* 32 (3): 228–48. https://doi.org/10.1108/03068290510580788.

Button, H. Warren, and Eugene F. Provenzo Jr. 1983. *History of Education and Culture in America.* Englewood Cliffs, NJ: Prentice-Hall.

Callan, Eamonn. 1982. "Dewey's Conception of Education as Growth." *Educational Theory* 32 (1): 19–27.

——— 2016. "Education in Safe and Unsafe Spaces." *Philosophical Inquiry in Education* 24 (1): 64–78.

Carsley, Dana, and Nancy L. Heath. 2015. "How Can Educational Leaders Promote Mental Health in Schools?" In *Key Questions for Educational Leaders*, edited by Darin Griffiths and John P. Portelli, 241–50. Burlington, ON: Word & Deed Publishing Inc., and Edphil Books.

Chan, Sin Yee. 2006. "The Confucian Notion of *Jing* (Respect)." *Philosophy East & West* 56, no. 2 (April): 229–52.

Chomsky, Noam. 2000. *Chomsky on MisEducation.* Lanham, MD: Rowman & Littlefield Publishers.

Cunningham, Frank. 2002. *Theories of Democracy: A Critical Introduction.* London: Routledge.

Darling-Hammond, Linda. 1996. "The Quiet Revolution: Rethinking Teacher Development." *Improving Professional Practice* 53, no. 6 (March): 4–10.

Deen, Phillip, ed. 2012. *Unmodern Philosophy and Modern Philosophy* by John Dewey. Carbondale: Southern Illinois University Press.

DeFalco, Anthony. 2010. "An Analysis of John Dewey's Notion of Occupations – Still Pedagogically Valuable?" *Education and Culture* 26, no. 1 (January): 82–99.

Delgado, Richard, and Jean Stefancic. 2017. *Critical Race Theory: An Introduction.* 3rd edn. New York: New York University Press.

DeWall, C. Nathan. 2013. "Looking Back and Forward: Lessons Learned and Moving Ahead." In *The Oxford Handbook of Social Exclusion*, edited by C. Nathan DeWall, 301–3. New York: Oxford University Press.

Dillon, Robin S. 1992. "Respect and Care: Toward Moral Integration." *Canadian Journal of Philosophy* 22, no. 1 (March): 105–32.

——— 2003. "Respect." *Stanford Encyclopedia of Philosophy.* Last revised February 18, 2018. https://plato.stanford.edu/entries/respect/.

Eames, S. Morris. 1969. "Introduction." In *Early Essays and Outlines of a Critical Theory of Ethics.* Vol. 3 of *John Dewey: The Early Works, 1882–1898*, edited by Jo Ann Boydston, xxix–xxxviii. Carbondale and Edwardsville: Southern Illinois University Press.

Edgar, Eugene, James M. Patton, and Norma Day-Vines. 2002. "Democratic Dispositions and Cultural Competency: Ingredients for School Renewal." *Remedial and Special Education* 23, no. 4 (July/August): 231–41.

Edmondson III, Henry T. 2006. *John Dewey & the Decline of American Education: How the Patron Saint of Schools Has Corrupted Teaching and Learning.* Wilmington, DE: ISI Books.

Eisenbeiss, Silke A. 2012. "Re-thinking Ethical Leadership: An Interdisciplinary Approach." *The Leadership Quarterly* 23 (5): 791–808. http://dx.doi.org/10.1016/j.leaqua.2012.03.001.

Enomoto, Ernestine K., and Bruce H. Kramer. 2007. *Leading through the Quagmire: Ethical Foundations, Critical Methods, and Practical Applications for School Leadership.* Lanham, MD: Rowman & Littlefield Education.

Fenstermacher, Gary. 2013. "The Moral Work of Teaching in Teacher Education." In *The Moral Work of Teaching and Teacher Education: Preparing and Supporting Practitioners,* edited by Matthew N. Sanger and Richard D. Osguthorpe, 3–13. New York: Teachers College Press.

Fernald, Charles D. 1995. "When in London...: Differences in Disability Language Preferences among English-Speaking Countries." *Mental Retardation* 33 (2): 99–103.

Fesmire, Steven A. 1995. "Dramatic Rehearsal and the Moral Artist: A Deweyan Theory of Moral Understanding." *Transactions of the Charles S. Peirce Society* 31 (3): 568–97.

———. 2003. *John Dewey and Moral Imagination: Pragmatism in Ethics.* Bloomington: Indiana University Press.

———. 2015. *Dewey.* New York: Routledge.

Fine, Gary A. 1993. "Ten Lies of Ethnography: Moral Dilemmas of Field Research." *Journal of Contemporary Ethnography* 22 (3): 267–94.

Foreman-Peck, Lorraine. 2015. "Towards a Theory of Well-Being for Teachers." In *Philosophical Perspectives on Teacher Education,* edited by Ruth Heilbronn and Lorraine Foreman-Peck, 152–66. West Sussex, UK: John Wiley & Sons.

Fraser, Steve, and Gary Gerstle, eds. 2005. *Ruling America: A History of Wealth and Power in a Democracy.* Cambridge, MA: Harvard University Press.

Freire, Paulo. 1973. *Education for Critical Consciousness.* New York: Seabury Press.

———. 1998. *Teachers as Cultural Workers.* Boulder, CO: Westview Press.

———. (1970) 2003. *Pedagogy of the Oppressed.* New York: Continuum.

Galupo, M. Paz 2009. "Cross-Category Friendship Patterns: Comparison of Heterosexual and Sexual Minority Adults." *Journal of Social and Personal Relationships* 26 (6–7): 811–31.

Garrison, Jim. 1999. "John Dewey's Theory of Practical Reasoning." *Education Philosophy and Theory* 31 (3): 291–312.

Garrison, Jim, Stefan Neubert, and Kersten Reich. 2012. *John Dewey's Philosophy of Education.* New York: Palgrave Macmillan.

Gelfand, Michele J., and Jeanne M. Brett, eds. 2004. *The Handbook of Negotiation and Culture.* Stanford, CA: Stanford University Press.

Ghobash, Omar Saif. 2016. *Letters to a Young Muslim*. New York: Picador.

Gilmore, Grant. 1977. *The Ages of American Law*. New Haven, CT: Yale University Press.

Goodlad, John I., Roger Soder, and Kenneth A. Sirotnik, eds. 1990. *The Moral Dimensions of Teaching*. San Francisco: Jossey-Bass.

Gorecki, Jan. 2017. *Justifying Ethics: Human Rights and Human Nature*. New York: Routledge.

Gouinlock, James. 1972. *John Dewey's Philosophy of Value*. New York: Humanities Press.

1993. *Rediscovering the Moral Life*. New York: Prometheus Books.

Greene, Maxine. 1978. "Wide-Awakeness and the Moral Life." In *Landscapes of Learning*, 42–52. New York: Teachers College Press.

Gribble, James. 1969. *Introduction to Philosophy of Education*. Boston: Allyn & Bacon.

Gutek, Gerald L. 2013. *Philosophical, Ideological, and Theoretical Perspectives on Education*. 2nd edn. New York: Pearson.

Haidt, Jonathan. 2006. *The Happiness Hypothesis: Finding Modern Truth in Ancient Wisdom*. New York: Basic Books.

Hansen, David T. 1988. "Was Socrates a 'Socratic Teacher'?" *Educational Theory* 38 (2): 213–24. https://doi.org/10.1111/j.1741-5446.1988.00213.x.

1993. "From Role to Person: The Moral Layeredness of Classroom Teaching." *American Educational Research Journal* 30, no. 4 (December): 651–74.

2001. *Exploring the Moral Heart of Teaching: Toward a Teacher's Creed*. New York: Teachers College Press.

Harris, Sam. 2010. *The Moral Landscape: How Science Can Determine Human Values*. New York: Free Press.

Hauser, Marc D. 2006. *Moral Minds: How Nature Designed Our Universal Sense of Right and Wrong*. New York: HarperCollins.

Heft, James L., ed. 1999. *A Catholic Modernity? Charles Taylor's Marianist Award Lecture*. New York: Oxford University Press.

Hess, Diana E. 2009. *Controversy in the Classroom: The Democratic Power of Discussion*. New York: Routledge.

Hickman, Larry A., Matthew Caleb Flamm, and Krzysztof Piotr Skowronski, eds. 2010. *The Continuing Relevance of John Dewey: Reflections on Aesthetics, Morality, Science, and Society*. Leiden, Netherlands: Brill.

Higgins, Chris. 2011. *The Good Life of Teaching: An Ethics of Professional Practice*. West Sussex, UK: John Wiley & Sons.

Hook, Sidney. 1959. "John Dewey – Philosopher of Growth." *The Journal of Philosophy* 56, no. 26 (December): 1010–18.

hooks, bell. 2014. *Feminist Theory: From Margin to Center*. New York: Routledge.

Horrigan, Paul Gerard. 2015. "Critique of Dewey's Instrumentalist Pragmatism." www.academia.edu/9966424/Critique_of_Deweys_Instrumentalist_Pragmatism.

House, Robert J., Paul J. Hanges, Mansour Javidan, Peter W. Dorfman, and Vipin Gupta, eds. 2004. *Culture, Leadership, and Organizations: The GLOBE Study of 62 Societies*. Thousand Oaks, CA: Sage Publications, Inc.

Ioannidis, John P. A. 2012. "Why Science Is Not Necessarily Self-Correcting." *Perspectives on Psychological Science* 7, no. 6 (November): 645–54. https://doi.org/10.1177/1745691612464056.

Johnston, James Scott. 2006. *Inquiry and Education: John Dewey and the Quest for Democracy*. Albany, NY: State University of New York Press.

2009. *Deweyan Inquiry*. Albany, NY: State University of New York Press.

Jonsen, Albert, and Stephen Toulmin. 1988. *The Abuse of Casuistry: A History of Moral Reasoning*. Oakland, CA: University of California Press.

Keltner, Dacher. 2009. *Born to Be Good: The Science of a Meaningful Life*. New York: W. W. Norton & Company.

Kestenbaum, Victor. 1996. "Preface." In *Theory of the Moral Life* by John Dewey, edited by Arnold Isenberg. New York: Irvington Publishers.

Kim, Jeong-Hee. 2011. "Teacher Inquiry as Phenomenological Bildungsroman." In *Practitioner Research in Teacher Education: Theory and Best Practices*, edited by Issa M. Saleh and Myint Swe Khine, 219–36. Frankfurt am Main: Peter Lang.

Kozol, Jonathan. 1991. *Savage Inequalities: Children in America's Schools*. New York: Crown Publishers.

Kunzman, Robert. 2006. *Grappling with the Good*. Albany, NY: State University of New York Press.

Kunzman, Robert. ed. 2011. *Philosophy of Education 2011*. Urbana, IL: Philosophy of Education Society.

2012. "How to Talk about Religion." *Educational Leadership* 69 (7): 44–8.

2016. "Navigating Religious Differences." *Educational Leadership* 74, no. 4 (December/January): 22–3.

Kurzban, Robert. 2010. *Why Everyone (Else) Is a Hypocrite: Evolution and the Modular Mind*. Princeton, NY: Princeton University Press.

Ladson-Billings, Gloria, ed. 2003. *Critical Race Theory Perspectives on the Social Studies: The Profession, Policies, and Curriculum*. Greenwich, CT: Information Age Publishers.

Lee, Valerie E., and Julia B. Smith. 1997. "High School Size: Which Works Best and for Whom?" *Educational Evaluation and Policy Analysis* 19, no. 3 (Autumn): 205–27.

Levitsky, Steven, and Daniel Ziblatt. 2018. *How Democracies Die*. New York: Crown Publishing Group.

Manne, Kate. 2018. *Down Girl: The Logic of Misogyny*. New York: Oxford University Press.

Margolis, Joseph. 1986. *Pragmatism without Foundations: Reconciling Realism with Relativism*. Oxford: Blackwell.

Martin, Jay. 2002. *The Education of John Dewey: A Biography*. New York: Columbia University Press.

Maxwell, Bruce. 2008. *Professional Ethics Education: Studies in Compassionate Empathy*. Dordrecht, Netherlands: Springer.

McAllister, Gretchen, and Jacqueline Jordan Irvine. 2002. "The Role of Empathy in Teaching Culturally Diverse Students: A Qualitative Study of Teachers' Beliefs." *Journal of Teacher Education* 53, no. 5 (November): 433–43.

McDermott, John J. 1991. "Introduction." In *Essays and Liberalism and Social Action*. Vol. 11 of *John Dewey: The Later Works, 1925–1953*, edited by Jo Ann Boydston, 1935–7. Carbondale and Edwardsville: Southern Illinois University Press.

McDonald, Hugh P. 2003. *John Dewey and Environmental Philosophy*. New York: State University of New York Press.

McVea, John F. 2007. "Constructing Good Decisions in Ethically Charged Situations: The Role of Dramatic Rehearsal." *Journal of Business Ethics* 70, no. 4 (February): 375–90.

Mehta, Jal. 2016. "Toward Pragmatic Educational Ethics." In *Dilemmas of Educational Ethics: Cases and Commentaries*, edited by Meira Levinson and Jacob Fay, 18–21. Cambridge, MA: Harvard Education Press.

Menand, Louis. 2002. *The Metaphysical Club: A Story of Ideas in America*. New York: Farrar, Straus and Giroux.

Miller, Franklin G., Joseph J. Fins, and Matthew D. Bacchetta. 1996. "Clinical Pragmatism: John Dewey and Clinical Ethics." *Journal of Contemporary Health Law & Policy* 13 (1): 27–51.

Murphey, Murray G. 1988. "Introduction." In *Human Nature and Conduct*. Vol. 14 of *John Dewey: The Middle Works, 1899–1924*, edited by Jo Ann Boydston, ix–xxiii, 1922. Carbondale and Edwardsville: Southern Illinois University Press.

Myles, Brenda Smith, Melissa L. Trautman, and Ronda L. Schelvan. 2004. *The Hidden Curriculum: Practical Solutions for Understanding Unstated Rules in Social Situations*. Shawnee Mission, KS: Autism Asperger Publishing Co.

Nias, Jennifer. 2005. "Why Teachers Need Their Colleagues: A Developmental Perspective." In *The Practice and Theory of School Improvement*, edited by David Hopkins, 223–37. Dordrecht, Netherlands: Springer.

Noddings, Nel. 1984. *Caring: A Feminine Approach to Ethics and Moral Education*. Berkeley: University of California Press.

1988. "An Ethic of Caring and Its Implications for Instructional Arrangements." *American Journal of Education* 96, no. 2 (February): 215–30.

2003. *Happiness and Education*. New York: Cambridge University Press.

2011. *Peace Education: How We Come to Love and Hate War*. New York: Cambridge University Press.

Pappas, Gregory Fernando. 1997a. "Dewey's Moral Theory: Experience as Method." *Transactions of the Charles S. Peirce Society* 33, no. 3 (Summer): 520–56.

1997b. "To Be or To Do: John Dewey and the Great Divide in Ethics." *History of Philosophy Quarterly* 14, no. 4 (October): 447–72.

2008. *John Dewey's Ethics: Democracy as Experience*. Bloomington and Indianapolis: Indiana University Press.

Peters, R. S. 1966. *Ethics and Education*. Oxford: Allen & Unwin.

Pinar, William F., William M. Reynolds, Patrick Slattery, and Peter M. Taubman. 1995. *Understanding Curriculum: An Introduction to the Study of Historical and Contemporary Curriculum Discourses*. New York: Peter Lang Publishing, Inc.

Pinker, Steven. 2002. *The Blank Slate: The Modern Denial of Human Nature*. New York: Viking.

2009. *How the Mind Works*. 2nd edn. New York: W. W. Norton & Company.

2011. *The Better Angels of Our Nature: Why Violence Has Declined*. New York: Viking.

2016. *The Blank Slate: The Modern Denial of Human Nature*. 2nd edn. New York: Viking.

Pring, Richard. (2007) 2017. *John Dewey: A Philosopher of Education for Our Time?* New York: Continuum.

Rawls, John. 1991. "Justice as Fairness: Political Not Metaphysical." In *Equality and Liberty*, edited by J. Angelo Corlett, 145–73. London: Palgrave Macmillan.

Rice, Suzanne, and Nicholas C. Burbules. 2010. "Listening: A Virtue Account." *Teachers College Record* 112 (11): 2728–42.

Rockefeller, Steven. 1991. *John Dewey: Religious Faith and Democratic Humanism*. New York: Columbia University Press.

Rogers, Melvin L. 2009. *The Undiscovered Dewey: Religion, Morality, and the Ethos of Democracy*. New York: Columbia University Press.

Ruitenberg, Claudia W. 2007. "'That's Just Your Opinion!' *American Idol* and the Confusion between Pluralism and Relativism." *Paideusis* 16 (1): 55–9.

2011. "The Empty Chair: Education in an Ethic of Hospitality." In *Philosophy of Education*, edited by R. Kunzman, 28–36. Urbana, IL: Philsophy of Education Society.

2016. *Unlocking the World: Education in an Ethic of Hospitality*. New York: Routledge.

2017. "Location, Location, Locution: Why It Matters Where We Say What We Say." *Philosophical Inquiry in Education* 24 (3): 211–22.

Ryan, Allen. 1995. *John Dewey and the High Tide of American Liberalism*. New York: W. W. Norton.

Shusterman, Richard. 2000. *Pragmatist Aesthetics: Living Beauty, Rethinking Art*. Lanham, MD: Rowman & Littlefield Publishers.

Simpson, Douglas J. 2006. *John Dewey*. New York: Peter Lang Publishing, Inc.

2011. "Neo-Deweyan Moral Education." In *Character and Moral Education: A Reader*, edited by Joseph L. DeVitis and Tianlong Yu, 207–26. New York: Peter Lang Publishing, Inc.

2017. "The Consciously Growing and Refreshing Life." In *John Dewey's Democracy and Education: A Centennial Handbook*, edited by Leonard J. Waks and Andrea R. English, 237–44. New York: Cambridge University Press.

Simpson, Douglas J., and Michael B. Jackson. 1995. "Glorious Dreams and Harsh Realities: The Roles and Responsibilities of the Teacher from a Deweyan Perspective." *Paideusis* 8 (2): 15–31.

———. 1997. *Educational Reform: A Deweyan Perspective.* New York: Garland.

———. 1998. "The Multiple Loves of the Successful Teacher: A Deweyan Perspective." *Educational Foundations* 12 (1): 75–82.

Simpson, Douglas J., and D. Mike Sacken. 2014. "The Sympathetic-and-Empathetic Teacher: A Deweyan Analysis." *Journal of Philosophy & History of Education* 64 (1): 1–20.

———. 2015. "The Ethical Principle of Regard for People: Using Dewey's Ideas in Schools." *International Journal of Progressive Education* 11 (1): 41–58.

———. 2016. "Ethical Principles and School Challenges: A Deweyan Analysis." *Education and Culture* 32 (1): 63–86.

Simpson, Douglas J., and Xiaoming Liu. 2007. "John Dewey's Theory of Learning: A Holistic Perspective." In *The Praeger Handbook of Education and Psychology: Volume 3*, edited by Joe L. Kincheloe and Raymond A. Horn Jr., 558–64. Westport, CT: Praeger Publishers.

Simpson, Douglas J., Michael B. Jackson, and Judy C. Aycock. 2005. *John Dewey and the Art of Teaching: Toward Reflective and Imaginative Practice.* Thousand Oaks, CA: Sage.

Sorrell, Kory. 2014. "*Our Better Angels*: Empathy, Sympathetic Reason, and Pragmatic Moral Progress." *The Pluralist* 9, no. 1 (Spring): 66–86.

Starratt, Robert J. 2003. *Centering Educational Administration: Cultivating Meaning, Community, Responsibility.* Mahwah, NJ: Lawrence Erlbaum Associates, Inc., Publishers.

Stein, Bradley D., Lisa H. Jaycox, Sheryl H. Kataoka, Marleen Wong, Wenli Tu, Marc N. Elliott, and Arlene Fink. 2003. "A Mental Health Intervention for Schoolchildren Exposed to Violence: A Randomized Controlled Trial." *Journal of the American Medical Association* 290 (5): 603–11. https://doi.org/10.1001/jama.290.5.603.

Stengel, Barbara S. 2009. "More Than 'Mere Ideas': Deweyan Tools for the Contemporary Philosopher." *Education and Culture* 25 (2): 89–100.

Stengel, Barbara S., and Alan R. Tom. 1995. "Taking the Moral Nature of Teaching Seriously." *Educational Forum* 59 (2): 154–63.

Stewart, Douglas. 2012. "Thinking about Forgiveness: A Philosophical Preamble to its Cultivation in Schooling." *Journal of Thought* 47 (1): 66–95. https://doi.org/10.2307/jthought.47.1.66.

Strike, Kenneth A. 2010. *Small Schools and Strong Communities: A Third Way of School Reform.* New York: Teachers College Press.

Strike, Kenneth A., and Jonas F. Soltis. 2009. *The Ethics of Teaching.* 5th edn. New York: Teachers College Press.

Stout, Jeffrey. 2004. *Democracy and Tradition.* Princeton, NJ: Princeton University Press.

Taylor, Charles. 1996. "A Catholic Modernity?" Paper presented at the Marianist Award Lecture at the University of Dayton, Dayton, OH.

Terchek, Ronald J., and Thomas C. Conte, eds. 2001. *Theories of Democracy: A Reader*. Lanham, MD: Rowman & Littlefield Publishers, Inc.

Thompson, Leigh, Margaret Neale, and Marwan Sinaceur. 2004. "The Evolution of Cognition and Biases in Negotiation Research: An Examination of Cognition, Social Perception, Motivation, and Emotion." In *The Handbook of Negotiation and Culture*, edited by Michele J. Gelfand and Jeanne M. Brett, 7–44. Stanford, CA: Stanford University Press.

Urban, Wayne J., and Jennings L. Wagoner Jr. 2009. *American Education: A History*. 4th edn. New York: Routledge.

Waddington, David L. 2015. "Dewey and Video Games: From Education through Occupations to Education through Simulations." *Educational Theory* 65 (1): 1–20. https://doi.org/10.1111/edth.12092.

——— 2020. "Time War: Paul Virilio and the Potential Educational Impacts of Real-Time Strategy Video Games." *Philosophical Inquiry in Education* 27 (1): 46–61.

Wagner, Paul A., and Douglas J. Simpson. 2009. *Ethical Decision Making in School Administration: Leadership as Moral Architecture*. Thousand Oaks, CA: SAGE Publications, Inc.

Waks, Leonard J., and Andrea R. English. 2017. *John Dewey's Democracy and Education: A Centennial Handbook*. New York: Cambridge University Press.

Warnick, Bryan, Douglas Yacek, and Shannon Robinson. 2018. "Learning to Be Moved: The Modes of Democratic Responsiveness." *Philosophical Inquiry in Education* 25 (1): 31–46.

Warren, Donald. 1985. "Learning from Experience: History and Teacher Education." *Educational Researcher* 14, no. 10 (December): 5–12.

Warren, Donald, and John J. Patrick, eds. 2006. *Civic and Moral Learning in America*. New York: Palgrave Macmillan.

Welchman, Jennifer. 1995. *Dewey's Ethical Thought*. Ithaca, NY: Cornell University Press.

West, Cornel. 1994. *Race Matters*. 2nd edn. New York: Vintage Books.

Westbrook, Robert B. 1991. *John Dewey and American Democracy*. New York: Cornell University Press.

Williams, Kipling D., Joseph P. Forgas, and William von Hippel, eds. 2005. *The Social Outcast: Ostracism, Social Exclusion, Rejection, and Bullying*. New York: Psychology Press.

Zhao, Yong. 2010. "Preparing Globally Competent Teachers: A New Imperative for Teacher Education." *Journal of Teacher Education* 61, no. 5 (November): 422–31. https://doi.org/10.1177/0022487110375802.

Zins, Joseph E., Roger P. Weissberg, Margaret C. Wang, and Herbert J. Walberg, eds. 2004. *Building Academic Success on Social and Emotional Learning: What Does the Research Say?* New York: Teachers College Press.

Index

Made in the USA
Middletown, DE
27 June 2021